WE'M...

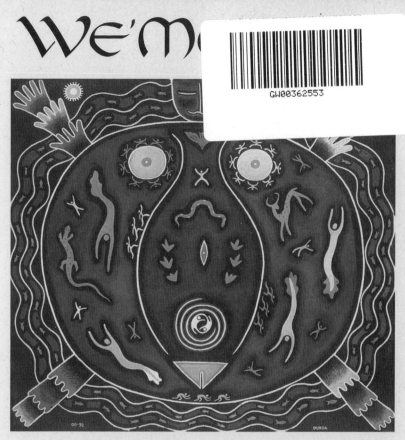

The Beginning World © *Durga Bernhard 1992*

EARTH MATTERS

GAIA RHYTHMS: AN ASTROLOGICAL MOON CALENDAR, APPOINTMENT BOOK, AND DAILY GUIDE TO NATURAL RHYTHM FOR WE'MOON

 published by
Mother Tongue Ink

WE'MOON '96: GAIA RHYTHMS FOR WOMYN
© Mother Tongue Ink 1995

P.O. Box 1395-A
Estacada, Oregon 97023
USA (tel: 503-630-7848)
E-mail: Wemoon@teleport.com

Created by the **We'Moon** Matrix
Creatrix and Crone Consultant: Musawa
We'Moonager and Graphics Editor: Beth Freewomon
Writing Editor and Contributor Hag: Pandora Cate
Production Initiate, Databaser, and Admoonistrator: Linda Meagaen

© *Sonja Shahan 1994*

Front cover art by Michelle Waters. Back cover art by Durga Bernhard. See "Cover Notes" on p. 188.

Distributed directly by the publisher, Mother Tongue Ink, on We'Moon land, and by our other fine distributors:

> **USA:** Abyss, Bookpeople, Ingram, Inland, Ladyslipper, Moving Books, New Leaf, Pacific Pipeline, Small Changes, and Vision Works. **Canada:** Dempsey (Vancouver). **International:** Airlift (London), Bookpeople (Oakland, CA), and Rotation (Berlin).

Astro-data reprinted with permission from Astro Communications Services, Inc., P.O. Box 34487, San Diego, CA 92163-4487.

Printed with soy-based ink on 100% recycled paper made entirely from de-inked newspapers and magazines, with a minimum of 50% post-consumer fiber. No chlorine bleach was used in this process. By using this paper, we saved about 97 trees and 51 cubic feet of landfill space.

Individuals can order this book directly from Mother Tongue Ink @ $16.00 postage paid. See p. 198 for complete ordering information.

$13.95 ISBN 0-9510661-7-X

TABLE OF CONTENTS

I. INTRODUCTION

Year at a Glance 4
Declaration of the Four Sacred
   Things 5
What is *WE'MOON*? 6
Introduction to the Theme 9
Earth Matter/Earth Body 13
How to Use This Book 14
Planets, Goddesses, Aspects 17
Sun Signs 18

Moon Signs: Transits 22
Lunar Rhythm 25
The Eight Lunar Phases 25
Where's That Moon? 27
The Sixty-Year Wheel Turns 28
Wheel of the Year: Holy Days 29
How to Use 1996 Predictions 30
Planetary Movements in 1996 30
World Time Zones 31

II. MOON CALENDAR*

I .... Creator/Destroyer Moon
II .. Listening/Understanding Moon
III .... Darkness/Magic Moon
IV .... Earth Action Moon
V .... Earth Body Moon
VI .... Earth Art Moon
VII .... Earth Tending Moon

VIII .... Provider Moon
IX .... Mundane Moon
X .... Weather/ing Moon
XI .... Sexy Mama Moon
XII .... Interconnectedness Moon
XIII........................... Shelter Moon

*Each Moon features herbal lore by Colette Gardiner
and astrological predictions by Gretchen Lawlor.

III. APPENDIX

Cover Notes 188
Acknowledgments 188
Copyrights/Contacts 189
Contributor Bylines 189
Becoming a Contributor 198
Ordering a **We'Moon** 198
Our Cosmic Clock 199

Mercury Retrograde 200
Eclipses 1996 201
Why Asteroids? 202
Asteroid Ephemeris 203
Planetary Ephemeris 204
Month at a Glance Calendars ... 210
Doodle Pages 222

1996 9996

JANUARY
M	T	W	T	F	S	S
1	2	3	4	5	6	7
8	9	10	11	12	13	14
15	16	17	18	19	20	21
22	23	24	25	26	27	28
29	30	31				

FEBRUARY
M	T	W	T	F	S	S
			1	2	3	4
5	6	7	8	9	10	11
12	13	14	15	16	17	18
19	20	21	22	23	24	25
26	27	28	29			

MARCH
M	T	W	T	F	S	S
				1	2	3
4	5	6	7	8	9	10
11	12	13	14	15	16	17
18	19	20	21	22	23	24
25	26	27	28	29	30	31

APRIL
M	T	W	T	F	S	S
1	2	3	4	5	6	7
8	9	10	11	12	13	14
15	16	17	18	19	20	21
22	23	24	25	26	27	28
29	30					

MAY
M	T	W	T	F	S	S
		1	2	3	4	5
6	7	8	9	10	11	12
13	14	15	16	17	18	19
20	21	22	23	24	25	26
27	28	29	30	31		

JUNE
M	T	W	T	F	S	S
					1	2
3	4	5	6	7	8	9
10	11	12	13	14	15	16
17	18	19	20	21	22	23
24	25	26	27	28	29	30

JULY
M	T	W	T	F	S	S
1	2	3	4	5	6	7
8	9	10	11	12	13	14
15	16	17	18	19	20	21
22	23	24	25	26	27	28
29	30	31				

AUGUST
M	T	W	T	F	S	S
			1	2	3	4
5	6	7	8	9	10	11
12	13	14	15	16	17	18
19	20	21	22	23	24	25
26	27	28	29	30	31	

SEPTEMBER
M	T	W	T	F	S	S
						1
2	3	4	5	6	7	8
9	10	11	12	13	14	15
16	17	18	19	20	21	22
23	24	25	26	27	28	29
30						

OCTOBER
M	T	W	T	F	S	S
	1	2	3	4	5	6
7	8	9	10	11	12	13
14	15	16	17	18	19	20
21	22	23	24	25	26	27
28	29	30	31			

NOVEMBER
M	T	W	T	F	S	S
				1	2	3
4	5	6	7	8	9	10
11	12	13	14	15	16	17
18	19	20	21	22	23	24
25	26	27	28	29	30	

DECEMBER
M	T	W	T	F	S	S
						1
2	3	4	5	6	7	8
9	10	11	12	13	14	15
16	17	18	19	20	21	22
23	24	25	26	27	28	29
30	31					

Declaration of the Four Sacred Things

The earth is a living, conscious being. In company with cultures of many different times and places, we name these things as sacred: air, fire, water and earth.

Whether we see them as the breath, energy, blood and body of the Mother, or as the blessed gifts of a Creator, or as symbols of the interconnected systems that sustain life, we know that nothing can live without them.

To call these things sacred is to say that they have a value beyond their usefulness for human ends, that they themselves become the standards by which our acts, our economics, our laws and our purposes must be judged. No one has the right to appropriate them or profit from them at the expense of others. Any government which fails to protect them forfeits its legitimacy.

For it is everyone's responsibility to sustain, heal and preserve the soil, the air, the fresh and salt waters, and the energy resources that can support diverse and flourishing life.

All people, all living things, are part of the earth-life, and so sacred. No one of us stands higher or lower than any other. Only justice can assure balance; only ecological balance can sustain freedom. Only in freedom can that fifth sacred thing that we call spirit flourish in its full diversity.

To honor the sacred is to create conditions in which nourishment, sustenance, habitat, knowledge, freedom and beauty can thrive. To honor the sacred is to make love possible.

To this we dedicate our curiosity, our will, our courage, our silences and our voices. To this we dedicate our lives.

WHAT IS *WE'MOON*?
A HANDBOOK IN NATURAL CYCLES

We'Moon: Gaia Rhythms for Womyn is more than an appointment book. It is a way of life! **We'Moon** is a *handbook in natural rhythm*. As we chart our days alongside other heavenly bodies, we begin to discover patterns in how we interrelate. **We'Moon** comes out of an *international womyn's culture*. Art and writings by we'moon from many lands give a glimpse of the great diversity and uniqueness of a world we create in our own image. **We'Moon** is about *womyn's spirituality* (spirit'reality). We share how we live our truth, what inspires us, how we envision our reality in connection with the whole earth and all our relations.

We'moon means "we of the moon." The moon, whose cycles run in our blood, is the original womyn's calendar. Like the moon, we'moon circle the earth. We are drawn to one another. We come in different shapes, colors, and sizes. We are continually transforming. With all our different hues and points of view, we are one.

We'moon means "women." Instead of defining ourselves in relation to men (*woman* means "wife of man" in Old English; *female* is a derivative of "male"), we use the word *we'moon* to define ourselves by our primary relation to the natural sources of cosmic flow ("we of the moon"). Other terms we'moon use are *womyn, wimmin, womon, womb-one.* **We'Moon** is a moon calendar for we'moon. As we'moon, we seek to be

© *Hope Swann 1990*

Queen of Heaven II

whole in ourselves, rather than dividing ourselves in half and hoping that some "other half" will complete the picture. We see the whole range of life's potential embodied by we'moon, and do not divide the universe into sex-role stereotypes according to the heterosexual model. Instead,

We'Moon is a sacred space in which to explore and celebrate the diversity of she-ness on earth. The calendar is we'moons' space. We see the goddess equally in the sun and the moon, in the earth and the sky.

We'moon culture exists in the diversity and the oneness of our experience as we'moon. *We honor both.* We come from all cultures, from very different ways of life. At the same time, we have a culture of our own as we'moon, sharing a common mother root. We are glad when we'moon from many different cultures contribute art and writing. When material is borrowed from cultures other than your own, we ask that it be acknowledged and something given in return. Being conscious of our sources keeps us from engaging in the divisiveness of either *cultural appropriation* (taking what belongs to others) or *cultural fascism* (controlling creative expression). We invite every we'moon to share how the "Mother Tongue" speaks to her, with respect for both cultural integrity and individual freedom.

We'moon look into the mirror of the sky to discover patterns regarding how we move here on earth. Like all native and natural earth-loving people since ancient times, we naturally assume a connection with a larger whole of which we are a part.

We show the natural cycles of the moon, sun, planets, and stars as they relate to earth. By recording our own activities side by side with those of other heavenly bodies, we may notice what connection, if any, there is for us.

Gaia Rhythms: The earth revolves around her axis in one day; the moon orbits around the earth in one month ($29^1/_5$ days); the earth orbits around the sun in one year. We experience each of these cycles in the alternating rhythms of day and night, waxing and waning, summer and winter. The earth/moon/sun are our inner circle of kin in the universe. We know where we are in relation to them at all times by the dance of lights and shadows as they circle around one another.

The Eyes of Heaven: As seen from earth, the moon and the sun are equal in size: "the left and right eye of heaven," according to Hindu (Eastern) astrology. Unlike the solar-dominated calendars of Christian (Western) patriarchy, the **We'Moon** looks at our experience through both eyes at once, with stars for our third eye. The **lunar eye** of heaven is seen each day in the phases of the moon as she is both reflector and shadow, traveling her 28-day path through all of the zodiac. The **solar eye** of heaven is apparent at the turning points in the sun's cycle. The year begins with the nearest new moon to Winter Solstice (in the Northern Hemisphere), the dark renewal time, and journeys through many seasons and balance points (solstices, equinoxes, and the cross-quarter days in between). The **third eye** of heaven may be seen in the stars. Astrology measures the cycles by relating the sun, moon, and all other planets in our universe through the *star signs,* helping us to tell time in the larger cycles of the universe.

Measuring Time and Space: Imagine a clock with many hands. The earth is the center from which we view our universe. The sun, moon, and planets are like the hands of the clock. Each one has its own rate of movement through the cycle. The ecliptic, a band of sky around earth within which all planets have their orbits, is the outer band of the clock where the numbers are. Stars along the ecliptic are grouped into constellations forming the signs of the zodiac—the twelve star signs are like the twelve numbers of the clock. They mark the movements of the planets through the 360° circle of the sky, the clock of time and space.

Whole Earth Perspective: It is important to note that all natural cycles have a mirror image from a whole earth perspective. The seasons (summer/winter, spring/fall) are always opposite in the Northern and Southern Hemispheres. Day and night are at opposite times on opposite sides of the earth, east to west. Also, each hemisphere sees a different side of the moon, hence waxing crescent moon in Australia faces right (e.g., ☽). The **We'Moon** calendar, produced in the northwestern United States, has a Northern Hemisphere perspective regarding times and seasons.

Whole Sky Perspective: It is also important to note that all over the earth, in varied cultures and times, the dome of the sky has been interacted with in countless ways. *The* zodiac we speak of is one of the many ways that hu-moons have pictured, counted, and related to the stars. In this calendar, we are using the tropical zodiac.   ✷ *Musawa*

© *Lin Karmon 1994*

Introduction to the Theme:
Earth Matters

Earth Matters, as a calendar theme, is many-fold. It is about being alive on this beautiful planet, this writhing green and blue ball of wonder! It is a celebration of our Mother Earth: creator, healer, teacher, provider, lover. It is a song calling forth planetary healing. It is an acknowledgement of earth's power and wisdom beyond any we could even understand. As hu-moonkind has become fragmented, separated from both earth and spirit, more interested in power and materialism, we are called to awareness. As the trees rapidly become toothpicks and toilet paper, as the wild spaces dwindle and the pavement expands, we are called to recognize the damage we have done. At the same time, as we acknowledge the wonders of every moment, we are called to heal and be healed.

Earth Matter. Earth Mater. Earth Mother. Like a mother who gives birth, the earth has the power to bring spirit into form—to *mater-realize*. The material level is not separate from the spiritual level. Matter is spirit embodied. Earth and spirit matters are intertwined. Earth is a living, self-regulating, self-healing organism, a sentient being. The Gaia hypothesis which affirms this principle is named after the ancient Greek goddess of earth. Earth science is finally beginning to "discover" what earth-loving peoples have always known: the earth is alive. The art and writing in each moon month in **We'Moon '96** reflect we'moon experiences of different aspects of the Mother, as in **Creator/Destroyer Moon**, **Darkness/Magic Moon**, **Earth Body Moon**, **Weather/ing Moon**, and **Sexy Mama Moon**. See Table of Contents for complete listing of moon themes.

Every being, every particle on and in and around this planet is intricately connected. We are all literally flesh of the same flesh. We breathe air that moves in our blood, eat food from the earth that then becomes soil. Rocks turn to pebbles to sand and to soil that grows plants that drink the sun, purify the air, and feed us. The water goes from sky to land to ocean, through deer and birds and fish. We are one being, eating our ancestors from our gardens. Earth-based spiritualities recognize this interconnection, valuing *all* entities as holy, equal, and intrinsic. What happens to her, happens to us. Loving her, we love ourselves;

hurting her, we hurt ourselves. Moon themes reflect this interconnection, in **Listening/Understanding Moon**, **Provider Moon**, and **Interconnectedness Moon**.

© S. J. Hugdahl 1994

Otter's Painting

Patriarchy inherently opposes this interconnection, dividing one from another on every level of existence—creating a world of people fragmented inside themselves, divided against each other, and alienated from the earth and all other beings. "Forgetting" our oneness has made it possible for us to pollute the ground, the rivers, the sky; forgetting it is all alive, forgetting it is us. When her wholeness is endangered, all who are part of her are endangered. Technology is an attempt to imitate her intelligence—in bits and pieces. In the hands of patriarchal culture, technology becomes a tool of destruction. You cannot take a living organism apart and hope to keep it alive, no matter how hard you try to put the pieces back together again. Her wisdom is in her wholeness—and it must be honored in order for the web of life to be mended. Only then can the balance be restored that Gaia maintains naturally. To heal the earth, we must heal ourselves and our fragmented relationships with her back into wholeness. If we do not, the earth changes she undertakes to heal herself may be even more cataclysmic.

Countless essential movements are striving to recover the balance, such as the struggles for indigenous peoples' lands and cultural rights, for the environment, as well as the work to attain peace, justice, and equality for all beings. It is *all* the same struggle. Womyn's groups have been a backbone of these movements. An example of the power inherent in womyn standing together is the Chipko movement of womyn "tree-huggers" in India. Many trees were saved by Indian womyn and children performing nonviolent civil disobedience, risking their lives in front of the lumber companies' instruments of destruction. There are examples around the world of indigenous peoples rising up to reclaim their lands and cultures, such as the Shoshone Nation organizing around the Nevada Nuclear Test Site and the Hawaiian Sovereignty Movement. Womyn's peace camps sit on the edges of military areas. There are environmental groups such as Earth First!, Nature Conservancy, and Sierra Club that use a wide variety of tactics on behalf of the earth. **Earth Action Moon** and **Earth Tending Moon** reflect some of the ways we'moon are mending the web.

Ecofeminism and womyn's spirituality are important contributions to this restoration, connecting womyn and the earth as entities bound up with each other. Womyn and the earth are intimately connected and suffer parallel exploitations under patriarchy. In Western/Christian worldviews, and others as well, womyn, earth, and people of color are "low" and "dark"; bodies, sensuality, and physical existence are inherently "evil." Heaven is "up above," far away from earth, not of this life; and all good is seen as coming from "the light." Ecofeminism brings a feminist perspective to the causes of and approaches to healing the environmental crisis. Deep ecology brings a consciousness of the sanctity of the natural world. Womyn's spirituality renews our ancient connection with the living goddess in ourselves, each other, the earth, and all beings. We'moon are gathering in circles and/or working alone to heal the patriarchal splits through a vision of wholeness, providing inspiration, support, and creative forms for magic and spiritual activism.

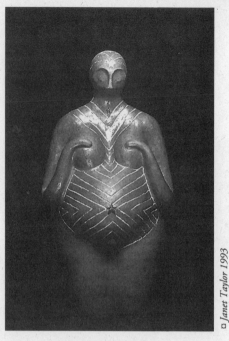

□ *Janet Taylor 1993*

Earth Mother of Mine

Moons such as **Mundane Moon**, **Earth Art Moon**, and **Shelter Moon** have to do with the sacred ways womyn are living and expressing themselves day to day, and with the overlooked sources of inspiration within the physical plane. Many of these sources are rarely noticed, or are considered to be unimportant, while in reality they are blessed miracles that keep us not only alive, but filled with holiness. How incredible that we walk, pulled down by gravity to the center of the earth! Every entity we come in contact with is an aspect of the living goddess, a wild mystery, unique unto itself. We can re-infuse all we do with spirit and all we witness with wonder. May we tend our visions with care, enjoy and share the fruits of our labor, replenish and be replenished by the sustainable garden of earth.

The **We'Moon** is yet another thread that connects us to each other. Thank you to Mother Gaia for birthing us out of the ocean, the ground, out of the fruitful darkness. Thank you for taking us into you when we are ready, folding us back into your bosom. This **We'Moon** is in your honor. Blessed be.

□ *Pandora and Musawa*

Earth Matter/Earth Body

In Hawaiian, the word *aina* means both "earth" and "body." To approach the Great Mother, we'moon go down deep, and do not seek to detach from earth, to transcend or rise above her. We do not look down on earth; we go inside to find the spirit who lives within. Earth is alive. She dances under our feet—not only does she spin and orbit through space, but she also churns and transforms underground. Earth matter is the most solid, densest form of energy; yet the earth flows and grows, as earth-air-fire-water constantly transform one element into another.

Two-thirds of the earth's crust is ocean floor, averaging 3-4 miles in thickness. The continental crust is thicker, averaging 18 miles (40-50 miles under the mountains) with deep taproots descending like the keel of a boat, as continents float in the rocky sea of the earth's mantle. Below the crust is a thin, rigid layer of twelve tectonic plates (similar to our skull bones) that slide over and under each other.

The mantle of the earth, extending 1,800 miles below the crust, is an ocean of rocky material slowly churning as in a giant cauldron, causing the tectonic plates welded to its upper rigid layer to move slowly. Heat rises from the molten center, lifting rocks that cool and harden as they near the surface and then sink back down. This thermodynamic action powers the massive movements within the earth. Huge swirls of rocky earth matter slowly circle out from the center of the earth causing the shifts in tectonic plates that produce earthquakes and volcanoes.

The mantle gets progressively hotter and more liquid the deeper we go until we reach a molten ring of liquid fire surrounding what is currently believed to be an iron-hard core in the center—the super dense center of gravity. What is inside the innermost core of earth is unknown; the tracking system fails at this point. Seismic waves passing through the layers of earth (from earthquakes or underground nuclear testing) momentarily shake rocks apart which then snap back into place, affecting the trajectory of the waves in measurable ways. Once the waves reach the pure molten rock layer around the hard core, they cannot penetrate further. What is hidden inside her core is a well-guarded secret: one of the earth's deepest mysteries. *Aloha aina: Love the earth, love the body.*

◻ *Musawa*

HOW TO USE THIS BOOK: KEY TO THE *WE'MOON*

Below and on the following two pages you will find terms and symbols, with explanations keyed to their uses in the **We'Moon**.

Astrology Basics

Planets: Planets are like chakras in our solar system, allowing for different frequencies or types of energies to be expressed.

Signs: The twelve signs of the zodiac are a mandala in the sky, marking off 30° segments in the 360° circle around the earth. Signs show major shifts in planetary energy through the cycles.

Glyphs: Glyphs are the symbols that represent planets and signs.

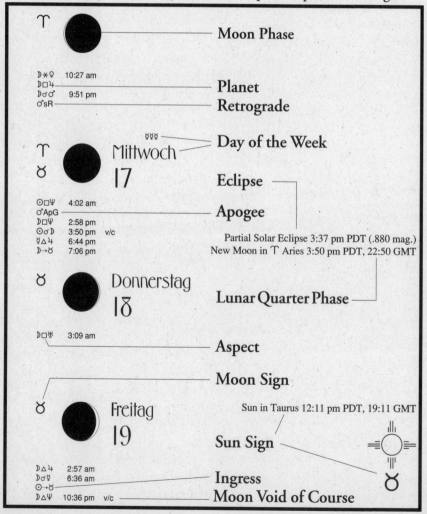

♈ — **Moon Phase**

☽⚹♀ 10:27 am
☽□♃
☽♂♂ 9:51 pm — **Planet**
♂sR — **Retrograde**

♈ — ☿☿☿ — **Day of the Week**
♉ Mittwoch
17 — **Eclipse**

⊙□♆ 4:02 am
♂ApG — **Apogee**
☽□♆ 2:58 pm
⊙♂☽ 3:50 pm v/c
☿△♃ 6:44 pm
☽→♉ 7:06 pm

Partial Solar Eclipse 3:37 pm PDT (.880 mag.)
New Moon in ♈ Aries 3:50 pm PDT, 22:50 GMT

♉ Donnerstag
18 — **Lunar Quarter Phase**

☽□♅ 3:09 am — **Aspect**

— **Moon Sign**

♉ Freitag
19

Sun in Taurus 12:11 pm PDT, 19:11 GMT

Sun Sign

☽△♃ 2:57 am
☽♂♅ 6:36 am
⊙→♉ — **Ingress**
☽△♆ 10:36 pm v/c — **Moon Void of Course**

♉

Features of the Calendar Pages

Sun Sign: The sun enters a new sign once a month (around the 20th or so), completing the whole cycle of the zodiac in one year. For a description see "Sun Signs" (pp. 18–21).

Moon Sign: The moon changes signs approximately every $2^1/_2$ days, going through all twelve signs of the zodiac every $29^1/_5$ days (the sidereal month). The moon sign reflects qualities of your core inner self. For descriptions of these energies see "Moon Signs: Transits" (pp. 22–24).

Moon Phase: Each calendar day is marked with a graphic representation of the phase that the moon is in. Although the moon is not actually visible in the sky during the new or dark moon, we take some artistic license with her representation. For the days before and after the *actual* new moon, we use miniscule crescent moon graphics. For more information about the moon see "The Eight Lunar Phases" and "Where's That Moon?" (pp. 25–27).

Lunar Quarter Phase: At the four quarter points of the lunar cycle (when the moon is new, waxing half, full, and waning half) we indicate the phase, sign, and exact time for each.

Day of the Week: Each day is associated with a planet whose symbol appears in the line above it (e.g., DDD is for Moon: Moonday, Monday, Luna Day, lundi, lunes). Each week the names of the days of the week are in one of four languages (English, German, French, Spanish). You will find Monday through Friday on the left-facing page, Saturday and Sunday on the right-facing page.

Eclipse: The time of greatest eclipse is given, which in general is not the exact time of the conjunction or opposition. For lunar and partial solar eclipses, the magnitude is given, in decimal form (e.g., .881 mag.), which denotes the fraction of the moon's diameter obscured by the shadow of the earth. For total and annular solar eclipses, the duration of the eclipse, in minutes and seconds, is given. For a more detailed explanation see "Eclipses 1996" (p. 201).

Daily Aspectarian

For each calendar day there is a listing of symbols that indicates a variety of planetary movements and relationships. Following are explanations of the various symbols found there.

Aspects: The little squiggles that show the angle of relation between different planets are aspects. An aspect is like an astrological weather forecast for the day, indicating which energies are working together easily and which combinations are more challenging. See "Aspects" (p. 17) for a brief explanation.

Ingresses: Arrows, in between planetary and sign glyphs, indicate planets moving into new signs.

☽ v/c—**Moon Void of Course:** The time just before the moon changes into a new sign is a good time to ground and center yourself, otherwise it can be a bit disorienting. The moon is said to be void of course from the last significant lunar aspect until the moon enters a new sign.

ApG—Apogee: This is the point in the orbit of a planet or the moon that is farthest from earth. The effects of transits at this time may be less noticeable immediately, but may appear later on. A good time to plant root crops.

PrG—Perigee: This is the point in the orbit of a planet or the moon that is nearest to earth. Transits with the moon or other planets when they are at perigee will be more intense. A good time to plant above-ground crops.

sR or sD—Retrograde or Direct: These are times when a planet moves backward (**sR**) or forward (**sD**) through the signs of the zodiac (an optical illusion, as when a moving train passes a slower train which appears to be going backward). When a planet is in direct motion, planetary energies are more straightforward; in retrograde, planetary energies turn back in on themselves, are more involuted.

Other Useful Features of the We'Moon

Annual Predictions: For an astrological portrait of this year for you, you might want to turn to Gretchen Lawlor's prediction for your sun sign, even before the year begins. These are located in the calendar pages around the month of your birthday, on the same page where the sun enters a new sign (see p. 30 for an introduction).

Time Zones: All aspects are in Pacific Standard/Daylight Time. To calculate for your area, see "World Time Zones" (p. 31).

Ephemerides are tables that show the exact position of heavenly bodies in degrees, using tabulations of latitude and longitude.

Planetary Ephemeris: Exact planetary positions, for every day, are given in the Ephemeris (pp. 204–209), showing where each planet is in the zodiac at noon GMT (Greenwich Mean Time).

Asteroid Ephemeris: Exact asteroid positions for every ten days are given (p. 203), showing where sixteen asteroids are in the zodiac at midnight GMT.

◻ *Musawa and Beth Freewomon*

PLANETS

Personal Planets are the ones closest to Earth.

    Mercury ☿: communication, conscious thought, inventiveness

    Venus ♀: relationship, love, sense of beauty and sensuality, empathy

    Mars ♂: will to act, initiative, ambition

Asteroids are found between Mars and Jupiter. They bridge the personal and the social planets. They reflect the rebirth of the goddess, and the awakening of feminine-defined energy centers in the human consciousness. See "Why Asteroids?" (p.202).

Social Planets are in between the personal planets and the outer planets.

    Jupiter ♃: expansion, opportunities, leadership

    Saturn ♄: limits, structure, discipline

Chiron ⚷ is situated between Saturn and Uranus and bridges the social and transpersonal planets. Chiron represents the wounded healer, the core wound that leads us to our path of service.

Transpersonal Planets are the outer planets. They are slow moving and influence generational issues.

    Uranus ♅: revolutionary change, cosmic consciousness

    Neptune ♆: spiritual awakening, cosmic love, all one

    Pluto ♇: death and rebirth, purification, takes us to the depths where total change is possible

* In the matriarchal zodiac, the planets are named after goddesses.

© *Blue Moonfire 1985, excerpted from* Matriarchal Zodiac

GODDESSES*

Metis: counsel, wisdom
Aphrodite: grace and love
Dione: sexuality, growth, struggle

Themis: time, justice, prophecy
Rhea: natural order and peace

Urania: heaven and earth
Tethys: the seas
Persephone: death in life, life in death

ASPECTS

Aspects show the angle between planets in the 360° circle of the sky. This relationship informs how the planets, and the signs they are in, influence each other. The **We'Moon** lists only the significant aspects:

♂ CONJUNCTION (planets are 0–5° apart)
    linked together, energy of aspected planets is mutually enhancing

✶ SEXTILE (planets are 60° apart)
    cooperative, energies of this aspect blend well

□ SQUARE (planets are 90° apart)
    challenging, energies of this aspect are different from each other

△ TRINE (planets are 120° apart)
    harmonizing, energies of this aspect are in the same element

☍ OPPOSITION (planets are 180° apart)
    polarizing or complementing, energies are diametrically opposite

⚼ QUINCUNX (planets are 150° apart)
    variable, energies of this aspect combine contrary elements

Sun Signs

There are twelve signs in the zodiac, marking off 30° segments in the 360° circle of the sky. As seen from earth, the sun travels through one sign every month, coming full circle around the zodiac in a year. What sign the sun was in when you were born is your *sun sign*. The zodiac starts at Spring Equinox when the sun moves into the sign of Aries.

© Mara Friedman 1994
Messenger

There are different *elements* associated with each sign (*air*—mind, *fire*—spirit, *water*—feelings, *earth*—body) and each element is in a different *modality* (*cardinal*—initiating, *fixed*—sustaining, *mutable*—transforming). These qualities are italicized at the beginning of each sun sign description.

□ *Musawa*

♈ ARIES (March 20–April 19). A *cardinal fire* sign ruled by Mars. Aries we'moon love adventure and believe that they are destined to achieve success and make a huge impact on the world. They are passionate, direct, and ruled by their hearts. They are extremely independent and require an environment that allows them to express their creativity and nurture their personal growth. But they must not allow their idealism or enthusiasm to turn into indolent daydreams. In Chinese astrology, Aries the Ram correlates to the magnificent Dragon.

♉ TAURUS (April 19–May 20). A *fixed earth* sign ruled by Venus. Taurus we'moon are creative and talented, sensitive, humorous, and caring. They love making friends and creating networks and contacts.

18

They are determined and often strive for things they desire, regardless of circumstances. Yet they have patience. Their clothing reflects their artistry and fine tastes. They can be frugal if necessary, but prefer the luxuries of the materially rich life if they can afford them. They must avoid being too stubborn or narrow-minded. In Chinese astrology, Taurus the Bull correlates to the wise Snake.

♊ GEMINI (May 20–June 20). A *mutable air* sign ruled by Mercury. Gemini we'moon possess a sunny disposition, are bright, open, and cheerful. They are full of charm and alert in action, and dislike hidden agendas. They find people and crowds exciting for they love parties and are not loners. Because of their carefree nature, they need ample room for self-expression. Gemini we'moon like to tell you what is on their minds. Care must be taken to not let their quick opinions alienate others. In Chinese astrology, Gemini the Twins correlates to the popular, fun-loving Horse.

♋ CANCER (June 20–July 22). A *cardinal water* sign ruled by the Moon. Cancer we'moon have a gentle, patient, and graceful nature. They are artistic and creative, and have exquisite taste, especially in decorating their home. With a tendency to be introverted, Cancer we'moon resolve problems by contemplating in seclusion. They need solitary peaceful moments to replenish their souls. They make decisions based on their accumulated experiences as well as their highly developed intuition. A negative trait could be overindulgence or overspending on luxuries. In Chinese astrology, Cancer the Crab correlates to the kind, artistic Sheep (Ram, Goat).

♌ LEO (July 22–August 22). A *fixed fire* sign ruled by the Sun. Leo we'moon are quick-witted, alert, romantic, playful, and extremely talented. In addition to being mentally active, they are full of physical stamina. They are uninhibited and express themselves fearlessly in all areas of life. They are generous and sensitive, and love to help others. They win trust easily and have strong leadership potential. But problems could develop from their being too self-centered and forgetting the big picture. In Chinese astrology, Leo the Lioness correlates to the ingenious, brilliant Monkey.

♍ **VIRGO** (August 22–September 22). A *mutable earth* sign ruled by Mercury. Virgo we'moon possess a sense of duty and pride. They are equipped with keen judgment and sharp wit, and are good planners. They can predict the outcome of any situation and act accordingly. They are quick and flexible, and if thrown into a situation at a moment's notice come out winners. They are perfectionists who care what others think of them. They desire praise for doing a great job. Care must be taken because their criticizing tendencies may drive away others, especially their partner. In Chinese astrology, Virgo the Virgin correlates to the impeccable Rooster.

♎ **LIBRA** (September 22–October 22). A *cardinal air* sign ruled by Venus. Libra we'moon are honest and trustworthy, and make excellent friends because they are always on your side. They won't hesitate to make sacrifices for people and ideas they believe in. When they fall in love, they fall hard. They are dedicated to their partners and therefore are selective in the beginning stages of dating. Once they find the right person, they are ready to devote themselves to them. Care must be taken to remain balanced and not go to extremes. In Chinese astrology, Libra the Scales correlates to the loyal Dog.

♏ **SCORPIO** (October 22–November 21). A *fixed water* sign ruled by Pluto and Mars. Scorpio we'moon make great friends and hurry to the aid of people they love. They have a strong sense of responsibility, and once their mind is set on something they don't easily change their direction. They are devoted to their chosen paths and careers. They don't like to be alone and will actively look for their "other half." Psychic and intuitive, they are attracted to the shamanic and otherworldly. Care must be taken to not become too intense in interactions with others. In Chinese astrology, Scorpio the Scorpion correlates to the sensual Pig (Boar).

♐ **SAGITTARIUS** (November 21–December 21). A *mutable fire* sign ruled by Jupiter. Sagittarius we'moon are clever, sharp, athletic, and humorous. They are observant and quick to take action. They are popular in social circles for they adapt easily to different environments, and their quick wit and broad smiles win admiration wherever they go. They trust their instincts over logic and reality. They are free souls who love adventure and travel. Being in nature is healing for them. Care must be taken to not become scattered or irresponsible. In Chinese astrology, Sagittarius the Archer correlates to the clever Rat.

♑ CAPRICORN (December 21–January 20). A *cardinal earth* sign ruled by Saturn. Capricorn we'moon are hardworking, methodical, independent, and ethical. They are noted for their perseverance in attaining their goals and in their ability to get the job done. They are self-reliant, and believe deeply in what they are doing. They achieve success step by step. They believe that as long as they apply themselves and perform, they will be recognized and rewarded. They must watch out to not become bitter or frustrated, for their temperament either enhances or hinders the success of their endeavors. In Chinese astrology, Capricorn the Sea Goat correlates to the patient, diligent Ox.

♒ AQUARIUS (January 20–February 19). A *fixed air* sign ruled by Uranus. Aquarius we'moon are courageous, sensitive, determined, and charismatic. They aim high and pursue their goals with passion. They stand out in a crowd because they are freethinkers and do not conform to the actions of the masses. Once they make a promise or declaration, count on them to pursue their goal with vigor and speed. They must take care that their loner attitude does not prevent them from seeking assistance when they are faced with an endeavor that requires the resources of another. In Chinese astrology, Aquarius the Water Bearer correlates to the daring, impulsive Tiger.

♓ PISCES (February 19–March 20). A *mutable water* sign ruled by Neptune. Pisces we'moon are intuitive, romantic, friendly, and adaptable. They long for companionship and dislike being alone, so they make every effort to conform. Their kindness and diplomacy make them welcome in social circles. They appreciate and strive to create peaceful and harmonious work and social environments. Because they love peace and beauty and dislike making enemies, they go out of their way to avoid arguments and conflicts. They are extremely intuitive and can sense danger, and will take quick action to protect themselves. Care must be taken that their fear of conflict does not make them weak or indecisive. In Chinese astrology, Pisces the Fishes correlates to the gentle, diplomatic Rabbit (Cat).

© Susan Levitt 1995

Moon Signs: Transits

Every two and a half days the moon shines her light through one of the twelve signs. This monthly cycle of the moon through the signs is reflected in subtle shifts in our feelings, moods, responses, and expression. When we attune our activities with the lunar flow, we become a channel for the wisdoms of the natural world. Approach each moon cycle as a journey and a teaching.

When the moon is in the same sign as our natal moon sign, we can look within more clearly, center in with our intuitive self, and reconnect with our primary mode of emotionality. Follow the moon around your birth chart, and try to cooperate with and utilize the energies offered with each sign.

During the year, each sign occurs only once as the dark/new moon, and only once as the full moon (except for the periodic doubling of signs); e.g., there is just one full moon in Leo, usually in February when the sun is in the opposite sign of Aquarius, and one dark/new moon in Leo during August when the sun is also in Leo. Expression of a sign is stronger at these times, so watch and celebrate. (Moon sign gardening tips are also included here.)

♈ MOON IN ARIES—This initiating fire sign awakens our creative urges. Our physical energy increases, and restlessness fuels our explorations. We may be quicker to express feelings, attitudes, and desires. Try new approaches, and discover new outlets. Spirit is moving, so channel moon in Aries with your vital willingness to be and to do. (Watch the sun's path over your garden spot, sense the fairies, clear brush and weeds, pioneer your plot.)

♉ MOON IN TAURUS—Earthy, appreciative Taurus concentrates our energies on the physical plane. This is a good moontime to beautify surroundings and acquire belongings. Our senses are keen, and our intuitive touch can inspire works of art, massage, or lovemaking. We find extra patience to stand our ground. Tend to body needs and pleasures. (Good planting time; cultivate your garden soil, dig mounds, set intentions, feed roots.)

♊ **MOON IN GEMINI**—Plan on play during airy, communicative Gemini. Watch verbal possibilities for witty exchanges! This is a good time to put energy into friendships, to attend meetings, or study some interest by yourself. Let your curiosity keep you on the move and in the moment. (Study companion planting, make plans for setting out the garden, exchange stories with neighbors, talk to your plants.)

♋ **MOON IN CANCER**—Our sensitivity rises to the surface during this watery moon of the Great Mother. Cancerian love for inclusiveness and nurturance feeds our inclinations toward home affairs, family needs, and solitude with ourselves. Tend to emotional needs and healing spaces. Use long baths or walks to center yourself. Cook and share good food. (Mother the garden, plant seeds or seedlings freely, plant trees and vines, fertilize, and water deeply.)

♌ **MOON IN LEO**—A generous warmth and vitality comes more easily during this fiery sign of the proud heart. Use Leo's energetic and extroverted energy to inspire self-confidence. Let any dramatic outbursts entertain and feed your creative appetite. Leo generates feelings of being special. Bring home treats for your inner child. (Fuss over plants, harvest, clip blooms for bouquets, show off the big ones, clear overgrowth.)

♍ **MOON IN VIRGO**—Process-oriented and earthy Virgo gets us motivated in the material world. Virgo favors focused intent and self-improvement, so direct your agenda accordingly. Use your critical eye, or someone else will. While cleaning up your act, assess and shore up projects. Tend to health and dietary needs, and address the stress factors in your life. (Clean up the garden, fertilize plants, outwit pests, weed out weaker growth, harvest the best.)

♎ **MOON IN LIBRA**—Venus-ruled, airy Libra is a mentor of the arts. Beauty, harmony, cooperation, and poetic flow are her gifts. It's a good social-gathering time when the moon entertains Libra. Both friendly attractions and love connections can be delightful. Balance bonds within yourself and significant others in your life. (Plant flowers, trim plants, clip blooms and make artful arrangements, tend houseplants.)

♏ **MOON IN SCORPIO**—We are intuitive and intense when this fixed water sign surfaces each month. This is a good time for dowsing out the mysteries, using divination and ritual. There is a tendency toward self-absorption; taking private space assists our deep reflection. Intimacies may lead to personal disclosures. Our masks come on or off as passions well up. (Fertile planting time; water deeply, transplant, compost, feed, and prune.)

♐ **MOON IN SAGITTARIUS**—Fiery Sagittarius inspires our independence, free expression, and gregariousness. Teaching, preaching, and promotional activities come easier during this extroverted sign. Time to move our bodies, so enjoy dance, sports, and travel. With our philosophical, high-minded aspirations, leaps of faith come easily! Keep a sense of humor. (Weed, till, make clearings, plan and do chores, harvest to dry, cut firewood.)

♑ **MOON IN CAPRICORN**—We can ground our intentions with right action in the material world during earthy Capricorn. Let your strength of will and commitment to purpose rise up to meet the occasion. While feelings may be guarded now, channel your ambitions with effort and diligence toward duty. When in doubt, assume importance. Seriously. (Plant, especially roots and bulbs, take cuttings, cultivate, dig weeds, harvest, clean up.)

♒ **MOON IN AQUARIUS**—Airy Aquarius catalyzes intellectual pursuits and the exchange of ideas. This is a good time for networking with friends, or for community activism. Leave room for impulsiveness. Expect some unique outpourings during this unconventional and offbeat sign. Create with the insightful, visionary qualities of Aquarius. Spread the word. (Plan ahead, clip and prune, weed, rid pests, cultivate new territory.)

♓ **MOON IN PISCES**—Our feelings and sensitivities flow during this changeable water sign. When not seeking solitude, we may feel the urge to merge into heart and spirit space. Our moods may be influenced by unconscious motivations or old hurts that surface now. Trust your tears. Channel the intuitive, imaginative energy of Pisces. Let the impressionable poet express herself. (Plant to your heart's content, water deeply, compost, meditate, play with fairies, make an altar in nature.)

© *Sandra Pastorius 1995*

Lunar Rhythm

Everything that flows moves in rhythm with the moon. She rules the water element on earth. She pulls on the ocean's tides, the weather, female reproductive cycles, the life fluids in plants, animals, and people. She influences the underground currents in earth energy, the mood swings of mind, body, behavior, and emotion. The moon is closer to the earth than any other heavenly body. The earth actually has two primary relationships in the universe: one with the moon who circles around her and one with the sun whom she circles around. Both are equal in her eyes. The phases of the moon reflect the dance of all three: the moon, the sun, and the earth, who together weave the web of light and dark into our lives. No wonder so much of our life on earth is intimately connected with the phases of the moon!

◻ *Musawa*

The Eight Lunar Phases

As above, so below. Look into the sky and observe which phase the moon is in. Then you will know where you are in the growth cycle of each lunar month. The phase that the moon was in when you were born reflects your purpose, personality, and preferences.

1. The **new moon** is like a SEED planted in the earth. We cannot see her but she is ready to grow, full of potential and energy for her new journey. We'moon born during the new moon are impulsive, passionate, and intuitive. They are risk takers and pioneers.

2. The **crescent moon** is the SPROUT. The seed has broken through the earth and reaches upward as she ventures from the dark, moist earth she has known. We'moon born during the crescent moon must break from the past, from the culture of their childhood, to create their own destiny. They represent the next generation, the new order that improves on the past.

3. The **first quarter moon** (waxing half moon) is the GROWTH phase. Roots go deeper, the stem shoots up, and leaves form as she creates a new strong body. We'moon born during the first quarter moon live a full life of much activity and excitement as old structures are cleared away to provide room for new developments.

4. The **gibbous moon** is the BUD of the plant, the pulse of life tightly wrapped, wanting to expand. For we'moon born during the gibbous moon, their talents lie in the ability to refine, organize, and purify.

They are seekers, utilizing spiritual tools as guides and allies on their journey to self-discovery.

5. She opens and blossoms during the **full moon** into the FLOWER, with the desire to share her beauty with others. We'moon born during the full moon enjoy companionship and partnership and have a desire to merge deeply. Fulfillment, abundance, and illumination are their goals.

6. As we go into the darkening phase of the **disseminating moon,** we get the FRUIT of the plant's life cycle, the fruits of wisdom and experience. For we'moon born during the disseminating moon, life must have meaning and purpose. They enjoy sharing their beliefs and ideas with others and are often teachers.

7. The **last quarter moon** (waning half moon) is the HARVEST phase, when the plant gives her life so that others may continue theirs. We'moon born during the last quarter have a powerful internal life of reflection and transformation. They can assume different roles and wear many masks while balancing their internal and external worlds.

8. The **balsamic moon** is the COMPOST phase, when the nutrients remain in the soil, providing nourishment for the next new seed. We'moon born during the balsamic moon possess the potential to be wise, insightful, understanding, and patient. They are prophetic and unique, and march to the beat of their own drummer.

© *Susan Levitt 1995*

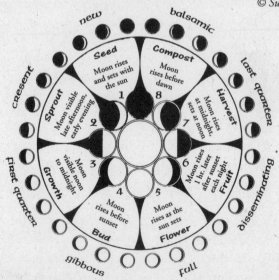

WHERE'S THAT MOON ?

Why is the moon sometimes visible during the day? And why does the moon sometimes rise very late at night? The answers lie in what phase the moon is in, which reflects the angle between the sun and moon as seen from earth. For each of the eight moon phases, the angle between the sun and moon progresses in 45° increments. Each phase lasts approximately 3–4 days of the moon's entire 29^1/$_5$ day cycle.

The **new moon** (or dark moon) rises at sunrise and sets at sunset. Astrologically, the sun and the moon are in *conjunction*. Because the sun's light overpowers the nearby moon in the day, and the moon is on the other side of the earth with the sun at night, she is not visible in the sky at all.

The **crescent moon** (or waxing crescent moon) rises midmorning and sets after sunset. She is the first visible sliver of moon, seen in the western sky in the late afternoon and early evening.

The **first quarter moon** (or waxing half moon) rises around noon and sets around midnight. Astrologically, the moon is *square* to the sun. She is visible from afternoon, when she is high in the eastern sky, until she sets in the west.

The **gibbous moon** rises midafternoon and sets before dawn. She is the bulging moon getting ready to be full, visible soon after she rises until she sets.

The **full moon** rises at sunset and sets at sunrise. Astrologically, the sun and moon are in *opposition* (ie., opposite each other in the sky and in opposite signs of the zodiac). She is visible all night long, from moonrise to moonset.

The **disseminating moon** is the waning full moon getting visibly smaller. She rises midevening and sets midmorning. She is visible from the time she rises almost until she sets.

The **last quarter moon** (or waning half moon) rises around midnight and sets around noon. Astrologically, the moon is *square* to the sun. She is visible from the time she rises until midmorning, when she is high in the western sky.

The **balsamic moon** (or waning crescent moon) rises before dawn and sets midafternoon. She is the last sliver of moon, seen in the eastern sky in the very early morning and late dawn.

THE SIXTY-YEAR WHEEL TURNS
Year of the Fire Rat:
February 19, 1996–February 6, 1997*

Western astrology, based on the four elements of fire, water, air, and earth, is derived from the cultures of ancient Egypt and the Mediterranean. Vedic astrology, based on the three elements of vata, pitta, and kapha, is derived from the cultures of ancient India. Chinese astrology, based on the five elements of fire, earth, metal, water, and wood, is derived from the ancient Chinese nature religion of Taoism.

The Chinese system has twelve signs, like Western astrology, but each sign, which is an animal, stands for a year, not just for a month. Each of the twelve Chinese animals experiences each of the five elements, making a sixty-year cycle. 1996 is the Fire Rat year, which is when this sixty-year cycle begins anew, so this once-in-a-lifetime event is definitely a time for new beginnings.

The Rat year is a time of plenty, bringing abundance and good fortune. Although there may be fluctuation in world economies, it is an excellent time to start a business, buy property, invest in long-term plans, or accumulate wealth. All ventures begun in the Rat year will prosper if well prepared, but it is not a time for foolish risks. (Save these for the Monkey year.) The Rat loves her pack, so the Rat year is also a time for socializing, entertaining, and enjoying ourselves.

© *Susan Levitt 1995*

*Chinese New Year begins the second new moon after Winter Solstice.

◻ *Mau Blossom 1993*

Moon Rat

THE WHEEL OF THE YEAR: HOLY DAYS

The seasonal cycle of the year is created by the tilt of the earth's axis as she leans towards the sun in the north or south at different points in her annual dance. *Solstices* are the extremes in the sun cycle (like new and full moon) when days and nights are either longest or shortest. At *equinoxes*, days and nights are equal (like the waxing or waning half moons). The four *cross-quarter days* roughly mark the

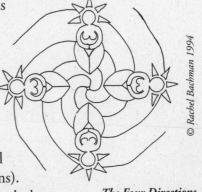

© *Rachel Bachman 1994*

The Four Directions

midpoints in between the solstices and equinoxes, giving eight seasonal "holy days" based on the natural cycles.

If you do not find your traditional holiday in the **We'Moon**, do not be upset. Just look for the nearest lunar or solar cycle turning point, and it is bound to be very close. At the root of all people's cultures—if you dig far enough—is a reverence for Mother Earth and a celebration of the natural cycles throughout the seasons of earth's passage in relation to her closest relatives in the universe. Only the names, dates, and specific events of the holidays have changed through the ages according to the prevailing culture. There are still some cultures today (such as Hindu, Jewish, Muslim, and Buddhist) that honor the lunar cycles by celebrating many holidays on new and full moons.

We use the fixed dates from the Gregorian calendar for the cross-quarter days, although traditionally they are lunar holidays. Beltane (May Day) and Lammas (Lugnasadh) are full moon festivals at which fertile, abundant, creative energy is celebrated. Samhain (Hallowmas) and Imbolc (Candlemas) are traditionally dark moon festivals, when death and rebirth, the crone, and the underworld journey are celebrated. The cross-quarter days are fire festivals celebrating the height of each season, when the subtle shifts in energy, initiated at the balance points of solstice and equinox, begin to be visible in nature. For example, the increasing amount of daylight that begins at Winter Solstice begins to be noticeable by Imbolc.

◻ *Musawa*

29

HOW TO USE THE 1996 PREDICTIONS

Sun sign predictions are surprisingly accurate. They seem to tap into the archetype of the sign, reflecting well the challenges and opportunities provided by the year's planetary movements. Some women also read the predictions for their rising sign. Consult your astrologer for more specific information and timing, as reflected by your own horoscope's transits and progressions.

This year I have added flower essence suggestions to each prediction. Flower essences are subtle liquid extracts, akin to homeopathic remedies, which heal on the emotional or soul level. They are truly mind-body remedies. I have been using them in my astrological work for years, to assist the healing opportunities in specific planetary configurations.*

Thank you for your continued enthusiastic response to my work. I love to play the sibyl for you.

¤ *Gretchen Lawlor 1995*

PLANETARY MOVEMENTS IN 1996

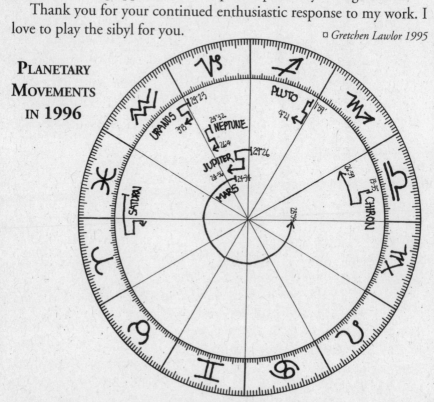

*I have referred only to the Bach Flower Remedies and the essences of the Flower Essence Society (FES) in California. There are many other excellent essences around, but these are the best documented and most widely available (both available from FES, P.O. Box 459, Nevada City, CA 95959).

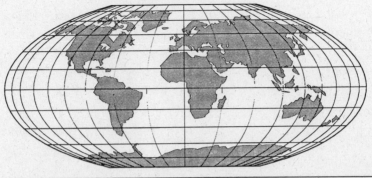

ID LW	NT BT	CA HT	YST	PST	MST	CST	EST	AST	BST	AT	WAT	GMT	CET	EET	BT	USSR Z3	USSR Z4	USSR Z5	SST	CCT	JST	GST	USSR Z10	ID LE
-12	-11	-10	-9	-8	-7	-6	-5	-4	-3	-2	-1	0	+1	+2	+3	+4	+5	+6	+7	+8	+9	+10	+11	+12
-4	-3	-2	-1	0	+1	+2	+3	+4	+5	+6	+7	+8	+9	+10	+11	+12	+13	+14	+15	+16	+17	+18	+19	+20

STANDARD TIME ZONES FROM WEST TO EAST CALCULATED FROM PST AS ZERO POINT:

IDLW:	International Date Line West	-4	BT:	Bagdhad Time	+11
NT/BT:	Nome Time/Bering Time	-3	IT:	Iran Time	+11 1/2
CA/HT:	Central Alaska & Hawaiian Time	-2	USSR	Zone 3	+12
YST:	Yukon Standard Time	-1	USSR	Zone 4	+13
PST:	Pacific Standard Time	0	IST:	Indian Standard Time	+13 1/2
MST:	Mountain Standard Time	+1	USSR	Zone 5	+14
CST:	Central Standard Time	+2	NST:	North Sumatra Time	+14 1/2
EST:	Eastern Standard Time	+3	SST:	South Sumatra Time & USSR Zone 6	+15
AST:	Atlantic Standard Time	+4	JT:	Java Time	+15 1/2
NFT:	Newfoundland Time	+4 1/2	CCT:	China Coast Time	+16
BST:	Brazil Standard Time	+5	MT:	Moluccas Time	+16 1/2
AT:	Azores Time	+6	JST:	Japanese Standard Time	+17
WAT:	West African Time	+7	SAST:	South Australian Standard Time	+17 1/2
GMT:	Greenwich Mean Time	+8	GST:	Guam Standard Time	+18
WET:	Western European Time (England)	+8	USSR	Zone 10	+19
CET:	Central European Time	+9	IDLE:	International Date Line East	+20
EET:	Eastern European Time	+10			

HOW TO CALCULATE TIME ZONE CORRECTIONS FOR YOUR AREA:

ADD if you are **east** of PST (Pacific Standard Time); **SUBTRACT** if you are **west** of PST on this map (see right-hand column of chart above).

.All times in this calendar are calculated from the West Coast of North America where it is made. Pacific Standard Time (PST Zone 8) is zero point for this calendar except during Daylight Savings Time (April 7–October 27, 1996, during which times are given for PDT Zone 7). If your time zone does not use Daylight Savings Time, add one hour to the standard correction during this time. Time corrections for GMT are also given for major turning points in the moon and sun cycles. At the bottom of each page EST/EDT (Eastern Standard or Daylight Time) and GMT (Greenwich Mean Time) times are also given. For all other time zones, calculate your time zone correction(s) from this map and write it on the inside cover for easy reference.

Sheela na Gig

◻ *Monica Sjöö 1978*

I. CREATOR/DESTROYER MOON

In the beginning, according to the Wise Woman tradition, everything began, as everything does, at birth. The Great Mother of All gave birth and the earth appeared out of the void. Then the Great Mother of All gave birth again, and again, and again, and people, and animals, and plants appeared on the earth. They were all very hungry. "What shall we eat?" they asked the Great Mother. "Now you eat me," she said, smiling. Soon there were a very great many lives, but the Great Mother of All was enjoying creating and giving birth so much that she didn't want to stop. "Ah," she said smiling, "now I eat you." and so she still does.

□ *Susun S. Weed 1989, modified and excerpted from* Healing Wise

© *Corvus Conjunctio 1991*

Kali

December

♏︎   **Monday**
18

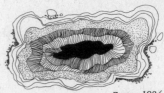

☐ *zana 1984*

☽✶☿   10:48 am
☉☌♃   1:44 pm
☽✶♂   5:08 pm

♏︎   **Tuesday**
♐︎   **19**

☽△♄   12:42 am
☽✶♆   9:52 am
☽✶♀   3:40 pm
☽✶♅   5:08 pm   v/c
☽→♐   7:14 pm
☽☌♇   9:43 pm

♐︎   **Wednesday**
20

☿☐♄   1:43 am
♀☌♅   9:50 am

♐︎   **Thursday**
♑︎   **21**

☽☐♄   1:09 am
♀→♒   10:24 am
☽☌♃   2:23 pm
☉☌☽   6:23 pm   v/c
☽→♑   6:47 pm

New Moon in ♐ Sagittarius 6:23 pm PST

2:23 GMT

♑︎   **Friday**
22

Solstice

♑︎

☉→♑   12:18 am
☽PrG   2:04 am
♀✶♇   6:16 pm
☽☌♅   9:33 pm
☽☌♂   9:57 pm

Sun in Capricorn 12:18 am PST, 8:18 GMT

All aspects in Pacific Standard Time; add 3 hours for EST; add 8 hours for GMT

The ancients knew that life and death are merely facets of the same creative power and process. Spirits of the dead are close to the waters of knowledge and the generative, fertilizing fires within the bowels of the earth; they can therefore give healing and prophetic powers. The ancestors were always thought to be accessible if invoked with the right rituals, to give help and advice.

Initiation is an active choice to enter into darkness, the deeper parts of one's being. In Greece, at the oracle cave, the seekers or initiates had to lower themselves into a cave through a hole similar to a birth canal and there they had to stay for three nights and days, after which they were helped out by therapeutes/helpers. If we avoid this experience of descent because of fear of our deeper selves, we block ourselves from powerful, transformative processes. This has been the shaman's way in all ages. Initiations always took place in caves, within mounds, in underground chambers like the Hopi kivas, reproducing the dark womb and involving death and rebirth experiences. The temple is a late development of the cave and is a symbol of the Goddess as house and shelter. The temple gate is the yoni or entrance into Her womb.

© *Monica Sjöö 1992, excerpted from* New Age and Armageddon: The Goddess or the Gurus? Towards a Feminist Vision of the Future

---

ᛉᛉᛉ

♑
♒

Saturday
23

☽⚹♄	12:19 am				
☿☌♂	5:42 am				
☽☌♆	8:59 am				
☽☌♅	4:09 pm	v/c	☽⚹♇	8:33 pm	
☽→♒	5:53 pm		☽☌♀	10:50 pm	

◎◎◎

♒

Sunday
24

☿⚹♄	2:56 am
♂⚹♄	11:50 pm

Mother Wolf Giving Birth to the Moon and Sun

□ *Webber 1994*

Winter Solstice/Yule

Winter Solstice marks the longest night of the year and the beginning of winter. The midwinter celebration has traditionally honored solar saviors and dying gods.

Among our earliest records of human spirituality are the animal cave paintings in France. Images of ice age hunting magic express the need in shamanic tribal religion to identify with and appease the spirits of animals killed for the survival of the tribe. Two thousand years ago many human societies had replaced hunting and gathering with farming and agriculture. At this time a new religion was born. The birth of Jesus in a stable where he lay in a manger and was surrounded by domestic farm animals and beasts of burden reflected a significant change in human relationships with the animal kingdom. The Christian mysteries have their root in shamanic hunting magic and culminate with high-tech televangelists ministering to the psychological needs and collective guilt of factory farm fed consumers.

Modern nature and goddess worship arise embracing feminism, animal liberation, and vegetarianism. The Earth Goddess reaches into our divided psyche to heal us and guide us back into the garden. Winter Solstice celebrates her rebirth and renewal.

□ *Peggy Sue McRae, reprinted and excerpted from* Earth First! Journal *(Yule 1994)*

Jane

Half-pint dragon
pug nostrils flaring
you blustered through your teens
fighting everything
except the one who left you pregnant.

We knew nothing of stone circles,
of girls turned to stone for dancing on Sundays.
Fearing the slow creep of granite in our mother's lips
that parried love with warnings against dead things
we danced naked in cornfields, wishing for wings, felt
their buds itch between our outstretched shoulders.

Before an ambulance could pass we sang
"Touch our knees, touch our toes, never go in one of those."
The chant "Touch collar, never have fever" charmed us
for drinking from the same mountain streams as dead sheep.
Exploring their gelid remains with sticks we read
the rainbow's shadow, the serpent spectrum of entrails
as wonderful as uncovering our own awkward, tender flesh.

You menstruated early, child-frame bent
by heavy breasts and stomach, hating
my dread fascination that followed you
to the toilets as to a cave of bones.

Though no one told me you were dying,
all week I have been making dragons,
small at first, crimson origami,
a larger sky-dragon, sun-yellow with orange fire,
then, with my daughter, an earth-dragon,
its scales of honesty and Christmas foil,
huge as your spirit walking.

□ *Llinora Milner 1993*

Dezember

ᴅᴅᴅ

♒
♓

Montag
25

☽✶♃	3:36 pm	v/c
☽→♓	6:46 pm	
☽□♇	9:43 pm	

♂♂♂

♓

Dienstag
26

☉✶☽	1:45 am

☿☿☿

♓
♈

Mittwoch
27

☽♂♄	3:39 am	
☽✶♂	6:33 am	
☽✶☿	11:55 am	
☽✶♆	1:16 pm	
☽□♃	8:36 pm	
☽✶♅	9:33 pm	v/c
☽→♈	11:07 pm	

♃♃♃

♈
Donnerstag
28

☿♂♆	1:29 am
☽△♇	2:26 am
☉□☽	11:08 am
☽✶♀	3:25 pm

♀♀♀

Waxing Half Moon in ♈ Aries 11:08 am PST, 19:08 GMT

♈
Freitag
29

☽□♂	5:16 pm
☽□♆	9:00 pm

All aspects in Pacific Standard Time; add 3 hours for EST; add 8 hours for GMT

© Corre Mott 1994

Creation

ᛃᛃᛃ

♈ ♉   🌓   **Samstag**
             30

☽□☿   1:59 am
☽△♃   5:44 am
☽□♅   5:57 am   v/c
☽→♉   7:22 am

☉☉☉

♉   🌒   **Sonntag**
             31

☉△☽   1:18 am
☽□♀   7:05 am
☿♂♅   8:34 pm
☽⚹♄   9:24 pm

MOON I

janvier 1996

ᗊᗊᗊ

♉
♊   **lundi**
       1

☽△♂	7:53 am			
☽△Ψ	7:55 am			
♂☌Ψ	8:27 am			
♅→≈	10:07 am			
♀△♄	11:33 am			
☽△♅	5:19 pm	v/c	☽△♀	7:21 pm
☽→♊	6:30 pm		☽☍♇	10:29 pm

♂♂♂

♊   **mardi**
       2

♃→♑   11:23 pm

☿☿☿

♊   **mercredi**
       3

☽△♀   1:49 am
☽□♄   9:54 am   v/c
☿⚹♇   9:59 am

♃♃♃

♊
♋   **jeudi**
       4

☽→♋   6:57 am
☽☍♃   7:33 am
☉□♄   12:41 pm

♀♀♀

♋   **vendredi**
       5

☽ApG   3:33 am
☉☍☽   12:52 pm
☽△♄   10:54 am

Full Moon in ♋ Cancer 12:52 pm PST, 20:52 GMT

All aspects in Pacific Standard Time; add 3 hours for EST; add 8 hours for GMT

Rock Recycling

Mother Earth includes everything in her spiral of change. Biological biodegrading and human remelting or remaking are not the only forms of recycling. Rocks recycle and recombine constantly. Molten material makes its way up through the crust to either erupt in fiery splendor as lava from a volcano *(extrusive igneous)* or cool slowly underground to form rocks with crystals of various sizes *(intrusive igneous)*. Particles of gravel or sand from all kinds of rocks weathering at the surface are deposited and buried, and under pressure become *sedimentary* rocks. Any of these basic rock types under high heat and pressure become *metamorphic* rocks. Each of these types may be reworked into any of the others in a continuous dance that recombines the elements!

□ *Guida Veronda 1995*

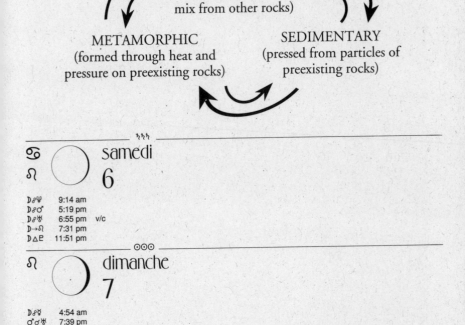

IGNEOUS
(formed by fire; a molten
mix from other rocks)

METAMORPHIC
(formed through heat and
pressure on preexisting rocks)

SEDIMENTARY
(pressed from particles of
preexisting rocks)

♋ ☌ ☊ ☽

♋
♌ ⃝ samedi
6

☽☍♆   9:14 am
☽☍♂   5:19 pm
☽☍♅   6:55 pm   v/c
☽→♌   7:31 pm
☽△♇   11:51 pm

⊙⊙⊙

♌ ⃝ dimanche
7

☽☍♉   4:54 am
♂♂♅   7:39 pm

enero

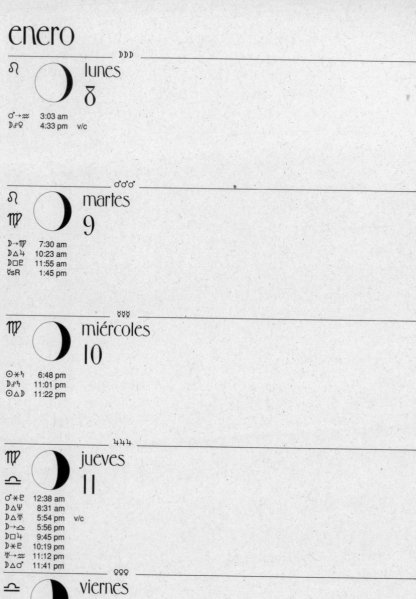

ꝺꝺꝺ

♌ ⬤ lunes
8

♂→♒ 3:03 am
☽☌♀ 4:33 pm v/c

♂♂♂

♌ ⬤ martes
♍   9

☽→♍ 7:30 am
☽△♃ 10:23 am
☽□♇ 11:55 am
☿sR 1:45 pm

☿☿☿

♍ ⬤ miércoles
10

☉⚹♄ 6:48 pm
☽☍♄ 11:01 pm
☉△☽ 11:22 pm

♃♃♃

♍ ⬤ jueves
♎   11

♂⚹♇ 12:38 am
☽△♆ 8:31 am
☽△♅ 5:54 pm v/c
☽→♎ 5:56 pm
☽□♃ 9:45 pm
☽⚹♇ 10:19 pm
♅→♒ 11:12 pm
☽△♂ 11:41 pm

♀♀♀

♎ ⬤ viernes
12

☽△☿ 2:34 am

All aspects in Pacific Standard Time; add 3 hours for EST; add 8 hours for GMT

River, Back, Bones

© *Julie Higgins 1993*

Comfrey
Symphytum officinale

Capricorn rules bones and joints, the structure of our physical being. Comfrey is an excellent herb for healing and strengthening bones and tissue. Recent claims of comfrey's liver damaging properties are controversial at best. Fortunately, comfrey is just as useful externally as internally. The constituents in question can't be absorbed through the skin. For any injury, lightly steam fresh comfrey leaves. Apply to a new injury  cool, to an old injury warm. Or mix dried leaves with water or olive oil to make a paste and apply. If you have concerns about taking comfrey internally, don't use it long-term or during pregnancy. Comfrey heals by reducing inflammation and encouraging cell regeneration. It is high in vitamins C and A, calcium and other minerals, and amino acids.

© *Colette Gardiner 1995*

♎ sábado
13

♉♂♂	3:21 am
☉□☽	12:46 pm
☽□♇	4:48 pm
☽△♀	11:36 pm v/c

Waning Half Moon in ♎ Libra 12:46 pm PST, 20:46 GMT

♎ ♏ domingo
14

☽→♏	1:31 am		
☽□♅	1:44 am		
☽✶♃	6:01 am		
☽□♉	6:55 am	♀→♓	8:31 pm
☽□♂	10:20 am	☿✶♇	10:58 pm

January

□ Lucy Steel 1994

♏ ♌♌♌ **Monday**
15

☽△♄	1:29 pm
☉☌♆	6:55 pm
☽✶♆	9:27 pm
☉✶☽	9:39 pm v/c
♆ApG	10:31 pm

♏ ♂♂♂ **Tuesday**
♐ **16**

☽→♐	5:26 am
☽✶♅	5:51 am
☽✶♉	6:59 am
☽□♀	8:29 am
☽☌♇	9:28 am
☽✶♂	4:35 pm
♉♂♅	8:03 pm
♀□♇	8:31 pm

♐ ☿☿☿ **Wednesday**
17

☿R→♒	1:38 am
♀✶♃	12:22 pm
☽□♄	3:21 pm v/c

♐ ♃♃♃ **Thursday**
♑ **18**

☽→♑	6:08 am
☽☌♃	11:36 am
☽✶♀	1:15 pm
☉☌☿	1:41 pm

♑ ♀♀♀ **Friday**
19

☽✶♄	3:01 pm
☽PrG	3:20 pm
☿PrG	6:45 pm
☽☌♆	10:03 pm
☽☌♉	11:23 pm

All aspects in Pacific Standard Time; add 3 hours for EST; add 8 hours for GMT

Year at a glance for AQUARIUS ♒ (Jan. 20–Feb. 19)

Aquarians even look different in 1996. Maybe it's the electricity in your eyes or just the wild clothing. Uranus has moved into your sign, where it is most at home, and will be there for seven years. You are now the perfect vessel for this unorthodox, inspired awakener. The part of you that has been waiting in the wings insists on erupting into your life—now. In 1996 you may occasionally feel awkward or out of control. It may take time to integrate this new self gracefully. There is increased voltage going through your system; Epsom salt baths and herbal nerve tonics calm and nourish your nerves. You respond well to acupuncture and vibrational medicines (homeopathy, gem and flower essences). Dill or Lavender essence (FES) allays the sense of being over-whelmed. Lotus essence (FES) helps integrate newly emerging aspects of self.

Aquarians (especially if born in January) will make some major change this year—either move, get married, give birth, break up, switch jobs.... Here's an opportunity to break free of old patterns, to move closer to your essential self. You will feel more lively and sociable than you have felt for the past five years (and there's more money around too).

Saturn indicates how you can constructively discharge some of the extra energy you've got this year. Look for educational opportunities and work that make use of your mental abilities, communication skills, and ability to be succinct. Shasta Daisy essence (FES) helps synthesize parts of an issue into a cohesive whole. Pluto brings challenges and changes through friendships, group involvements, and long-term goals in the next few years. Friendships deepen with shared experiences. Power struggles in groups ultimately encourage better understanding and increased commitment.

◻ *Gretchen Lawlor 1995*

♑
♒

Saturday

20

☉☌☽	4:52 am	v/c		
☽→♒	5:16 am			
☽☌♅	6:01 am	♂☌♆	3:00 pm	
☽✶♇	9:14 am	☽☌♂	9:02 pm	v/c
☉→♒	10:54 am	☉☌♅	11:22 pm	

Sun in Aquarius 10:54 am PST, 18:54 GMT

☼

♒

Lunar Imbolc

New Moon in ♑ Capricorn 4:52 am PST, 12:52 GMT

♒

Sunday

21

♅ApG   6:47 pm

---

it's a free cunt tree

As much in the Earth as in the Sky
this ancient longing to be free
not free in the abstract
but daily—free of fear
free of violence   free of poverty

I pour my blood to feed the tree
blood flows from me
I bleed but do not die
I bleed but do not die
the tree grows in me   my cunt is the tree
roots that can split concrete   if given time
give me a chance and I will split the walls of prisons
let out the womyn held for prostitution
held as Lesbians   held for not being "white"
held as crazy as ugly as fat and too noisy
as angry and charged with the history of this   cunt tree

Oh but her story   Oh but herstory
my girlfriend says they want to decorate me
as a christmas tree with pretty things
that catch the light and break so easily
under the boot of their self-proclaimed authority
We laugh defiantly   like girls
(before they have learned to mumble insecurity)
knowing   we are a forest growing
in cities and suburbs on reservations
and in small rural communities   we have always grown back
never perfect or without mistakes   but persistent
and alive!   hearing the rocks sing   listen!
this cunt tree wasn't planted here with patriarchy
when european invaders came to this land   babbling discovery
distorting matriarchy   a bird cannot fly with one broken wing
committing genocide   an ongoing atrocity

II. LISTENING/UNDERSTANDING MOON

If we are, indeed, like nerve cells in the mind of an all-encompassing being, then out of this web we cannot fall. No failure, or stupidity can sever us from that living because that is what we are.

– Joanna Macy

Collage and handlettering © Rashani 1991, quote © Joanna Macy 1991

this cunt tree is older than we are
this cunt tree is older than rape
older than shame
older than hate
this is the tree of life
this tree does not belong to us
we come from this   cunt tree.

© Ellen Marie Hinchcliffe 1994

inspired by Jen Johnson's amazing painting *it's a free cunt tree* and dedicated to her and to Norma Jean Croy, an Indigenous Lesbian unjustly serving a life prison term in California. May she soon be free! ! ! !

Januar

♒ Montag
♓ 22

☽→♓	5:03 am
☽□♇	9:15 am
☽✳♃	12:07 pm
☽☌♀	9:05 pm

♂♂♂

♓ Dienstag
23

☽☌♄	4:34 pm
☽✳♅	5:46 pm
☽✳♆	11:54 pm v/c

☿☿☿

♓ Mittwoch
♈ 24

☽→♈	7:38 am
☽✳♅	8:54 am
☿✳♄	11:02 am
☽△♇	12:15 pm
☉✳☽	3:07 pm
☽□♃	4:04 pm

♃♃♃

♈ Donnerstag
25

☽✳♂	7:45 am
☽□♅	8:18 pm

♀♀♀

♈ Freitag
♉ 26

☽□♆	6:05 am v/c
♂△♇	8:18 am
☽→♉	2:17 pm
☽□♅	3:55 pm

All aspects in Pacific Standard Time; add 3 hours for EST; add 8 hours for GMT

© *Leslie Foxfire Stager 1994*

Time to Hear

If we take time and silence
to listen
to the unsilencing of Nature,
we can hear the stories of the stones,
the cry of the sea,
the tales told by trees,
the breath of the wind.
We rush to speak for them,
but wait.
Take time and silence
and listen
to the voice of the earth.

© *Jo Pacsoo 1994*

♉   Samstag
27

☽△♃	12:21 am
☉□☽	3:15 am
☽□♂	8:08 pm
☽✳♀	8:37 pm

Waxing Half Moon in ♉ Taurus 3:15 am PST, 11:15 GMT

♉   Sonntag
28

☽△♅	3:40 am
☽✳♄	8:22 am
⚷ʂR	2:26 pm
☽△♆	4:15 pm	v/c

janvier

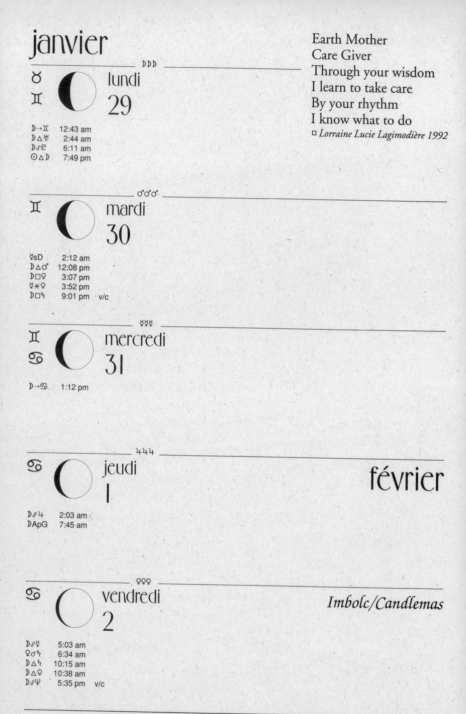

Earth Mother
Care Giver
Through your wisdom
I learn to take care
By your rhythm
I know what to do
☐ *Lorraine Lucie Lagimodière 1992*

ᛞ ᛞ ᛞ

♉
Ⅱ
☿

lundi
29

D→Ⅱ   12:43 am
D△♅   2:44 am
D☍P   6:11 am
☉△D   7:49 pm

♂ ♂ ♂

Ⅱ

mardi
30

♉sD   2:12 am
D△♂   12:08 pm
D□♀   3:07 pm
☿⚹♀   3:52 pm
D□♄   9:01 pm v/c

☿ ☿ ☿

Ⅱ
♋

mercredi
31

D→♋   1:12 pm

♃ ♃ ♃

♋

jeudi
1

février

D☍♃   2:03 am
DApG   7:45 am

♀ ♀ ♀

♋

vendredi
2

Imbolc/Candlemas

D☍♉   5:03 am
♀♂♄   6:34 am
D△♄   10:15 am
D△♀   10:38 am
D☍♆   5:35 pm v/c

All aspects in Pacific Standard Time; add 3 hours for EST; add 8 hours for GMT

Waiting Woman

□ *S. J. Hugdahl 1981*

Imbolc/Brigid/Candlemas

Beneath the ice blue landscape of winter we have contracted, grieving losses and letting the healing earth touch our wounds. Held within the vastness of eternal darkness we have touched the edge of an endless void. Sparks from Brigid's anvil, like shooting stars in a black velvet night, initiate our return to the surface: Celtic Goddess of poetry, smithcraft, and healing, she forges us anew, kindling the flame of creativity and life.

Mature Douglas Fir Seed

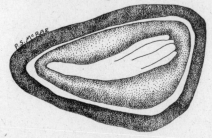

□ *Peggy Sue McRae 1994*

Seeds that fell from the withered blossoms of autumn begin to stir. Pale new sprouts push against the solidarity of inner walls until the imprisoning shell gives way. The clear song of Brigid sinks deeply into the dream of winter to hearken the coming spring.

□ *Peggy Sue McRae, reprinted from* Earth First! Journal *(Brigid 1994)*

Earth Energies

□ *Audrey Nichols 1993*

In the Name of the Mother

Resurrected from her
uterine underworld
ever-green Persephone
pours her blessings

& when no one is looking
dips her brush
scratches a tiny sun
a tiny talisman
—like the one
you lost last winter—
into the city sky

& when no one is listening
she speaks the true names

La Va Ya Ra Ma

Saying it all
saying nothing
speaking the true names

La Va Ya Ra Ma

> earth
> water
> air
> fire
> Mother

La Va Ya Ra Ma

yours & mine

¤ *Gail D. Whitter 1992*

ᏏᏏᏏ

♋
♌   ( )   samedi
          3

D→♌   1:47 am
D♂♅   4:23 am
D△♇   7:27 am
☉△♋   12:36 pm

⊙⊙⊙

♌   ( )   dimanche
          4

☉♂D   7:59 am
D♂♂   9:23 pm   v/c

Full Moon in ♌ Leo 7:59 am PST, 15:59 GMT

febrero

patriarchy—
a little toxic tangent in time
□ Becky Bee 1994

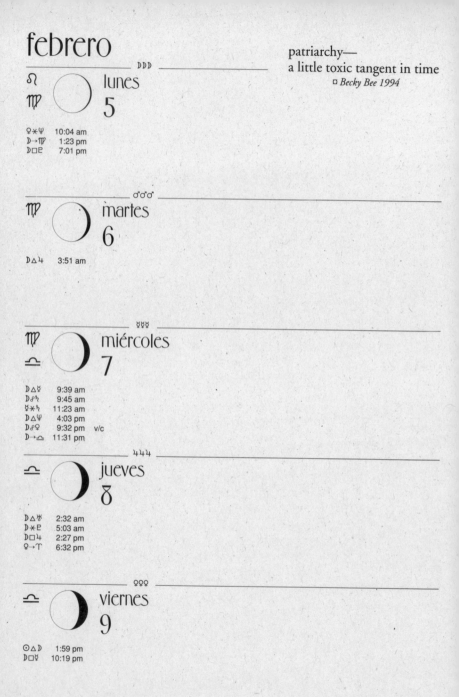

♌
♍ ◖ lunes
5

ΔΔΔ

♀✶♆ 10:04 am
☽→♍ 1:23 pm
☽□♇ 7:01 pm

♍ ◖ martes
6

♂♂♂

☽△♃ 3:51 am

♍
♎ ◖ miércoles
7

☿☿☿

☽△♅ 9:39 am
☽☍♄ 9:45 am
☿✶♄ 11:23 am
☽△♆ 4:03 pm
☽☍♀ 9:32 pm v/c
☽→♎ 11:31 pm

♎ ◖ jueves
8

♃♃♃

☽△♅ 2:32 am
☽✶♇ 5:03 am
☽□♃ 2:27 pm
♀→♈ 6:32 pm

♎ ◖ viernes
9

♀♀♀

☉△☽ 1:59 pm
☽□☿ 10:19 pm

All aspects in Pacific Standard Time; add 3 hours for EST; add 8 hours for GMT

□ zana 1986

Ginkgo   *Ginkgo biloba*

To stand under a mature ginkgo tree is to listen to ancient herstory.
Ginkgo's story originated millions of years ago. Today, the leaves are
used to aid in memory retention (Aquarius rules the mind). One of the
keynotes of the coming Aquarian era may well be information overload.
Aquarius also deals with circulation, which ginkgo increases. Ginkgo is
a nonstimulating brain tonic and can be used on a regular basis by people
studying or by people concerned with memory loss. As with any herb
used regularly, take periodic breaks from ginkgo and reevaluate your
current state of health.

© Colette Gardiner 1995

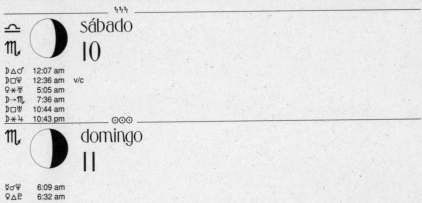

♄♄♄

♎		sábado
♏	☽	10

☽△♂	12:07 am	
☽□♆	12:36 am	v/c
♀✶♅	5:05 am	
☽→♏	7:36 am	
☽□♅	10:44 am	
☽✶♃	10:43 pm	

⊙⊙⊙

♏	☽	domingo
		11

♉♂♆	6:09 am	
♀△♇	6:32 am	

February

© Judith Burros 1991

Mending Heart

DDD

♏

♐

Monday
12

☉□☽	12:38 am
☽△♄	1:22 am
☽✶♆	6:29 am
☽✶♅	8:22 am
☽□♂	9:10 am v/c
☽→♐	12:59 pm ☽♂♇ 6:07 pm
☽✶♅	4:10 pm ☽△♀ 9:21 pm

Waning Half Moon in ♏ Scorpio 12:38 am PST, 8:38 GMT

♂♂♂

♐

Tuesday
13

♀♀♀

♐

♑

Wednesday
14

☽□♄	4:54 am
☉✶☽	7:38 am
☽✶♂	2:48 pm v/c
☽→♑	3:30 pm
♅→♒	6:45 pm

♄♄♄

♑

Thursday
15

☽□♀	3:49 am
♂→♓	3:51 am
☽♂♃	6:28 am

♀♀♀

♑

♒

Friday
16

☽✶♄	6:06 am
☽♂♆	10:15 am v/c
♅♂♅	1:01 pm
☽→♒	4:01 pm
☽♂♅	7:19 pm
♀□♃	7:21 pm
☽♂♅	7:51 pm
☽✶♇	8:51 pm

All aspects in Pacific Standard Time; add 3 hours for EST; add 8 hours for GMT

Globe Shield

© Corre Mott 1994

spirit speaks through wood water fire earth and air.
heart song longs to manifest in many ways nearly lost: listen
matters very dear to our soul: common good, creaturehood.

▭ *Lorraine Lucie Lagimodière 1993*

≈ ## Saturday
17

☽PrG	12:38 am
☽✳♀	8:08 am
☿✳♇	8:21 am

○○○

≈
♓ ## Sunday
18

☉☌☽	3:31 pm	v/c
☽→♓	4:10 pm	
☽☌♂	8:56 pm	
☽□♇	9:07 pm	

New Moon in ≈ Aquarius 3:31 pm PST, 23:31 GMT

Louisiana Voodoun Memories

Smell the crispy bread frying?
Feel the sultry depths of the Louisiana lagoon?
Make a tea, slippery,
out of green hanging moss
Suck it down whole
like a snake consuming its
prey.
Root your genitals in thick,
black mud, there in the lusty swamp.
Sink down into the silky silt slit
Gripped by the walls of muscle and
memory, give up, child,
to the power of the source.
Tinkling windchime breeze
the cotton sheets ripple on the Cajun backcountry
Screen door squeaking
flies swarming noisily
a metal pan, magic is being
brewed into the solid, summer air.
Ancestors remembered
Forces of Elders consulted
Swirling, boiling salt call,
Inhabit us now, Black Mother of All!
Screeching chant of ecstasy
power raw and red
light no more fires of misconception
we are dealing with vast tracts of
energy crackling.
The sweat on her upper lip
flies into the boiling cauldron
as she rips her dark, dancing body into
the Other Side

¤ *Webber 1994*

III. DARKNESS/MAGIC MOON

White Ink
I write
in white ink
on cave walls
in basalt tunnels
in slot canyons

white spirals
circle
inward
spin me
to my shadow
the knower
dark mother
whose milk
is my ink
my white ink
sweet tasting
on her walls

Februar

♓ Montag
19

Sun in Pisces 1:02 am PST, 9:02 GMT

♓

♂□♇	12:13 am
☉→♓	1:02 am
☽✱♃	8:22 am

♂♂♂

♓
♈ Dienstag
20

☽♂♄	8:17 am	
☽✱♆	12:06 pm	v/c
♀♌♅	1:19 pm	
☽→♈	5:59 pm	
☽✱♅	9:55 pm	
☽△♇	11:14 pm	

☿☿☿

♈ Mittwoch
21

☽✱♉	7:58 am
☽□♃	11:50 am
☽♂♀	8:40 pm

♃♃♃

♈
♉ Donnerstag
22

☉□♇	2:05 am	
☽□♆	4:57 pm	v/c
☽→♉	11:09 pm	

♀♀♀

♉ Freitag
23

☽□♅	3:36 am
☉✱☽	7:05 am
☽✱♂	11:20 am
☽△♃	7:09 pm
☽□♉	8:39 pm

All aspects in Pacific Standard Time; add 3 hours for EST; add 8 hours for GMT

Year at a glance for PISCES ♓ (Feb. 19–Mar. 20)

Saturn finally leaves Pisces on April 7, 1996. For the last 2½ years you were presented with opportunities to discipline your free-flowing nature, to accomplish goals and make long-range plans. In the process, you may have experienced frustration, isolation, or lowered energy.

In April Saturn enters your house of assets and resources. In the next 2½ years you will need to accomplish a lot with minimal outlay. Don't waste energy in self-criticism; channel the temptation to do so into efficient management of the resources and talents you've got. Use Larch (Bach) to channel self-criticism into confident action. You may have more physical energy than you've had in the last three years.

Pluto, planet of regeneration, continues to dominate your solar chart. From 1993 to March 1996 it conspired with Saturn to redirect you to new goals. Now you need to specialize, to focus upon who you are and why you are here. You will be most happy if you can totally commit yourself to a cause. Scotch Broom essence (FES) helps to transform social despair into social action. Power issues may surface; you may be the victim or the perpetrator, so stay conscious. February-born Pisces will feel this most acutely; all Pisceans will experience potential solution/resolution on the heels of any crisis. Someone acknowledges your potential and provides opportunities to move forward. Trillium essence (FES) helps individuals collaborate for collective gain.

Jupiter brings opportunities through friends and brings exciting insights into long-term goals. Uranus, the awakener, and Neptune, the visionary, bring receptivity to collective trends and encourage social service. Take time alone; your secret selves want to come out and play.   □ *Gretchen Lawlor 1995*

♉ ◐   ♄♄♄
    Samstag
    24

☽✶♄   10:09 pm

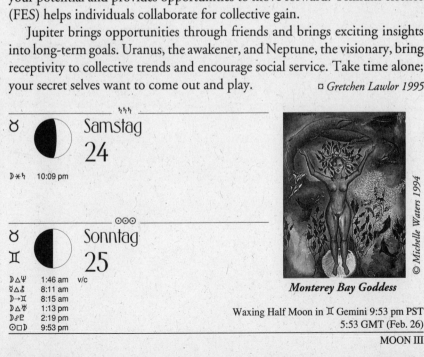

© *Michelle Waters 1994*

Monterey Bay Goddess

♉ ◑   ☉☉☉
♊   Sonntag
    25

☽△♆   1:46 am   v/c
☿△♃   8:11 am
☽→♊   8:15 am
☽△♅   1:13 pm
☽☍♇   2:19 pm
☉□☽   9:53 pm

Waxing Half Moon in ♊ Gemini 9:53 pm PST
5:53 GMT (Feb. 26)

MOON III

février

ⅠⅠ)))

♊ 🌓 **lundi**
26

☽□♂ 1:14 am
☽△♅ 2:49 pm

□ *Isabel F. Vargas 1993*

Grounding Myself

♂♂♂

♊
♋ 🌗 **mardi**
27

☽⚹♀ 2:47 am
☽□♄ 10:21 am v/c
☽→♋ 8:11 pm

☿☿☿

♋ 🌗 **mercredi**
28

☉△☽ 3:47 pm
☽△♂ 5:55 pm
☽☍♃ 7:40 pm
☽ApG 11:05 pm

♃♃♃

♋ 🌗 **jeudi**
29

☽□♀ 9:51 pm
☽△♄ 11:38 pm

♀♀♀

♋
♌ 🌗 **vendredi**
1

mars

☽☍♆ 2:26 am v/c
♂⚹♃ 2:49 am
☽→♌ 8:48 am
☽☍♅ 2:23 pm
☽△♇ 3:02 pm
☉⚹♃ 10:05 pm

All aspects in Pacific Standard Time; add 3 hours for EST; add 8 hours for GMT

Goddess Ritual

♌ ◯ ♄♄♄

samedi

2

♀□♆   11:29 pm

♌ ◯ ⊙⊙⊙
♍

dimanche

3

☽ ⚼ ♉   8:26 am
☽ △ ♀   3:38 pm   v/c
☽ → ♍   8:14 pm

---

marzo

□ *Lorraine Lucie Lagimodière 1993*

ⅮⅮⅮ

♍ ◯ **lunes**
4

Ɒ□♇   2:17 am
☉♂♂   6:03 am
Ɒ△♃   8:16 pm

♂♂♂

♍ ◯ **martes**
5

Ɒ☍♂   1:03 am
☉☍Ɒ   1:24 am
♇ʀʀ   8:12 pm
♀→♉   6:02 pm
Ɒ☍♄   10:14 pm
Ɒ△♆   11:59 pm   v/c

Full Moon in ♍ Virgo 1:24 am PST, 9:24 GMT

☿☿☿

♍ ◯
♎   **miércoles**
6

Ɒ→♎   5:41 am
Ɒ△♅   11:21 am
Ɒ⚹♇   11:32 am

♄♄♄

♎ ◯ **jueves**
7

♉→♓   3:54 am
Ɒ□♃   5:34 am
♃□♄   10:57 pm

♀♀♀

♎ ◯
♏   **viernes**
8

Ɒ□♆   7:43 am   v/c
♅⚹♇   12:39 pm
Ɒ→♏   1:06 pm
♀□♅   1:14 pm
Ɒ△♉   5:46 pm
Ɒ□♅   6:46 pm
Ɒ☍♀   7:15 pm

All aspects in Pacific Standard Time; add 3 hours for EST; add 8 hours for GMT

Alsia Well in Cornwall/Kernow

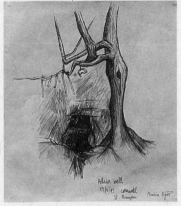

Alsia well
17/3/93 Cornwall
St. Bruyan   Monica Sjöö

□ *Monica Sjöö 1993*

Elder   *Sambucus* spp.

Pisces is a mutable sign. Her psychic abilities enable her to listen to the sounds of magic beneath the waters and to believe. Elder is one of the magical trees of the Wiccan tradition. Elder groves were considered sacred and were often destroyed by Christian fanatics. Elder well represents the dark mysteries. She is a strong herb and should not be used lightly in magic.

Her energy amplifies will to such an extent that she should only be used when your intent is completely clear, and never for selfish purposes. She can also be used for protection. When elder is taken internally, care is needed as some varieties are poisonous.

© *Colette Gardiner 1995*

♏ ☽ **sábado**
9

☿□♇	1:35 am
☽✶♃	12:46 pm
☽△♂	10:46 pm

♏ ☽ **domingo**
♐ **10**

☉△☽	1:06 am	
☿✶♀	2:03 am	
☽△♄	12:37 pm	
☽✶♆	1:28 pm	v/c
☽→♐	6:33 pm	
☽♂♇	11:59 pm	

MOON III

March

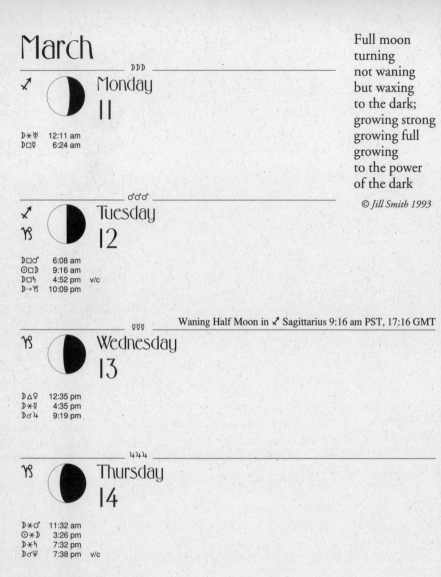

Full moon
turning
not waning
but waxing
to the dark;
growing strong
growing full
growing
to the power
of the dark

© *Jill Smith 1993*

♐ ⅅⅅⅅ

Monday
11

☽✶♅ 12:11 am
☽◻♀ 6:24 am

♐ ♂♂♂

Tuesday
12

♐
♑

☽◻♂ 6:08 am
☉◻☽ 9:16 am
☽◻♄ 4:52 pm v/c
☽→♑ 10:09 pm

Waning Half Moon in ♐ Sagittarius 9:16 am PST, 17:16 GMT

♑ ☿☿☿

Wednesday
13

☽△♀ 12:35 pm
☽✶♅ 4:35 pm
☽♂♃ 9:19 pm

♑ ♃♃♃

Thursday
14

☽✶♂ 11:32 am
☉✶☽ 3:26 pm
☽✶♄ 7:32 pm
☽♂♆ 7:38 pm v/c

♑ ♀♀♀
♒

Friday
15

☽→♒ 12:16 am
☽✶♇ 5:23 am
☽♂♅ 5:54 am
♄✶♆ 8:48 am
♀✶♃ 10:03 am
☽◻♀ 6:26 pm v/c
☽PrG 9:42 pm

All aspects in Pacific Standard Time; add 3 hours for EST; add 8 hours for GMT

© *Sandra Stanton 1993*

Raven Woman

─────── ᚼᚼᚼ ───────

 ≋ ● **Saturday**
16

♀⊼♅   11:06 pm

─────── ⊙⊙⊙ ───────

 ≋ ● **Sunday**
♓ **17**

☽→♓   1:51 am
☉⚹♆   5:51 am
☽□♇   6:57 am
♄ApG 10:03 am
☉♂♄ 11:05 am

MOON III

The Future Is Now

"We don't inherit the earth from our ancestors,
we borrow it from our descendents." Old Chinese saying.

If we don't buy another gadget, newspaper, stereo or TV;
If we wear out our clothes, dry our hair in the wind,
and learn to like our size, shape and smell;
If we don't drive on motorways or fly in aeroplanes;
If we count the cost of pollution instead of profits;
If we don't eat food out of season,
sprayed with chemicals & flown across the world;
If we conserve the resources of the earth
and recognize that they belong to all people;
If we don't idolize "free trade" & support multinationals;
If we cut out waste and reuse what we can;
If we don't continue to want;
If we refuse to consume;
If we be here and now and ourselves,
walk, talk to our neighbors,
grow food and communities,
Plant trees—end wars—
Then, perhaps there will be an earth for our children's children
And for all those who remain in poverty while the earth is wasted
        and polluted
in the name of "progress," "productivity" and "profit."   © *Jo Pacsoo 1994*

© *Beth Freewomon 1995*

IV. EARTH ACTION MOON

Madre del Mundo

Save the Mother
Save the Land
Honor Treaty Rights
Stop Nuclear Testing on Our Sacred Earth

This sculpture was originally installed on U.S.– occupied Shoshone Land across from the Missile Test Site in Mercury, Nevada. She was part of a Mother's Day Peace Action opposing the bombing and desecration of our Sacred Mother Earth.

März

♓ **Montag**
18

□ *Joanna Tamar 1992*

☽⚹♀	12:10 am
☽⚹♃	1:47 am
☽☌♅	10:20 am
☽☌♂	9:03 pm
☽⚹♆	11:39 pm

♂♂♂

♓
♈ **Dienstag**
19

☽☌♄	12:17 am	
♀△♃	12:49 am	
☉☌☽	2:46 am	v/c
☽→♈	4:16 am	
☽△♇	9:31 am	
☽⚹♅	10:24 am	

New Moon in ♓ Pisces 2:46 am PST, 10:46 GMT

☿☿☿

♈ **Mittwoch**
20

Sun in Aries 12:04 am PST, 8:04 GMT

Equinox

♈

☉→♈	12:04 am
☽□♃	5:38 am
♂⚹♆	9:15 pm

♃♃♃

♈
♉ **Donnerstag**
21

☽□♆	4:12 am	v/c
☽→♉	9:00 am	
☽□♅	3:38 pm	
♂☌♄	5:49 pm	

♀♀♀

♉ **Freitag**
22

☽△♃	12:25 pm
☿ApG	2:37 pm
☿⚹♆	3:30 pm
☽☌♀	7:00 pm

All aspects in Pacific Standard Time; add 3 hours for EST; add 8 hours for GMT

Year at a glance for ARIES ♈ (Mar. 20–Apr.19)

It's time; an old life ends. 1995 was a year of completion for you. In April 1996 Saturn enters Aries; you embark upon a fourteen-year cycle of inner strengthening. During the next two and one-half years you will slowly piece together a new self-image. Your internal revolution is helped by external reorganization—in your appearance, home, lifestyle, even location. Use Sage-brush essence (FES) to release old attachments, or Walnut (Bach) for protection and assistance during transitions.

Pluto in early Sagittarius nourishes your new identity through a deepening of your faith. Your current philosophy or spiritual path will be tested; you need guidelines for your metamorphosis. Travel (or foreigners), advanced studies, or the legal world are portals of this transformation. Pluto requires crisis to effect change; you may agonize or obsess over what is asked of you. Power struggles are empowerment struggles; use Mt. Pride essence (FES) for courage.

Jupiter is at your solar midheaven this year, so weigh carefully any professional opportunities offered you. There is danger of regressing into old roles, of being tempted by promises of recognition or financial gain. Any worthwhile opportunity must support your new self-image.

Uranus, the liberator, is strongly placed in your chart for the next seven years, encouraging your efforts to be more independent, unique, and unconventional. You'll find yourself with goals and ambitions that you never believed would be important to you—perhaps of a humanitarian or revolutionary nature. Use Buttercup essence (FES) to appreciate your uniqueness. Association with groups of people help to liberate you from the past. A friend may be the catalyst that alters your life, and/or you may decide to split from old social circles in order to grow.   ◻ *Gretchen Lawlor 1995*

♉
♊

Samstag
23

⊙△♇	1:15 am	☽✳︎♂	4:04 pm	v/c
♀☌♄	1:25 am	☽→♊	5:00 pm	
☽△Ψ	12:00 pm	⊙✳︎♅	6:22 pm	
☽✳︎♄	1:37 pm	♀☌♂	7:18 pm	
☽✳︎♀	3:42 pm	☽☍♇	10:50 pm	

⊙⊙⊙

♊
Sonntag
24

♀→♈	12:04 am
☽△♅	12:14 am
⊙✳︎☽	12:44 am
♂→♈	7:13 am

© Sudie Rakusin 1987

Spring Equinox/Eostar

Eostar is the Saxon goddess of death and rebirth, a Teutonic variation of the Babylonian goddess Ishtar and the Canaanite goddess Astarte. She brings about regeneration and the first signs of spring. Eggs and rabbits, both time-honored symbols of fertility, are the symbols of her feast. The hiding and hunting of brightly painted eggs is a fertility ritual in her honor.

The Christian celebration of Easter has taken its name from Eostar since the Middle Ages and is always on the first Sunday after the first full moon following the spring equinox. *Eostar* is from the same root word as the word *estrus*, the period of heat or rut in which females are in a maximum state of sexual receptivity. Rituals performed at this season blessed seeds and the fertility of the land.

◻ *Peggy Sue McRae, reprinted and excerpted from* Earth First! Journal *(Eostar 1992)*

Ecofeminism: The Intersection of Feminism and Ecology

> We live on the earth with millions of species, only one of
> which is the human species. Yet the human species in its
> patriarchal form is the only species which holds a conscious
> belief that it is entitled to dominion over the other species,
> and over the planet. Paradoxically, the human species is
> utterly dependent on nonhuman nature. We could not live
> without the rest of nature; it *could* live without us.

The special message of ecofeminism is that when women suffer through both social domination and the domination of nature, most of life on this planet suffers and is threatened as well. It is significant that feminism and ecology as social movements have emerged now, as nature's revolt against domination plays itself out in human history and in nonhuman nature at the same time. As we face slow environmental poisoning and the resulting environmental simplification, or the possible unleashing of our nuclear arsenals, we can hope that the prospect of extinction of life on the planet will provide a universal impetus to social change. Ecofeminism supports utopian visions of harmonious, diverse, decentralized communities, using only those technologies based on ecological principles, as the only practical solution for the continuation of life on earth.

Visions and politics are joined as an ecofeminist culture and politics begin to emerge. Ecofeminists are taking direct action to effect changes that are immediate and personal as well as long-term and structural. Direct actions include learning holistic health and alternate ecological technologies, living in communities that explore old and new forms of spirituality which celebrate all life as diverse expressions of nature, considering the ecological consequences of our lifestyles and personal habits, and participating in creative public forms of resistance.

© *Ynestra King 1989, reprinted and excerpted with permission from*
"The Ecology of Feminism and the Feminism of Ecology," from
Healing the Wounds: The Promise of Ecofeminism,
edited by Judith Plant and published by New Society Publishers

mars

DDD

♊ lundi
25

☿△♇ 12:43 pm
☿⚹♅ 10:31 pm

♂♂♂

♊
♋ mardi
26

☽□♄ 1:11 am   v/c
☽→♋ 4:07 am
☽□♂ 7:15 am
☽□♅ 2:26 pm
☉□☽ 5:32 pm

☿☿☿

Waxing Half Moon in ♋ Cancer 5:32 pm PST
0:32 GMT

♋ mercredi
27

☽☍♃ 11:21 am
☽ApG 6:33 pm
☉♂☿ 11:38 pm

♃♃♃

♋
♌ jeudi
28

♂△♇ 2:51 am
☽⚹♀ 4:27 am
☽☍♆ 11:33 am
☽△♄ 2:19 pm   v/c
☽→♌ 4:38 am
☽△♇ 10:35 pm
☽△♂ 11:59 pm

♀♀♀

♌ vendredi
29

☽☍♅ 12:31 am
♂⚹♅ 8:19 am
☉△☽ 11:29 am
☽△♅ 3:14 pm
☿☍♅ 3:36 pm

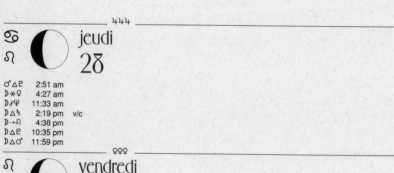

All aspects in Pacific Standard Time; add 3 hours for EST; add 8 hours for GMT

Supporting Organic Farming Is Direct Earth Action! ! !

By supporting organic farming I am casting a spell of healing for the Earth, my body, and all living creatures. Buying, growing, and eating organically is direct Earth action. It's a basic, daily ritual that honors and supports the entire ecosystem.

Organic farming is a system that nourishes soil and microbial life, while producing healthy food. Conventional (read: *chemical*) farming is a system that is harmful to all living creatures, including humans, soil, water, animals, and the Earth as a whole.

Cast a circle while you gather your food. Whether it be in your garden, at the Farmer's Market, in the co-op or local store, you have choices. Get to know your garden, a farmer, or the local produce manager. Your choices will have an effect on this planet.

Organic food may appear to be more expensive, until you examine the true costs of chemical farming with an eagle's eye view. When you pay "more" for an organic vegetable you are paying for the true cost of that item. When you pay "less" for a vegetable that was produced by agribusiness, by chemical methods, that is just the first installment. The further installments will come when we all pay for cleaning up ground water from pesticide poisoning, for birth defects, for the loss of topsoil, for general health problems, for the loss of wildlife, and so on.

To support local organic farming is to be part of the magical spell that is changing the destructive ways of feeding humans into a system that nourishes all living creatures and the Earth herself. ¤ *Liz Tree 1995*

ॐ ☾ ꜧꜧꜧ
samedi
30

☾□♀   9:46 pm   v/c

◌◌◌
ॐ ☾ dimanche
♏ 31

☾→♏   4:16 am
☉⚹♌   6:42 am
☾□♇   9:58 am
♀△♆   7:33 pm
♉□♃   11:09 pm

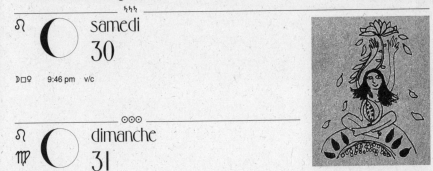

¤ *Joanna Tamar 1994*

abril

no trespassing:
but over the barbed wire
one crow flies
  □ *Gail D. Whitter 1994*

♍ ◯ **lunes**
    1

DDD

☿PrG   12:26 am
☽△♃   12:08 pm

ゞゞゞ

♍ ◯ **martes**
♎   2

♂♂♂

☽△♆   9:54 am
☽△♀   1:00 pm
☽☌♄   1:26 pm   v/c
☽→♎   2:27 pm
♀⚹♄   7:37 pm
☽⚹♇   7:49 pm
☽△♅   9:59 pm

♎ ◯ **miércoles**
    3

☿☿☿

☽☌♂   4:35 am
♀→♊   8:27 am
☉☌☽   5:08 pm
☽□♃   8:16 pm

Full Moon in ♎ Libra 5:08 pm PST, 0:08 GMT (Apr. 4)
Total Lunar Eclipse 5:10 pm PST (1.380 mag.)

♃♃♃

♎ ◯ **jueves**
♏   4

☽☌☿   8:20 am
☽□♆   4:40 pm   v/c
☽→♏   8:58 pm

♀♀♀

♏ ◖ **viernes**
    5

☽□♅   4:17 am
☉□♃   2:59 pm

Thistle
many genera and species

CUTTING THRU THE SMOG OF OPPRESSION ↭ INVOKING AIR SPIRITS ↭ FOR ALL TO BREATHE FREELY

□ *Debby Earthdaughter 1991*

Thistle represents taking a stand and making yourself visible—a quality which Aries and other action-oriented types embody. Thistle often grows in disturbed, even burned over ground. Thistle leaves are very nutritious and increase mother's milk. Remove the spines; then steam them or make tea. Most thistle leaves are bitter but some are sweet. The seeds and leaves are also

used to cleanse and support the liver. The liver is the organ associated with anger, and unexpressed anger can be hard on the liver. Fiery types in general can often use liver support. Use tincture (20–30 drops) or a cup of tea periodically as a tonic, more if the liver needs help. Take action, speak out, use your anger, and support your liver.

© *Colette Gardiner 1995*

ℳ ◗ ♄♄♄ **sábado**
6

☽✱♃	1:52 am	
♀☍♇	8:09 am	
♅□♆	3:36 pm	
☽✱♆	9:16 pm	

ℳ ◑ ○○○ **domingo**
♐ **7**

☽△♄	1:22 am	v/c	☽☍♀	7:50 am	
☽→♐	1:22 am		☽✱♅	8:34 am	
♂☍♄	1:28 am		♀△♅	7:11 pm	
♄→♈	1:50 am		☿→♉	8:17 pm	
☽♂♇	6:13 am		☽△♂	8:40 pm	

Daylight Savings Time begins 2:00 am PST

April

↗ Monday
8

☉△☽   10:06 am   v/c

Ceremonial Storm Pattern
(wool weaving)

© Selina Begay 1995

♂♂♂

↗
♑ Tuesday
9

�→♑   4:31 am
☽□♄   4:57 am
☽△☿   9:40 am

☿☿☿

♑ Wednesday
10

☿□♅   12:50 am
☽□♂   2:27 am
☽♂♃   8:51 am
☉□☽   4:37 pm
☽PrG   7:57 pm

Waning Half Moon in ♑ Capricorn 4:37 pm PDT, 23:37 GMT

♃♃♃

♑
♒ Thursday
11

☽♂♆   3:14 am   v/c
☽→♒   7:10 am
☽⚹♄   8:02 am
☽⚹♇   11:49 am
☽♂♅   2:25 pm
☽□☿   7:59 pm
☽△♀   8:26 pm

♀♀♀

♒ Friday
12

☽⚹♂   8:01 am
☉⚹☽   11:07 pm   v/c

All aspects in Pacific Daylight Time; add 3 hours for EDT; add 7 hours for GMT

The Weaving Project

In 1974, the federal government passed Public Law 93-531, authorizing the partitioning of the Hopi-Diné Joint Use Area and the removal of ten thousand Diné (Navaho) people. This led to livestock confiscation, water diversion, fencing of previously open land, the discontinuation of road and education improvements, clearing of land, and threats to ceremonial grounds. (The threatened lands are in the center of the Black Mesa of the Colorado Plateau in Arizona, known as Big Mountain.)

In 1984, The Weaving Project (also known as Women in Resistance, the Sovereign Diné Nation Textile Industry Weaving Collective) was organized to combat the abuses taking place in the Joint Use Area and to build a strong economic base by promoting self-sufficiency through the practice of traditional Diné art.

One of the project's most important aspects has been the encouragement of weavers to promote and support their traditional art and ceremonial ways at a time when these are threatened. The Weaving Project has also made a commitment to the weavers to support them in their long-term efforts to resist forced removal from the land and to support their traditional ceremonial life.

Through the sale of the collective's weavings, The Weaving Project directly supports the Diné women's resistance to forced relocation and genocide. The weaver receives 100 percent of the price she asks for her weaving. In this way, whenever someone buys a weaving, she is directly supporting the Diné women in their effort to stay on their ancestral lands and to keep their culture alive.

© *Marsha Gómez 1994, reprinted and excerpted from* woman of power *(issue 23)*
For more information about The Weaving Project contact:
Weaving Resource Center, P.O. Box 822, St. Michaels, AZ 86511.

ᕽᕽᕽ

♒
♓
🌑 **Saturday**
13

♉︎∏♃	6:54 am
☽→♓	10:01 am
☽□♇	2:38 pm

◯◯◯

♓
🌑 **Sunday**
14

☽□♀	2:49 am
☽✶♉	6:13 am
♀△♃	9:45 am
☽✶♃	3:15 pm

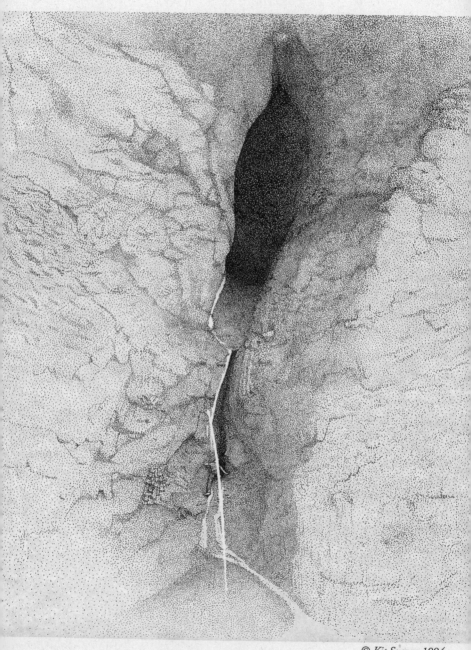

© *Kit Sugrue 1994*

Return to Mother Earth

V. EARTH BODY MOON

April

□ Sun Crow 1993

ⅮⅮⅮ

♓
♈

Montag
15

☽⚹♆ 9:43 am v/c
♂□♃ 11:28 am
☽→♈ 1:44 pm
☽♂♄ 3:30 pm
☽△♇ 6:23 pm
☽⚹♅ 9:23 pm

♂♂♂

♈

Dienstag
16

☽⚹♀ 10:27 am
☽□♃ 8:02 pm
☽♂♂ 9:51 pm

☿☿☿

♈
♉

Mittwoch
17

☉□♆ 4:02 am
♂ApG 12:33 pm
☽□♆ 2:58 pm
☉♂☽ 3:50 pm v/c
☿△♃ 6:44 pm
☽→♉ 7:06 pm

Partial Solar Eclipse 3:37 pm PDT (.880 mag.)
New Moon in ♈ Aries 3:50 pm PDT, 22:50 GMT

♃♃♃

♉

Donnerstag
18

☽□♅ 3:09 am

♀♀♀

♉

Freitag
19

Sun in Taurus 12:11 pm PDT, 19:11 GMT

♉

☽△♃ 2:57 am
☽♂☿ 6:36 am
☉→♉ 12:11 pm
☽△♆ 10:36 pm v/c

All aspects in Pacific Daylight Time; add 3 hours for EDT; add 7 hours for GMT

Year at a glance for TAURUS ♉ (Apr. 19–May 20)

An opportunity materialized April–June of 1995 for Taurus to further career aspirations. 1996 follows with the same electricity. It's a year of sudden, unexpected chances to share your special genius with the world. Your outlook is progressive and unique. It's a lot for Taurus to contain; nervous tension or bouts of exhaustion may give you pause, especially March–May 1996. Lavender or Chamomile essence (FES) soothes nerves; Vervain (Bach) lessens exhaustion from overstriving.

You are attracted to social, humanitarian, or revolutionary issues. Since mid-1993 you have been looking for the right cause to commit to. The more willing you have been to shoulder responsibilities, the more opportunities now come your way. There will be moments of illumination when you are the channel for the highest potential of a group. Don't expect to stay in the limelight; yours is an erratic power. Be courageous, seize your chance, and surrender your spot when the force has left you. Use Larkspur essence (FES) for inspired leadership. Jupiter expands your outlook through travel, foreigners, or politics. If you write, this would be an excellent time to publish or promote yourself through public speaking.

In the next few years you will face a loss or even a death in some form, which will force a reassessment of priorities and major changes in the way you manage your life. Another manifestation of Pluto could come through other people's money or values, or shared finances. Your life will be significantly affected by others' changes in fortune. There may be crises or power struggles where you pit your values against theirs. At the least, you will gain profound insight into yourself. Sage essence (FES) helps you to survey your life from a higher perspective.   □ *Gretchen Lawlor 1995*

♉ ●   **Samstag**
♊   **20**

☽→♊	2:55 am
☽⚹♄	5:52 am
☽⚻♇	7:49 am
☽△♅	11:26 am

♊ ●   **Sonntag**
    21

| ☽☌♀ | 9:16 am | |
| ☽⚹♂ | 9:36 pm | v/c |

Awakening
□ *Lori Nicolosi 1994*

avril

⟩⟩⟩

♊
♋ lundi
22

☽→♋ 1:26 pm
☽□♄ 5:04 pm
☉✶☽ 7:53 pm

© Julie Higgins 1993

Earth Rhythms

♂♂♂

♋ mardi
23

☿☿☿

♋ mercredi
24

☽☍♃ 12:29 am
☉□♅ 2:52 am
☽□♂ 1:42 pm
☽✶☿ 3:33 pm
☽ApG 3:33 pm
☽☍♆ 9:12 pm v/c

♃♃♃

♋
♌ jeudi
25

☽→♌ 1:45 am
☽△♄ 6:01 am
☽△♇ 6:42 am
☽☍♅ 10:52 am
☉□☽ 1:41 pm

Waxing Half Moon in ♌ Leo 1:41 pm PDT, 20:41 GMT

♀♀♀

♌ vendredi
26

☽✶♀ 5:04 pm
☽△♂ 6:03 am
☽□☿ 7:33 am v/c

All aspects in Pacific Daylight Time; add 3 hours for EDT; add 7 hours for GMT

□ *Becca 1993*

**The Serpent at the
Base of the Spine**

Trees

merging self to become
one with the Great Mother's grass.
womb-heavy:
>   i can feel the
>   trees' life growing,
>   growing,
>   in my belly.
i know you,
as your body lays across
my green grass.

© *Jen Breese 1994*

♌︎
♍︎   samedi
     27

☽→♍︎   1:50 pm
☽□♇   6:32 pm
♄△♇   7:41 pm

♍︎   dimanche
     28

☉△☽   6:33 am
☉⚹♃   8:07 pm
♆sR   10:23 pm

abril

—))) —

♍
♎ 　○　 **lunes**
29

☽△♃	12:03 am
☿△♆	4:53 am
☽□♀	6:55 am
♂□♆	11:42 am
☽△♆	7:16 pm
☽△♅	7:42 pm　v/c
☽→♎	11:28 pm

— ♂♂♂ —

♎ 　○　 **martes**
30

☽⚹♇	3:48 am
☽☍♄	4:23 am
☽△♅	7:56 am

— ☿☿☿ —

♎ 　○　 **miércoles**
1

mayo

☽□♃	7:47 am
☽△♀	4:43 pm

Beltane

— ♃♃♃ —

♎
♏ 　○　 **jueves**
2

☽□♆	1:46 am
☽☍♂	5:24 am　v/c
☽→♏	5:43 am
♂→♉	11:17 am
☽□♅	1:42 pm

— ♀♀♀ —

♏ 　○　 **viernes**
3

☉☍☽	4:49 am
☽⚹♃	12:14 pm
☿sR	3:35 pm

Lunar Beltane
Full Moon in ♏ Scorpio 4:49 am PDT, 11:49 GMT

All aspects in Pacific Daylight Time; add 3 hours for EDT; add 7 hours for GMT

Ginger

© Lin Karmon 1994

Beltane/May Day

Beltane is the dawn of desire. Fingers of sunlight sink heat into moist earth. Responding in a blush of apple blossom fragrance and frogsong, soil opens. Hard buds expanding. Silken petals part to a glowing golden core. With the passing motion of a green snake, a glistening reservoir of dew held suspended on a blade of grass is released. Running down the stem into the sweet dripping wetness of the earth.

¤ *Peggy Sue McRae 1993, reprinted from* Earth First! Journal *(Beltane 1993)*

□ *Sue Rice 1991*

Earth Bound

When the Moon is closer to the Earth than she has been for one hundred years, so close they could probably touch tongues, when the Moon is full and I am ovulating, when all this is true, I ask the Earth if I can plow Her, plow Her vulva, and She says, "Yes, yes, yes!" So I do and plant my seed, and monthly when my moon returns, I sacrifice my blood to the Earth, spreading my rose-colored water over the seeds that become plants and flower into the fruit of our creation. I pluck the fruit, harvest the bounty, and change it into food. I eat and drink of Her body and my own. We do this again and again, year after year, until finally, I go into the darkness, lay my body down next to Hers, and dissolve into Her. And when another who is ready to plant her seed asks the Earth, "May I plow you, plow your vulva," I say, "Yes, yes, yes!"

© *Kim Antieau 1994*

Mallows

Althaea spp., *Malva* spp.

From marshmallow to cheese-weed, the mallows embody soft, soothing energy. Their main property is producing copious amounts of mucilaginous (slippery) lubricant. Use leaves, flowers, and roots; all parts are good. They soothe, coat, and protect. Crush the fresh plant and apply externally to mild burns or dry, chapped skin.

© *Sierra Lonepine Briano 1988*

Make a tea using two teaspoons of powdered root per one quart of water; use as a gargle for sore throats, as a tea for irritated stomachs (ulcers) and intestines (after diarrhea), or as a sitz bath for dry vaginal tissue—all in all a great lubricant. Taurus rules the throat and tonsils, and embodies earthy sensuality.

© *Colette Gardiner 1995*

♏ ♐	🌔	sábado 4

☽⚹♆	5:18 am			
☽☍♅	6:47 am	v/c	☽☌♇	12:49 pm
♃sR	7:35 am		☽△♄	2:18 pm
☽→♐	9:06 am		☽⚹♅	4:46 pm

♐	🌔	domingo 5

May

Pebble Goddess

◻ *Hawk Madrone 1994*

⟫⟫⟫

♐
♑ ## Monday
6

☽☍♀	2:30 am	v/c
☽→♑	10:55 am	
☽PrG	2:54 pm	
☽△♂	4:07 pm	
☽□♄	4:24 pm	

♂♂♂

♑ ## Tuesday
7

☉△♃	3:53 pm
☽♂♃	4:05 pm
☉△☽	4:06 pm

☿☿☿

♑
♒ ## Wednesday
☷

♅sR	8:27 am		
☽♂♆	8:52 am		
☽△♅	8:54 am	v/c	
☿△♆	9:51 am		
☽→♒	12:40 pm	☽⚹♄	6:34 pm
♂□♅	2:03 pm	☽♂♅	8:20 pm
☽⚹♇	4:12 pm	☽□♂	8:41 pm

♃♃♃

♒ ## Thursday
9

| ☉□☽ | 10:05 pm |

♀♀♀

Waning Half Moon in ♒ Aquarius 10:05 pm PDT
5:05 GMT

♒
♓ ## Friday
10

☽△♀	9:42 am	
☽□☷	10:08 am	v/c
☽→♓	3:30 pm	
☽□♇	7:02 pm	

All aspects in Pacific Daylight Time; add 3 hours for EDT; add 7 hours for GMT

Essence

I am between worlds.
I am too small
for one and too big
for the other.
Gravity adheres to
my body wherever
it pleases. I orbit
myself and watch
the rotation of others.
It would be sensible
to form my ozone to
a more useful shape
but I like the dirt
on my knees, the
grass at my belly and
the stars in my hair.

© *Rachel Bachman 1992*

© *Sonja Shahan 1994*

♓ Saturday
11

♃♃♃

☽∗♂ 2:40 am
☽∗♃ 10:02 pm

○○○

♓ Sunday
♈ 12

☉∗☽ 5:57 am
☽∗♉ 12:32 pm
☽□♀ 3:13 pm
☽∗♆ 3:56 pm v/c
☽→♈ 8:01 pm
☽△♇ 11:35 pm

© Lycia Trouton 1992

Hogfuel Horns

This piece is an adjunct to the large mounds of wood debris in this research area. I have compressed the hogfuel (a waste product of cedar bark mulch from the lumber industry) into a U shape, an inversion of the piles of "waste" wood already at the site. It is also a bull's horn, symbolic of the Goddess (a bull's head shape corresponds to the uterus).   *© Lycia Trouton 1995*

© Lycia Trouton 1991

Spiral
(compressed peat moss bricks)

The organic materials and processes I use create a living artwork which has a life cycle of its own. The piece generally recycles/returns back into the Earth, part of the cycle of creation, death, and regeneration.

© Lycia Trouton 1995

VI. EARTH ART MOON

Illinois River, Southern Oregon

The "totem" images are significant to me, as a quintuplet water sign and as a womon who grew up in the Pacific Northwest. My inclination, if I can't be in or on WATER, is to lie down next to her. Thus, these are the images I see. These photos are a reflection of my spirituality—the deep soul of my love for the EARTH-SHE. They are my favorite works.

Mai

♈ 〉〉〉 Montag
13

☽♂♄	3:05 am
☽⚹♅	4:12 am
♂⚻☍	3:05 pm

Winged Goddess

□ *Bev Severn 1994*

♈ ♂♂♂ Dienstag
14

☽□♃	3:32 am
☉♂♉	6:13 am
☽□♆	10:10 pm
☽⚹♀	10:24 pm	v/c

♈
♉ ♀♀♀ Mittwoch
15

☽→♉	2:26 am
☽□♅	10:52 am
☽♂♂	9:01 pm

♉ ♃♃♃ Donnerstag
16

♉PrG	10:07 am
☽△♃	10:56 am
☽♂♉	9:54 pm

♉
♊ ♀♀♀ Freitag
17

☉♂☽	4:47 am
☽△♆	6:21 am	v/c
☽→♊	10:49 am
☽☍♇	2:24 pm
☽⚹♄	7:14 pm
☽△♅	7:33 pm

New Moon in ♉ Taurus 4:47 am PDT, 11:47 GMT

All aspects in Pacific Daylight Time; add 3 hours for EDT; add 7 hours for GMT

Goddess Beads

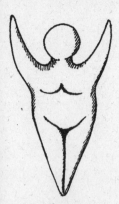

Celebrating Goddess

Spiral Goddess

I make and sell these small, modelled and carved images of the goddess out of porcelain and red clay.

To me these images symbolize many things: the earth, women's power, nurturance, healing, fertility, creativity, protection, celebration.

I've felt some unease around the issue of selling goddess images but now feel this is resolved for me—selling my work has enabled me to support my daughter and myself.

I love getting my work out and seeing my beads being worn daily by women in my community. I also place small goddess figures in ancient trees in areas which are threatened by logging. They remain there as guardians. ▫ *Bev Severn 1994*

Earth Mother
(red clay)

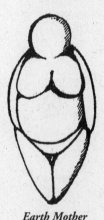

Earth Mother
(porcelain)

♄♄♄

♊ ● Samstag
18

☉△♆   1:02 am

○○○

♊ ● Sonntag
♋   19

♄⚹♅   9:51 am
☽♂♀   5:55 pm   v/c
☽→♋   9:17 pm
♀sR   11:04 pm

mai

♋ ## lundi
20

Sun in Gemini 11:24 am PDT, 18:24 GMT

☽□♄ 6:27 am
⊙→♊ 11:24 am

♊

♂♂♂

♋ ## mardi
21

☽⚹♂ 12:51 am
☽☍♃ 7:40 am
☽⚹♅ 3:02 pm

☿☿☿

♋
♌ ## mercredi
22

☽☍♆ 4:39 am   v/c
♇PrG 5:48 am
⊙☍♇ 6:50 am
☽ApG 9:23 am   ⊙⚹☽ 1:33 pm
☽→♌ 9:29 am   ☽☍♅ 6:35 pm
☽△♇ 12:59 pm   ☽△♄ 7:15 pm

♃♃♃

♌ ## jeudi
23

☽□♂ 5:27 pm

♀♀♀

♌
♍ ## vendredi
24

☽□♅ 2:04 am
☽⚹♀ 5:41 am   v/c
☽→♍ 9:59 pm

All aspects in Pacific Daylight Time; add 3 hours for EDT; add 7 hours for GMT

Year at a glance for GEMINI ♊ (May 20–June 20)

Since mid-1993 you have been working hard on professional goals and have been as focused as Gemini gets. 1995 should have been a very productive year. You experienced respect for your talents, along with added responsibilities. In April 1996 Saturn shifts into Aries, and you reap rewards from your diligence. You can ease up, delegate. If you didn't apply yourself under this influence, you may experience disappointments in 1996.

Rewards come from cooperating in team efforts, using the group's talents and resources to accomplish collective goals. The demands of others may seem onerous; team ventures may feel overly complicated. Perseverance furthers; you are developing a new place in your group or community. Impatiens (Bach) furthers tolerance of group process, Quaking Grass essence (FES) helps harmonize individual identity with group spirit.

Uranus takes you to different cultures and customs in a search for new inspiration. A chance encounter with a truly wise person may liberate you from old prejudices on the spot. Sudden opportunities for specialized studies or even teaching, lecturing, or publishing give vent to your genius self. You can be a catalyst in education with your unorthodox outlook; you are way ahead of the times. You have extra energy during June and July; September and October are excellent months to start new projects.

Someone appears who will significantly alter your life. If you are already involved in a relationship, you will experience stormy confrontations as you renegotiate your roles. In 1996 you must not lose sight of yourself in your efforts to integrate with others. Use Goldenrod essence (FES) to balance the polarities of self and other. A partnership that is still around in three or four years will last a long time.

□ Gretchen Lawlor 1995

© Mara Friedman 1994

♍ 🌓 **samedi**
25

☽□♇	1:19 am
☉△♅	3:02 am
☉□☽	7:14 am
♂△♃	7:52 am
☉✳♄	6:09 pm

Waxing Half Moon in ♍ Virgo 7:14 am PDT, 14:14 GMT

♍ 🌓 **dimanche**
26

☽△♃	7:23 am
☽△♂	9:00 am
☽△♅	12:47 pm

mayo

© Lycia Trouton 1994

**Painting Pâté for
Forest Inhabitants**

〉〉〉

♍
♎ lunes
27

☽□♀	3:22 am	
☽△♆	3:54 am	v/c
☽→♎	8:34 am	
☽✶♇	11:36 am	
♅sD	11:58 am	
☽△♅	4:57 pm	
☽☍♄	6:27 pm	
☉△☽	10:02 pm	

♂♂♂

♎ martes
28

☽□♃	3:44 pm	
☉△♄	5:55 pm	

☿☿☿

♎
♏ miércoles
29

☿♂♂	3:03 am	
☽△♀	9:21 am	
☽□♆	11:07 am	v/c
☽→♏	3:31 pm	
☽□♅	11:15 pm	

♃♃♃

♏ jueves
30

☽✶♃	8:13 pm	

♀♀♀

♏
♐ viernes
31

☽☍♉	2:14 am	
☽☍♂	4:06 am	
☽✶♆	2:33 pm	v/c
☽→♐	6:44 pm	
☽♂♇	9:10 pm	

All aspects in Pacific Daylight Time; add 3 hours for EDT; add 7 hours for GMT

Words into Hands

Words change into hands;
Hands stretch to the four corners of the world,
     stitch a sail,
     spin wool into thread,
     throw clay on a wheel,
     knead dough into bread
     build ships out of steel.

I name the boundaries,
     choose the elements.
I say the word,
     extending my hand,
     transforming the sea,
          the fish,
          the tree,
          the wild berries,
          myself
Into me.

© Leeala 1991

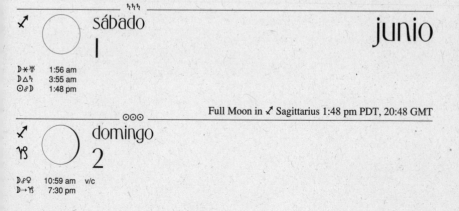

♐   ♄♄♄   **sábado**
1

☽✶♅   1:56 am
☽△♄   3:55 am
☉☌☽   1:48 pm

junio

Full Moon in ♐ Sagittarius 1:48 pm PDT, 20:48 GMT

♐   ☉☉☉   **domingo**
♑   **2**

☽☌♀   10:59 am   v/c
☽→♑   7:30 pm

June

DDD

♑ ◐ Monday
3

D□♄ 4:41 am
DPrG 9:23 am
D♂♃ 9:34 pm

♂♂♂

♑ ◐ Tuesday
♒ 4

♄sD 1:55 am
D△♅ 6:39 am
D△♂ 10:35 am
D♂♆ 3:34 pm v/c
D→♒ 7:46 pm
D✳E 9:59 pm

☿☿☿

♒ ◐ Wednesday
5

D♂♅ 2:43 am
D✳♄ 5:18 am
☉△D 9:32 pm

♄♄♄

♒ ◐ Thursday
♓ 6

D△♀ 8:47 am
D□♅ 10:01 am
D□♂ 2:25 pm v/c
D→♓ 9:20 pm
D□E 11:34 pm

♀♀♀

♓ ◐ Friday
7

© *Georgiann Carlson 1994*

Mullein *Verbascum thapsus*

Gemini rules the nervous system and the lungs. Women who are artists are often exposed to excess dust and fumes from dyes, paints, clays, sawdust, and fabrics. All of us face more air pollution than was common a few generations ago. Although mullein leaf can't undo the effects of air pollution, it can help the lungs clean out some of the heavier debris and strengthen the lungs, ensuring better overall body function and elimination. Leaves should be picked before the plant sends up a flower stalk. Use dried or fresh to make tea or tincture. Take twice a day during times of high dust or pollen levels to keep lungs clear. Drink extra water too. Take two to three times a week as a tonic for chronic lung problems such as asthma. Mullein also helps to remove excess mucus.

© *Colette Gardiner 1995*

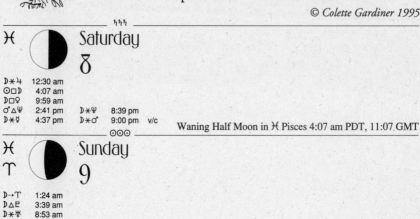

ℋ Saturday ♉

☽✶♃	12:30 am
☉□☽	4:07 am
☽□♀	9:59 am
♂△♅	2:41 pm
☽✶♅	4:37 pm

☽✶♆	8:39 pm	
☽♂♂	9:00 pm	v/c

Waning Half Moon in ℋ Pisces 4:07 am PDT, 11:07 GMT

ℋ Sunday ♈ 9

☽→♈	1:24 am
☽△♇	3:39 am
☽✶♅	8:53 am
☽♂♄	12:24 pm

Juni

DDD

♈ ## Montag
10

☽□♃	5:38 am
♀PrG	7:19 am
⊙♂♀	9:20 am
☽✳♀	1:32 pm
⊙✳☽	2:05 pm

♂♂♂

♈
♉ ## Dienstag
11

☿△♆	2:21 am	
☽□♆	3:08 am	v/c
☽→♉	8:12 am	
☽□♅	3:55 pm	

☿☿☿

♉ ## Mittwoch
12

♂→♊	7:43 am
☽△♃	1:13 pm

♃♃♃

♉
♊ ## Donnerstag
13

☽△♆	11:57 am	v/c
☿→♊	2:46 pm	
☽→♊	5:17 pm	
☽♂☿	5:32 pm	
☽♂♂	7:20 pm	
☽☊♇	7:29 pm	
♂☊♇	9:53 pm	

♀♀♀

♊ ## Freitag
14

☽△♅	1:10 am
☽✳♄	5:45 am
☿☊♇	1:38 pm

¤ Oshun Coyotë 1994, photos by Michelle

These Rock Women have been inspired by the stone circles of Avebury, the spirals of New Grange, the Grimes Grave Goddess and the Tel Brak Eye Goddesses. These solid, powerful, earthed shapes come into form out of the clay body of Mother Earth herself, continuing the archetypal journey from Neolithic times through to the present.

¤ Oshun Coyotë 1994

♊ **Samstag**
15

☽☌♀ 2:45 am
♅☌♂ 12:14 pm
☉☌☽ 6:37 pm   v/c

New Moon in ♊ Gemini 6:37 pm PDT
1:37 GMT

♊
♋ **Sonntag**
16

☽→♋ 4:09 am
☽□♄ 5:13 pm
☿△♅ 7:59 pm

Sanctuary

Six womyn gather for three weeks in a mountain valley in southern British Columbia. We have come to live in harmonious retreat with each other and with the Earth Mother; we seek respectful sanctuary in her. Four of us are physically debilitated by chronic illness of some kind. Four out of six is a provocative ratio, representative of the exponential increase of chronic health problems among womyn during the last two decades.

Through my own experience with chronic fatigue syndrome, I have come to view this development as an adaptive response at the individual human level to a tortured dying planet. We hold her pain in our bodies. As her pain intensifies, we manifest illness as a way to demand wakefulness, to reestablish appropriate connectedness with ourselves and with her. As our bodies reflect the Earth's suffering, we can contact our rage, in a most personal and urgent way, at the utterly unacceptable state of her disease.

Herein lies a healing space, an opportunity—indeed a necessity—to transform the energy of our despair and anger into creative, proactive concrete changes in our lives. Healing the Earth involves healing our relationship to her, and we must begin with ourselves. We must begin with our connection to our own Earthbodies by bounding into them with an openhearted attention and by attentive intention to live in balance. Each woman's attempts at harmonic living contribute to the planet's recovery. Our mutual healing comes through each other.

As we seek sanctuary in her, so we must provide sanctuary for her. We must practice spiritual activism by holding the circle of her potential wholeness in our minds and heart. We must feed the spark of life force in each of us in any way we can. "Like cells in the body of the Earth Mother, we are seeing her need, feeling her pain, hearing her call, sensing her message, and speaking her truths."

◻ *Virginia Neale 1994, quote from Vicki Noble,* Uncoiling the Snake, *p. 167*

VII. EARTH TENDING MOON

Dancing the Spiral

© *Jillian Player 1990*

juin

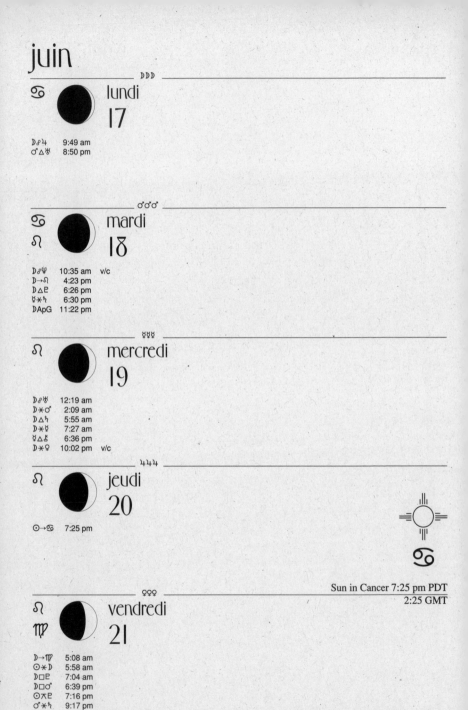

♋ 〉〉〉 **lundi**
17

☽☍♃ 9:49 am
♂△♅ 8:50 pm

♋ ♂♂♂ **mardi**
♌ **18**

☽☍♆ 10:35 am v/c
☽→♌ 4:23 pm
☽△♇ 6:26 pm
♀⚹♄ 6:30 pm
☽ApG 11:22 pm

♌ ☿☿☿ **mercredi**
19

☽☍♅ 12:19 am
☽⚹♂ 2:09 am
☽△♄ 5:55 am
☽⚹♀ 7:27 am
☿△♄ 6:36 pm
☽⚹♀ 10:02 pm v/c

♌ ♃♃♃ **jeudi**
20

☉→♋ 7:25 pm

Sun in Cancer 7:25 pm PDT
2:25 GMT

♋

♌ ♀♀♀ **vendredi**
♍ **21**

☽→♍ 5:08 am
☉⚹☽ 5:58 am
☽□♇ 7:04 am
☽□♂ 6:39 pm
☉⚻♇ 7:16 pm
♂⚹♄ 9:17 pm

All aspects in Pacific Daylight Time; add 3 hours for EDT; add 7 hours for GMT

Year at a glance for CANCER ♋ (June 20–July 22)

Cancers are highly visible in the public arena in 1996. You are reaching a personal peak, a culmination of aspirations, with Saturn at the apex of your chart from 1996 to 1998. You will gain status and receive both recognition and added responsibilities. In the last Saturn cycle (1993–1995) your focus was upon developing a vision of your future. 1996 is an optimum time to extend yourself, especially in March and April. There is need for flexibility; your efforts may need reorganizing to meet practical demands.

All this can be scary for Cancer-born souls, who feel adventurous only when operating from a secure foundation. You may need to free yourself from ancient fears of change in order to get the most from this year. Golden Yarrow essence (FES) helps you to be creative despite sensitivity.

Uranus has left its opposition to your sign and is solidly placed in your house of transformation during 1996. Relationships, which have been unsettled or undependable in the last seven years, begin to stabilize. You need to be willing to change habitual patterns of relating, to be open to unconventional collaborations (especially May–June) for new and unusual purposes. Use Beech (Bach) for tolerance; use Rock Water (Bach) to flow with circumstances. Someone foreign, religious, famous, or wealthy brings opportunities; you both gain from this association. Metamorphosis comes suddenly, and from unexpected places.

Pluto began a slow transit of Sagittarius in 1995, highlighting the mind-body link. You have the willpower and stamina to implement new health regimes or even to completely rebuild your health. Use Manzanita essence (FES) to feel at home in your body or Self-Heal essence (FES) to catalyze healing. Health problems are Pluto's way of pointing out critical imbalances in your life. ¤ *Gretchen Lawlor 1995*

♍ samedi
22

☽□♅	4:59 am
☽□♀	8:25 am
☽△♃	9:41 am

♍ dimanche
23
♎

♅☌♀	2:20 am		
☽△♆	10:50 am	v/c	
☽→♎	4:38 pm		
☽✶♇	6:24 pm	♂△♂	10:47 pm
☉□☽	10:24 pm	☽△♅	11:55 pm

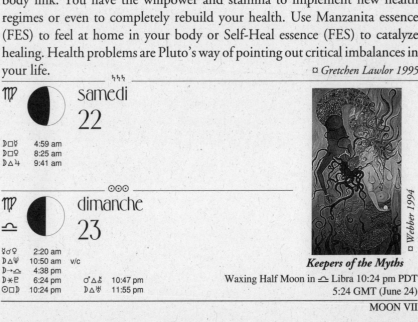

¤ *Webber 1994*

Keepers of the Myths
Waxing Half Moon in ♎ Libra 10:24 pm PDT
5:24 GMT (June 24)

□ Peggy Sue McRae 1994

Summer Solstice/Litha

Litha, European goddess of fertility, power, and order, is kin to Hera, Greek goddess of power, tradition, and childbirth.

At high summer the penetrating sun rises early and lingers, attending the pregnant earth. What blossomed with the spring is now imbued with power from the sun to grow fruit. Litha, crowned with roses, celebrates the longest day of summer with feasting and dancing. The ritual bonfire, which represents the sun, is kept burning through the night. Leaping through the flames will bring protection in the coming year. At the end of the feasting, wreaths of flowers worn by revelers are cast upon the flames. Midsummer is a traditional time to gather herbs for use in healing and magic throughout the year. Irish tradition holds that on Midsummer's Eve one's soul wanders from the body to the eventual place of death.

□ Peggy Sue McRae 1994, reprinted and excerpted from Earth First! Journal *(Litha 1993 and 1994)*

□ *Becca 1993*

Creating Cloth Moon Pads

Creating personal menstrual pads is a significant statement symbolizing how we feel about being a womb'an. We give our bodies, hearts, and souls the message that we honor and respect our cycles, and consider our blood our ally. We let our mother (Earth) know that we honor and respect her beauty and wisdom; therefore we do not pollute the planet with disposable waste.

The cloth represents our canvas that we paint our monthly story onto—all of our hopes, joys, disappointments, fears, resentments, elations, and dreams. Letting go of our pent-up energy opens way for renewed creativity and spontaneity. Our blood is the birth of creation.

Creating a cloth pad is a simple, yet incredibly empowering feat of freedom. My favorite is a folding one that measures approximately 9 x 14 inches. This is truly ecological since you simply fold the pad onto a dry side when one side becomes full.

You begin with a piece of washed flannel, approximately 18 x 28 inches (or size it to fit), fold in half lengthwise, then by hand or machine sew three sides, turn it inside out, then stitch the remaining edge. It's as simple as that!

excerpt □ Barbara J. Raisbeck 1994

junio

© Billie Miracle 1994

♎ ### lunes
24

☽☍♄   5:56 am
☽△♂   9:06 am
☽△♀   5:11 pm
☽□♃   7:19 pm

♎ ### martes
25

☽△♅   12:17 am
☽□♆   7:23 pm   v/c

♎
♏ ### miércoles
26

☽→♏   12:54 am
☽□♅   7:33 am
☉△☽   10:33 am

♏ ### jueves
27

☽✶♃   1:10 am
☽✶♆   11:50 pm   v/c

♏
♐ ### viernes
28

☉□♄   4:49 am
☽→♐   5:02 am
☽♂♇   6:23 am
☽✶♅   11:04 am
☽△♄   4:46 pm

All aspects in Pacific Daylight Time; add 3 hours for EDT; add 7 hours for GMT

Be a Prayer

May each step of this walk be a prayer
For Earth, for Water, Fire, and Air.

Let them know that we listen and care
For eagle, for whale, for bear.

May our work be of mending the tear
Where the planet has suffered cruel wear.

Sending hopes and good throughts for repair,
Singing praise for the life that's still there.

May each step of this walk be a prayer.
May each step of this walk

Be a prayer.

© Joules 1993

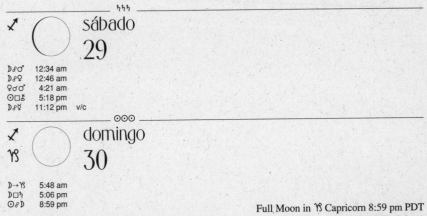

ħħħ

♐ ◯ sábado
29

☽☌♂   12:34 am
☽☍♀   12:46 am
♀☌♂   4:21 am
☉□♄   5:18 pm
☽☍♅   11:12 pm   v/c

☉☉☉

♐ ◯ domingo
♑   30

☽→♑   5:48 am
☽□♄   5:06 pm
☉☍☽   8:59 pm

Full Moon in ♑ Capricorn 8:59 pm PDT
3:59 GMT (July 1)

July

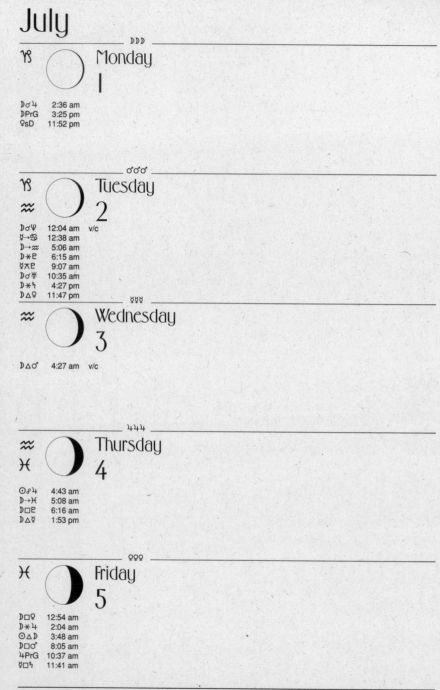

Monday 1
♑

- ☽♂♃ 2:36 am
- ☽PrG 3:25 pm
- ♀sD 11:52 pm

Tuesday 2
♑
♒

- ☽♂♆ 12:04 am v/c
- ☿→♋ 12:38 am
- ☽→♒ 5:06 am
- ☽⚹♇ 6:15 am
- ☿⊼♇ 9:07 am
- ☽♂♅ 10:35 am
- ☽⚹♄ 4:27 pm
- ☽△♀ 11:47 pm

Wednesday 3
♒

- ☽△♂ 4:27 am v/c

Thursday 4
♒
♓

- ☉☍♃ 4:43 am
- ☽→♓ 5:08 am
- ☽□♇ 6:16 am
- ☽△♅ 1:53 pm

Friday 5
♓

- ☽□♀ 12:54 am
- ☽⚹♃ 2:04 am
- ☉△☽ 3:48 am
- ☽□♂ 8:05 am
- ♃PrG 10:37 am
- ♅□♄ 11:41 am

All aspects in Pacific Daylight Time; add 3 hours for EDT; add 7 hours for GMT

Red Clover
Trifolium pratense

Cancer is a nurturing sign ruling the breasts, and red clover is a strong, yet nourishing herb. The lavender-pink flowers are the part of the plant that is used. For external use, fresh flowers are crushed or dried ones reconstituted to make a paste, which can be applied to breast lumps to reduce them. A tea of red clover increases mother's milk when taken daily. Studies have shown that the sprouts can increase estrogen levels in postmenopausal

women. Red clover is high in calcium and B vitamins. It also thins the blood slightly and helps the liver and other organs function better. Use once or twice a week as a tonic, or more frequently when healing from substance abuse or hepatitis. Gardeners often plant it as a cover crop to enrich the soil with nitrogen and organic matter.

© *Colette Gardiner 1995*

ᛊᛊᛊ

♓ **Saturday**
♈ **6**

☽✶♆	1:59 am	v/c
♀□♄	5:26 am	
☽→♈	7:43 am	
☽△♇	8:51 am	
☽✶♅	1:32 pm	
☽♂♄	8:30 pm	

○○○

♈ **Sunday**
7

☽□♀	2:39 am
☽✶♀	5:25 am
☽□♃	5:34 am
☉□☽	11:56 am
☽✶♂	3:23 pm
♀♂♃	7:57 pm

Waning Half Moon in ♈ Aries 11:56 am PDT, 18:56 GMT

Juli

♈ ♉ —))) — Montag ♉

☽□♆	7:31 am	v/c
☽→♉	1:44 pm	
☽□♅	7:47 pm	

♉ — ♂♂♂ — Dienstag 9

☽△♃	12:26 pm
☽✶♀	9:19 pm

♉ ♊ — ☿☿☿ — Mittwoch 10

☉✶☽	12:18 am	
☽△♆	4:14 pm	v/c
☽→♊	10:53 pm	

♊ — ♃♃♃ — Donnerstag 11

☽☍♇	12:01 am
☉♂☿	2:02 am
☽△♅	5:02 am
☽✶♄	1:16 pm

♊ — ♀♀♀ — Freitag 12

☽♂♀	1:35 am	
☽♂♂	4:49 pm	v/c

The Gift

© Nancy Bright 1991

꜀꜀꜀

♊
♋   **Samstag**
13

☿ApG 7:08 am
☽→♋ 10:09 am

☉☉☉

♋   **Sonntag**
14

☽□♄ 12:56 am
☽☍♃ 9:09 am
☿☍♆ 10:24 am

Cross Section Red Cabbage
(life forms)

© *Cilla Ericson 1993*

What She Grew and What She Saved

Over her head clouds sprouted cabbage leaves,
coarse and broad, cupped against a sky
colored like weak tea.
She pruned rose bushes to the shapes of stars.
When the rains came she misunderstood and placed umbrellas
over the rhubarb. She followed the moon.
Planted in circles a garden that grew
more like a tide as the summer waxed,
cresting at the edge of lawn.
In her fingers the muscles and bones crooked
into dense twigs until it was impossible
for her to know what she held in her hands:
dirt, dandelions, or honeybees?
When the sun came and stayed
sharp and hot for a month she remembered all the secrets
she kept closed in her heart
and lay down in her garden
to become as quiet as the earth.

¤ *Amy Schutzer 1994*

Leek Labyrinth
© *Cilla Ericson 1994*

VIII. PROVIDER MOON

A la Carrera

juillet

♋
♌

lundi
15

☉☌☽	9:16 am
☽☍♆	3:20 pm
☽☌♅	9:36 pm v/c
☽→♌	10:32 pm
☽△♇	11:34 pm

© *Sonja Shahan 1994*

New Moon in ♋ Cancer 9:16 am PDT, 16:16 GMT

♂♂♂

♌

mardi
16

☿→♌	2:57 am
☽☍♅	4:32 am
☽ApG	6:33 am
☿△♇	8:45 am
☽△♄	1:31 pm

☿☿☿

♌

mercredi
17

☽⚹♀	6:33 am
☿☍♅	12:56 pm

♃♃♃

♌
♍

jeudi
18

☽⚹♂	1:06 am v/c
♆PrG	7:02 am
☉☍♆	10:57 am
☽→♍	11:17 am
♄sR	11:52 am
☽□♇	12:15 pm

♀♀♀

♍

vendredi
19

☽△♃	9:10 am
☿△♄	6:46 pm
☽□♀	9:48 pm

All aspects in Pacific Daylight Time; add 3 hours for EDT; add 7 hours for GMT

Because the Earth Matters!

Sisters! Because the Earth matters,
we long to speak with you of the many gifts of the
Cannabis/Hemp/Marijuana plant,
used for thousands of years by people all over the world
as their primary resource for
food, fiber, fuel, oil, paper, medicine, and inspiration!

Sisters! Because the Earth matters,
we long to co-inspire with you in sacred Pagan-ja rituals
so powerful that we will disappear the fears that keep us complicit
with the modern day witchhunt against this God/dess-given plant,
the one plant with which we could replace
trees for paper and building materials,
petrochemicals for fuels, oils, and plastics,
pesticide-laced cotton for fiber, and
pharmaceuticals for medicine!

Sisters! Because the Earth matters,
we long to sit with you in sacred pipe circle,
sharing our prayers and visions for a world
where all plants are free to grow, and
where toxic chemicals are prohibited and hunted down.

Sisters! Because the Earth matters,
we long for you to remember that
Where there's Hemp, there's Hope!

© *The Holy Hemp Sisters 1995*

ᗁᗁᗁ

♍
♎

samedi
20

☽△♆	3:57 pm
☽□♂	4:52 pm
☉⚹☽	8:36 pm v/c
☽→♎	11:15 pm

⊙⊙⊙

♎

dimanche
21

☽⚹♇	12:07 am		
☿⚹♄	1:11 am		
☽△♅	4:40 am		
☿⊼♃	10:27 am	☽□♃	7:53 pm
☽☍♄	1:42 pm	☽⚹♄	9:43 pm

julio

♎︎

lunes
22

Sun in Leo 6:20 am PDT, 13:20 GMT

♌︎

☉→♌︎ 6:20 am
☽△♀ 11:22 am
☉△♇ 5:03 pm

♎︎
♏︎

♂︎♂︎♂︎

martes
23

☽□♆ 1:43 am
☽△♂ 5:55 am v/c
☽→♏︎ 8:44 am
☉□☽ 10:50 am
☽□♅ 1:40 pm

Waxing Half Moon in ♏︎ Scorpio 10:50 am PDT, 17:50 GMT

♏︎

☿☿☿

miércoles
24

☽✶♃ 3:39 am
♅PrG 3:50 am
☽□☿ 2:59 pm
☉☍♅ 11:50 pm

♏︎
♐︎

♃♃♃

jueves
25

♃□♊︎ 1:21 am
☽✶♆ 7:48 am v/c
♂︎→♋︎ 11:33 am
☽→♐︎ 2:25 pm
☽♂︎♇ 3:06 pm
☽✶♅ 6:50 pm
☉△☽ 8:16 pm

♐︎

♀♀♀

viernes
26

♂︎⚹♇ 1:39 am
☽△♄ 2:57 am

Year at a glance for LEO ♌ (July 22–Aug. 22)

Uranus, the awakener, is in your house of relationships this year. If you aren't presently involved in a relationship, you'll be meeting someone whose purpose is to wake you up and bring new energy into your life. People you meet now have the effect of changing your life dramatically. 1996 is a good time to get out and circulate, especially for July-born Leos.

If you are already involved in a relationship, it's time to change old patterns and breathe new life into your relationship. Uranus brings restlessness and frustration. Existing relationships need to become more spacious; roles and routines need to become less predictable. Morning Glory essence (FES) brings more of a "be here now" awareness.

Your partner may be the one who explodes in frustration, or walks out on you. This disruption helps develop parts of yourself you would have otherwise neglected. Beech essence (FES), Rock Water (Bach), and Impatiens (Bach) all promote flexibility and acceptance of differences in relationship. Quince essence (FES) assists loving empowerment of others.

In a general sense, Leos will be acting as agents of change in 1996, showing us new ways of looking at life. Your activities may be considered too radical by some members of your community. Saguaro essence (FES) brings understanding and respect for the past so that you can move forward with insight.

Pluto entered your house of creative self-expression in 1995 (staying until 2008). Powerful transformations occur through any creative extension of yourself—children, the arts, sports, romance. Saturn and Pluto create a grand trine with Leo from April 1996 through December. Exploring the creativity of other cultures through travel or study brings fresh perspective and inspiration to your own work.   ▢ *Gretchen Lawlor 1995*

♐ ◐ **sábado**
♑   **27**

☽△☿	1:43 am	
☽☍♀	2:44 am	v/c
☿⚹♀	3:03 pm	
☽→♑	4:18 pm	
☽☍♂	6:48 pm	

--- ⊙⊙⊙ ---

♑ ◐ **domingo**
      28

☽□♄	4:03 am
☽♂♃	8:06 am

▢ *Lucy Steel 1993*

Goddess of Marigolds

July

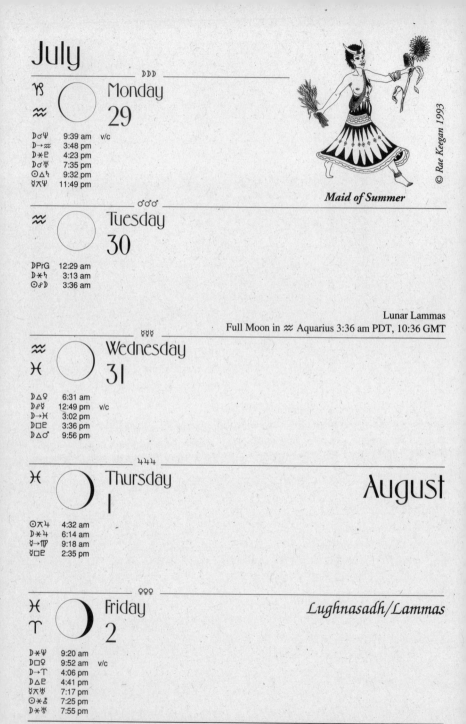

♑
♒ ○ ## Monday
29

☽☌♆	9:39 am	v/c
☽→♒	3:48 pm	
☽⚹♇	4:23 pm	
☽☌♅	7:35 pm	
☉△♄	9:32 pm	
☿△♆	11:49 pm	

Rae Keegan 1993

Maid of Summer

♒ ○ ## Tuesday
30

☽PrG	12:29 am	
☽⚹♄	3:13 am	
☉☍☽	3:36 am	

Lunar Lammas
Full Moon in ♒ Aquarius 3:36 am PDT, 10:36 GMT

♒
♓ ○ ## Wednesday
31

☽△♀	6:31 am	
☽☍♅	12:49 pm	v/c
☽→♓	3:02 pm	
☽□♇	3:36 pm	
☽△♂	9:56 pm	

♓ ◐ ## Thursday
1

August

☉⚻♃	4:32 am	
☽⚹♃	6:14 am	
♅→♍	9:18 am	
♅□♇	2:35 pm	

♓
♈ ◐ ## Friday
2

Lughnasadh/Lammas

☽⚹♆	9:20 am	
☽□♀	9:52 am	v/c
☽→♈	4:06 pm	
☽△♇	4:41 pm	
♅⚻♅	7:17 pm	
☉⚹♆	7:25 pm	
☽⚹♅	7:55 pm	

All aspects in Pacific Daylight Time; add 3 hours for EDT; add 7 hours for GMT

Lughnasadh/Lammas

Lughnasadh, or Lammas, marks the beginning of harvest. The wheat is cut. The sacrifice is made. Here in Idaho, in a forest slated to be cut, it becomes apparent that far too much is asked to be sacrificed for a harvest that feeds too few. We are called upon to make personal sacrifices in order to stop this carnage. Being here, if it can be considered a sacrifice, is also a privilege. Even imprisonment for the defense of this forest is an honor.

As Shelly Douglas, a longtime anti-nuclear activist, said, "The actual experience of jail, chosen in response to conscience, is comparative freedom. In choosing to make a statement of truth that puts us into jeopardy with the law, we deliberately break many of the bars that imprison us in our everyday lives." In choosing to resist the destructive power of the corporate state we sacrifice "business as usual" and what comforts and securities may be gained by our participation in such a system. What we harvest is freedom. Freedom for ourselves, for the wild, and for the Earth.

◻ *Peggy Sue McRae, reprinted from* Earth First! Journal *(Lughnasadh 1993)*

I am an observer: clay and loam, tomato and praying mantis. The weeds move underground like rivers. Persistent as morning glory, I spring back year after year. In their cabins and makeshift trailers, the women sleep and dream I am here but do not wake. In the morning they circle with their dew-wet boots and consider me.

In the hottest part of the day they leave me alone. I listen to the insects, cabbage moths with their muted flour wings, and to the earthmovers, worms tunneling, grinding stones, rearranging from below. Ladybugs settle on leaves like teacups. Above me a dragonfly purrs, her touch electric and startling. I beg her to come closer, to lick me with her turquoise tongue. But the dragonfly vanishes when the woman with tools returns with her tractors and tillers. For hours she claws and pulverizes me.

Dusk. I am ocher. Persian blue. The dimming light iridescent, forgiving of mistakes. Shadows inch across me like an incoming sea.

The lovers bring me pussy willows. They circle like taproots and kiss slowly. Their tongues vine. When they lay down I have every vantage point. Their mouths are dragonflies, whispering secrets into my heart. I lean close. They are a wildfire, smoldering, quick-burning. I feel what they feel and push against them, into their murmurs and undulations. I cannot help but watch. They are absorbed and unaware of how I touch them everywhere until they howl into my skin, ripe as anything I have ever grown.

Night like a crow's inked wings. In the cabins and trailers the women sleep and dream I am here but do not wake. I am an old woman in need of her rest. I push the moon over the horizon and close my eyes.

□ *Amy Schutzer 1994, excerpt from
"Musings on a Summer's Day at We'Moon 1994"*

Vegetables as Healers

We often forget simple things like food as medicine. Fresh greens raw or steamed and blended make a cleansing morning drink. Add steamed potatoes for more substance. Beets or carrots raw or cooked provide vitality, gently stimulate digestion, and are highly favored by the liver. Garlic in warm oil can be used for an earache. Cayenne opens the pores with a bang, and grated raw potato makes a good poultice for inflamed infections. We nourish our gardens and they nourish us.

♈  **Saturday**
3

☽□♂	1:53 am
☽♂♄	4:20 am
☽□♃	7:56 am
☉△☽	12:06 pm

♈
♉ **Sunday**
4

☽□♆	1:11 pm	
☽⚹♀	5:12 pm	v/c
☽→♉	8:34 pm	

August

ꝺꝺꝺ

♉ Montag 5

☽□♅	12:31 am
♂□♄	3:45 am
☽△♉	7:46 am
☽⚹♂	9:57 am
☽△♃	1:14 pm
☉□☽	10:26 pm

Waning Half Moon in ♉ Taurus 10:26 pm PDT
5:26 GMT

♂♂♂

♉ Dienstag 6

☿⚹♂	4:39 pm	
☽△♆	8:51 pm	v/c
♀→♋	11:16 pm	

☿☿☿

♉
♊ Mittwoch 7

☽→♊	4:50 am
☽☍♇	5:29 am
☿△♃	5:40 am
♀⚻♇	8:48 am
☽△♅	8:51 am
☽⚹♄	6:33 pm
♂☍♃	7:34 pm

♃♃♃

♊ Donnerstag 8

| ☽□♉ | 12:26 am | |
| ☉⚹☽ | 1:09 pm | v/c |

♀♀♀

♊
♋ Freitag 9

| ☽→♋ | 3:58 pm |
| ☽♂♀ | 8:58 pm |

All aspects in Pacific Daylight Time; add 3 hours for EDT; add 7 hours for GMT

© *Nancy Ann Jones 1994*

Ceres

♋   ♄♄♄

Samstag
10

♇sD	3:32 am
☽□♄	5:58 am
☽☌♃	9:28 am
☽☌♂	1:31 pm
☽✶⛢	8:04 pm

☉☉☉

♋

Sonntag
11

☽☍♆	7:51 pm	v/c

bringing in firewood

This Is Who I Am

These things I know: how to turn the damper just so, when to close the air vents, how to choose the right pieces of wood, when to open the oven damper so the warmed air circulates around the oven heating the entire body of the stove. I hold and examine each piece of wood to insure it will fit like a lover on a cold night curved tight to the next piece of wood. I'm partial to those quarter-round pieces of wood; they have just enough space between them to allow the fire breathing room. I twist the damper not quite shut. My cookstove is an 1881 Quick Meal that sucks air from its many cracks and holes, and a tightly shut damper would allow a steady curl of smoke to escape and fill the cabin in no time. I fall asleep to the hiss of water simmering on the stove, and if I'm careful enough the night before, I'll wake to hot coals the next morning. I am both servant and mistress of the stove. I serve it willingly for what it offers me. Heat and a sense of myself. This is who I am. A woman who cuts, carries, and stacks wood. A woman who has practiced and mastered the art of filling the cookstove firebox to last till morning.

□ *Terry Lee 1994*

IX. MUNDANE MOON

Saturday Night at the Laundromat

Five quarters fill the slots
like fingers, and they plunge
into the belly of the machine,
thrashing. The laundromat's deserted

except for seven or eight poets
a conga drum and
an old guitar.
No one came to play video games.

The soap is free,
one empty blue box of Cheer.
There's a number for Narcotics Anonymous
circled on the far wall.

We're somewhere in the spin cycle
and all the dryers are full
of leaping socks. Wet underwear
is particularly heavy, so we have time

to ponder great questions. The 100 uses
for a wire hanger. How to find
black socks in the dark belly
of a Speed Queen. We shout

encouragement. Only you can drown out
the dryers. Only you
can wring the truth
out of a towel. It seems

the ceiling fan is stuck
on middle C
and it's getting hard
to keep your knees warm.

¤ *Marcia Cohee 1992, reprinted from* Borderlands

août

♋ ♌ **lundi**
12

D→♌	4:30 am
D△♇	5:10 am
D☍♅	8:19 am
DApG	9:29 am
♂□♃	2:40 pm
D△♄	6:25 pm

ROCK

□ *Stephanie Gaydos 1994*

A Rock

♂♂♂

♌ **mardi**
13

☿☿☿

♌ ♍ **mercredi**
14

☉☌D	12:35 am	v/c
♀□♄	4:21 pm	
D→♍	5:08 pm	
D□♇	5:49 pm	

New Moon in ♌ Leo 12:35 am PDT, 7:35 GMT

♃♃♃

♍ **jeudi**
15

D✳♀	7:59 am
D△♃	9:58 am
D✳♂	9:39 pm

♀♀♀

♍ **vendredi**
16

♀☍♃	8:07 am	
D☌♅	11:08 am	
D△♆	8:17 pm	v/c

All aspects in Pacific Daylight Time; add 3 hours for EDT; add 7 hours for GMT

Her Own Salt

She had to scatter her own salt
because the city would not
because the road she took each day
from home to store
was not important enough
because the budget had been cut in half
because no one had been prepared for such extremity
because because because
And now she has to scatter her own salt
careful to secure each step
on the slippery expanse of asphalt and cement

It is the salt of the earth, falling from her own hands
that makes her feel safe.

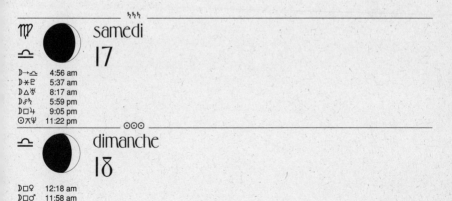

agosto

⊃⊃⊃ ──────────────

♎︎
♏︎   **lunes**
19

☽□♆ 6:26 am
☉∗☽ 9:04 am v/c
☽→♏︎ 2:51 pm
☽□♅ 5:55 pm

Earth

♂︎♂︎♂︎ ──────────────

♏︎   **martes**
20

☽∗♃ 6:05 am
☽△♀ 1:53 pm
☿△♆ 4:36 pm
☽△♂ 11:22 pm

☿☿☿ ──────────────

♏︎
♐︎   **miércoles**
21

♀□♄ 7:54 am
☽∗♆ 1:48 pm
☽∗♅ 3:29 pm
☉□☽ 8:37 pm v/c
☽→♐︎ 9:49 pm
☽♂♇ 10:29 pm

Waxing Half Moon in ♏︎ Scorpio 8:37 pm PDT, 3:37 GMT

♃♃♃ ──────────────

Sun in Virgo 1:24 pm PDT, 20:24 GMT

♐︎   **jueves**
22

☽∗♅ 12:33 am
☽△♄ 9:08 am
☉→♍︎ 1:24 pm
☉□♇ 10:49 pm

♍︎

♀♀♀ ──────────────

♐︎ **viernes**
23

☽□♀ 10:50 pm v/c

─────────────────────────────────

All aspects in Pacific Daylight Time; add 3 hours for EDT; add 7 hours for GMT

Year at a glance for VIRGO ♍ (Aug. 22–Sept. 22)

Saturn moved you out into the public arena in 1994 and 1995. You tested your skills after a long period of inner development. You had the courage and stamina to do something you really believed in. For some Virgoans this occurred within the setting of a partnership. You took a stance, agreements were made, your commitment was either firmed up or finished. Through interacting with others you gained a better sense of who you were and what you had to offer.

In April 1996, Saturn enters Aries. Pooling your resources with others can bring substantial progress, but also holds big lessons for you from 1996 to 1998. Be meticulous in understanding everyone's deeper motives (especially your own). Hold to your agreements; repay debts promptly. On a deeper level, you are learning to incorporate other people's values into your life, without losing your individuality. Goldenrod essence (FES) helps.

With the support of Uranus, you bring innovation to your work, contributing both insight and unusual techniques. If there is no place for your originality at work, move on. Jupiter provides self-assurance and expansion of creative expression in 1996. If you have become too attached to work and have neglected other areas of your life, circumstances (either job loss or ill health) may give you time to reassess your priorities. Iris essence (FES) supports creativity; Buttercup essence (FES) honors your uniqueness.

Pluto sits at the base of your chart. From 1995 onwards opportunities will arise to free yourself from the past, from early childhood patterns, even from unresolved issues in your ancestral line. Red Clover essence (FES) breaks unhealthy inherited patterns. On a mundane level, you could remodel your home, or decide to relocate.

¤ *Gretchen Lawlor 1995*

♐
♑ sábado
24

☽→♑   1:23 am
☉☌♅   2:08 am
☉△☽   3:57 am
☽□♄ 11:49 am
☽☌♃   2:34 pm

♑ domingo
25

☽☍♀   5:06 am
☽☍♂ 10:48 am
☽☌♆   6:52 pm v/c
♉→♎ 10:17 pm

© *Deborah Koff-Chapin 1983*

August

♑
♒ ○ Monday
26

☽→♒	2:11 am	
☽△♄	2:23 am	
☽✶♇	2:50 am	
☽♂♅	4:26 am	
☽✶♄	12:02 pm	v/c
☿✶♇	12:22 pm	

A River

□ *Stephanie Gaydos 1994*

♂♂♂

♒ ○ Tuesday
27

☽PrG   10:01 am

♅♅♅

♒
♓ ○ Wednesday
28

☿△♅	12:20 am
☽→♓	1:50 am
☽□♇	2:30 am
☉☍☽	10:53 am
☽✶♃	2:23 pm

Full Moon in ♓ Pisces 10:53 am PDT, 17:53 GMT

♃♃♃

♓ ○ Thursday
29

☽△♀	11:52 am	
☽△♂	2:56 pm	
☽✶♆	6:37 pm	v/c

♀♀♀

♓
♈ ◐ Friday
30

☽→♈	2:16 am
☽△♇	3:00 am
☽✶♅	4:23 am
☽☍♀	6:22 am
☽♂♄	12:07 pm
☽□♃	3:18 pm
☉△♃	4:23 pm

All aspects in Pacific Daylight Time; add 3 hours for EDT; add 7 hours for GMT

Ereshkigal

□ *Elizabeth Hunter 1991*

Burdock   *Arctium lappa*

Virgo rules the digestion, and digestion is central to good health. Many traditions hold that all systems are nourished by the stomach—our source of power. Burdock has many uses, one of which is to keep digestion functioning smoothly. Its slightly mucilaginous nature gently

stimulates the intestines. It's considered a "blood cleanser" and acts on all the digestive organs—liver, pancreas, and gall bladder. It's an energy mover for the abdominal-pelvic area and helps to stabilize blood sugar. Use the fresh root in a stir-fry, soup, or tea. The root also dries well for use in a tea or tincture.

© *Colette Gardiner 1995*

♈ ☾   Saturday
              31

☽□♀   6:01 pm
☽□♂   7:41 pm
☽□♆   9:07 pm   v/c

♈ ☾   Sunday   September
♉   1

☽→♉   5:21 am
☽□♅   7:30 am
☽△♃   7:15 pm
☉△☽ 11:16 pm

September ☽☽☽

♉ **Montag**
2

♂☍♆ 1:49 am
♀☍♆ 10:35 am

Oatmeal

17¢ a pound
cooked over hot coals
seasoned with wild currants
served with boiled thistle
under the broad wild
starry sky.

excerpt ▫ Harvest McCampbell 1989

♂♂♂

♉
♊ **Dienstag**
3

♀♂♂	12:33 am			
☽△♆	3:15 am			
☽✶♂	4:36 am			
☽✶♀	4:45 am	v/c	☽△♅	2:21 pm
♃sD	7:14 am		☽△♉	6:46 pm
☽→♊	12:09 pm		♀sR	10:42 pm
☽☍♇	1:06 pm		☽✶♄	10:54 pm

☿☿☿

♊ **Mittwoch**
4

☉□☽ 12:07 pm v/c

♃♃♃   Waning Half Moon in ♊ Gemini 12:07 pm PDT, 19:07 GMT

♊
♋ **Donnerstag**
5

☽→♋ 10:30 pm

♀♀♀

♋ **Freitag**
6

♾□♅ 4:57 am
☽□♄ 9:27 am
☽☍♃ 2:10 pm
♀→♌ 10:08 pm

All aspects in Pacific Daylight Time; add 3 hours for EDT; add 7 hours for GMT

Hazelnuts

¤ *S. J. Hugdahl 1994*

ꜛꜛꜛ

♋ Samstag
7

☉⚹☽	4:50 am
☉∠⚷	7:29 am
♀△♇	10:38 am
♀☍♅	9:43 pm

☉☉☉

♋
♌ Sonntag
8

☽☍♆	1:10 am				
☽♂♂	9:27 am	v/c			
☽→♌	10:55 am		☽⚹♅	3:39 pm	
☽△♇	12:04 pm		☽ApG	6:45 pm	
☽☍♅	1:00 pm		☽△♄	9:39 pm	v/c
☽♂♀	2:34 pm		☿⚹♀	11:00 pm	

Dry is old
Young is water.
Juice moistens flesh
the just-born leaf
the moist veined petal
fluid gelled for a moment of life.
Sun sucking all the while—
warming, yes, and flaming existence
but in the end baking dry.
Water leaves cells behind
and leaves curl,
edges thin
yellow and brown.
The colors of dry
crunch under my feet
snap is the sound of
no water
crumble is the texture
of age.
Dry is destination.
In the beginning,
is the water
and the water is god
until fire's slow burn
puckers us all.

© *Bethroot Gwynn 1994*

X. WEATHER/ING MOON

Lucy Steel 1994

Goddess of Dandelions

Goddess of Dandelions: Meadow Ritual

Thick, dark-smelling liquid of decomposed dandelions, I have let your summer blooms, your leaves, your roots and friendly soil all rot and mulch and turn into a stenchy pulp. Dare I smear your sticky juices on my skin? You grow about me in the grasses in abundance. I can touch your large succulent leaves and smell your sunshine flowers. Old Crone, Old Wise Woman, you have captured me and I yield to your power. Your cleansing spirit surrounds me and I grow old and wise with you. Give me your wrinkled hand and take me on a journey. The Beech Tree can watch us and the grasses conceal us.

Lucy Steel 1993

septembre

Mater Matters #1
Recent figures put the age of the Earth at 4.6 billion years; her earliest life forms appeared 3.2 billion years ago.

¤ *Guida Veronda 1995*

𝄢𝄢𝄢

♌  **lundi**
9

♂→♌ 1:03 pm

♂♂♂

♌
♍  **mardi**
10

♂△♇ 12:14 pm
☿△♅ 8:38 pm
☿⚹♂ 11:21 pm
☽→♍ 11:29 pm

☿☿☿

♍ **mercredi**
11

☽□♇ 12:43 am
♂☍♅ 2:20 am
☿⚹♇ 8:07 am
☽△♃ 3:20 pm
♀△♄ 4:04 pm

♃♃♃

♍ **jeudi**
12

☿R→♎ 2:33 am
☉☌☽ 4:08 pm

New Moon in ♍ Virgo 4:08 pm PDT, 23:08 GMT

♀♀♀

♍
♎ **vendredi**
13

☽△♆ 1:20 am
☽☌☿ 8:41 am   v/c
☽→♎ 10:52 am
☽⚹♇ 12:09 pm
☽△♅ 12:40 pm
☽⚹♂ 3:53 pm
☽☍♄ 8:28 pm

All aspects in Pacific Daylight Time; add 3 hours for EDT; add 7 hours for GMT

Bone Woman

© *Judith Anderson 1994*

♎︎

samedi

14

☽✶♀ 1:52 am
☽□♃ 2:24 am
♀⚹♃ 8:10 am
☿PrG 6:37 pm

⦿⦿⦿

♎︎
♏︎

dimanche

15

☽□♆ 11:06 am   v/c
☽→♏︎ 8:21 pm
☽□♅ 9:59 pm

septiembre

ᗃᗃᗃ

♏ lunes
16

☽□♂ 4:05 am
☽⚹♃ 11:28 am
☽□♀ 4:04 pm

Mater Matters #2
The weathering away of mountains almost exactly balances the
uplift of land forms—both
continents and ocean basins!
◻ *Guida Veronda 1995*

♂♂♂

♏ martes
17

♂△♄ 1:57 am
☿△♆ 2:21 am
☉♂♉ 6:06 am
☉△♆ 10:03 am
☽⚹♉ 5:27 pm
☽⚹♆ 6:38 pm
☉⚹☽ 7:19 pm v/c

☿☿☿

♏   miércoles
♐ 18

☽→♐ 3:32 am
☽♂♇ 4:53 am
☽⚹♅ 5:01 am
☽△♄ 11:45 am
☽△♂ 1:34 pm

♃♃♃

♐ jueves
19

☽△♀ 3:12 am
☽□☿ 7:04 pm

♀♀♀

♐ viernes
♑ 20

☉□☽ 4:24 am v/c
♅⚹♇ 6:17 am
☽→♑ 8:13 am
☽□♄ 3:47 pm
☽♂♃ 10:24 pm

Waxing Half Moon in ♐ Sagittarius 4:24 am PDT, 11:24 GMT

All aspects in Pacific Daylight Time; add 3 hours for EDT; add 7 hours for GMT

Year at a glance for LIBRA ♎ (Sept. 22–Oct. 22)

Saturn moves into Aries and above the Libran horizon in 1996. By April you complete a cycle of personal/inner development that began around 1981; in 1996 you shift your focus outward—into the public arena. In the last couple of years you have been preparing for this debut by fine-tuning your skills and learning to be more efficient. You are now ready to offer your knowledge and experience; people will notice you.

1996 is only the beginning of the outward cycle, which lasts for the next fourteen years. Personal and professional partnerships are the stage (battleground?) for your efforts to move out into the world. Partners may feel confining; it is easy to project your shadow onto a partner. Saturn sounds the alarm; you may have become too self-involved, and need to awake to accountability. On the flip side, you may have gotten so tied up in being accommodating that you are not being true to yourself. Either way you will need to negotiate boundaries. Use Centaury (Bach) for good boundary-making, especially if you have been overly adaptable, or Black-Eyed Susan essence (FES) for acknowledging your shadow projections. Chiron in Libra from September 1995 to early 1997 implies healing of relationship problems, which may require a crisis before renewal is possible.

Productive collaboration is stimulated by Uranus in Aquarius: you are beginning to tap into your creative genius self, revealing a playful, magnetic side. Pluto, planet of metamorphosis, is a creative stimulant in the lives of September-born Librans during 1996. Pluto's obsessive focus is best channeled into deepening your thinking and improving communication skills. Demanding new studies, research, or personal journaling help you bring secrets/mysteries out into the light. □ *Gretchen Lawlor 1995*

♑ sábado

21

☽△☿ 7:16 pm

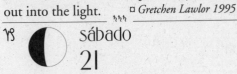

© *Sudie Rakusin 1993*

◌◌◌

♑
≈

domingo

22

Equinox

☽☌♆ 2:27 am
☉△☽ 10:39 am   v/c
☽→≈ 10:40 am
☉→♎ 11:01 am
☽☌♅ 11:56 am
☽⚹♇ 12:04 pm
☽⚹♄ 5:42 pm
♀⚹♂ 6:30 pm

♎

Sun in Libra 11:01 am PDT, 18:01 GMT

© Cilla Ericson 1994

Fall Equinox/Mabon

Giving and gratitude mark the season of harvest. Mother Earth begins her annual contraction—pulling life back into herself. Day and night are equal length as the balance shifts toward the deep blue quiet of winter's sleep. As she draws the velvet cloak of solitude around herself she does not retreat without first bestowing a bounty of treasure.

Thickets heavily laden with plump juicy blackberries sparkle like jewels in the morning dew. Apples, golden and russet, fill the air with spicy vapors as they bubble over wood fires. Harvest of hops coats our fingers with sweet sticky resin. Hops in tea or a pillow induce sleep and prophetic dreams. Set to brew, hops provide the foamy amber beverage of the coming season's celebrations.

Acknowledging her as the source of our sustenance, our gratitude is measured in the joy that we share in her gifts.

□ *Peggy Sue McRae, reprinted from* Earth First! Journal *(Mabon 1993)*

Days to Equinox

The apple tree before the house
has split and fallen under the weight of her own fruit.
I am struck dumb.
I remember catastrophe.

We stand, each of us, wondering if we caused her death
by pruning her too well,
and rejoicing, greedy, in her plentiful bearing.
I lament that I was not alive and listening well enough
to hear her groaning with her burden,
that I did not come running to ease her shoulders
with a little crutch, as I could have done.
We debate over her wound, gaping and white with fungus,
whether she was too ill, in any case, to stand longer,
or whether it was her first unnatural grafting
which brought her to such a fate,
to be brought down by her own bounty.
I am horrified that I ate her fruit,
yet did not taste in it her agony.
We speak, too late, of the need to care better
for the things with which we tamper.
I am like a child, unwilling to believe in the finality of this,
her crashing finish, too hard a loss to swallow—
not, so much, loss of her apples, but the sudden harshness in the yard,
which is the absence of her spreading self.
I think: It is her shade I'll miss most—her shadow-self.

It may be that she, old many-
autumned mother
to a million apple children,
was simply tired of cycling
gestation,
was ready to pass the duty to a
young and stronger wife.
It may be she chose her time.
I am selfishly wishing she would
speak more loudly this time,
and tell me that this was so.

But I will put away this selfishness,
and turn to the last respectful
harvest of her little ones,
see that they are cherished as the
precious beings they are,
and I will pledge to remember now,
with every pippin I take between
my teeth,
how some mother labored,
how she stood, with aching arms,
to make ready her children.

September

♒ 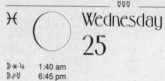 ☽ Monday
23

☽☌♂	12:24 am
♂⊼♃	4:10 am
☉△♅	5:31 am
☉✶♇	8:19 am
☽☌♀	4:53 pm v/c

♒
♓ ☽ Tuesday
24

☽→♓	11:44 am
☽□♇	1:11 pm
☽PrG	2:53 pm

♓ ☽ Wednesday
25

☽✶♃	1:40 am
☽☌☿	6:45 pm

♓
♈ ☽ Thursday
26

☽✶♆	4:33 am v/c
☿sD	10:03 am
☉☌♄	12:12 pm
♄PrG	12:31 pm
☽→♈	12:47 pm
☽✶♅	.1:57 pm
☽△♇	2:21 pm

☽☌♄	7:18 pm
☉☌☽	7:52 pm
♀♀♀	

♈ 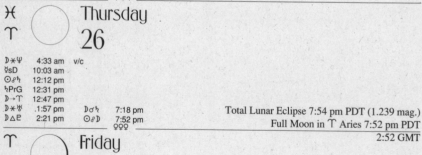 ○ Friday
27

☽□♃	3:14 am
☽△♂	6:59 am

Total Lunar Eclipse 7:54 pm PDT (1.239 mag.)
Full Moon in ♈ Aries 7:52 pm PDT
2:52 GMT

All aspects in Pacific Daylight Time; add 3 hours for EDT; add 7 hours for GMT

□ *Nic Beechsquirrel 1993*

Glastonbury Tor and the Wind

♈ ☽☽☽
♉ ◐ **Saturday**
28

☽△♀	4:12 am	
☽□♆	6:47 am	v/c
☽→♉	3:25 pm	
☽□♅	4:37 pm	

♉ ☉☉☉
  ◐ **Sunday**
29

☽△♃	6:55 am	
♀⚹♆	11:49 am	
☽□♂	12:59 pm	

September

Eyes & Water
The eye sees what is near:
Rain in the pool,
Water for the fields.
© *Laila Wah 1994*

♉ ☽ **Montag**
♊   **30**

☽△♉	3:02 am	
☽△♆	11:50 am	
☽□♀	2:08 pm	v/c
☽→♊	9:02 pm	
☽△♅	10:17 pm	
☽♂♇	11:00 pm	

♂♂♂

♊ ☽ **Dienstag**
         1

Oktober

☽✶♄	3:44 am
☉△☽	1:43 pm
☉□♃	5:02 pm
☽✶♂	10:51 pm

☿☿☿

♊ ☽ **Mittwoch**
         2

| ☽□☿ | 2:52 pm |

♃♃♃

♊ ☽ **Donnerstag**
♋   **3**

☽✶♀	4:47 am	v/c
☽→♋	6:15 am	
☽□♄	12:59 pm	
♀→♍	8:23 pm	

♀♀♀

♋ ☽ **Freitag**
         4

☽♂♃	12:36 am
☉□☽	5:05 am
♀☌♅	9:57 am
♀□♇	8:39 pm

Waning Half Moon in ♋ Cancer 5:05 am PDT, 12:05 GMT

All aspects in Pacific Daylight Time; add 3 hours for EDT; add 7 hours for GMT

水田 月月人雨沐

Nettles *Urtica dioica*

Libra rules the kidneys and embodies the balance that can come with age. Stinging nettles is a wonderful fluid balancer. It stimulates the kidneys without irritation to help the body reduce ·excess water retention, such as premenstrual water retention. The kidneys are also filters, and nettles helps them do their job more efficiently.

© Laila Wah 1994,
Chinese version of "Eyes & Water"

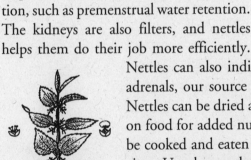

Nettles can also indirectly help to stimulate the adrenals, our source of energy after menopause. Nettles can be dried and powdered and sprinkled on food for added nutrients. Fresh nettles should be cooked and eaten like spinach. They are delicious. Use gloves to harvest the young tops for fresh food or the mature pre-flowering leaves for drying.

© Colette Gardiner 1995

ᛌᛌᛌ

♋
♌

Samstag
5

☿△Ψ	5:16 am	
☽⚹Ψ	8:04 am	
☽⚹♄	8:23 am	v/c
☽→♌	6:13 pm	
☽⚹♅	7:31 pm	
☽△♇	8:38 pm	

◉◉◉

♌

Sonntag
6

☽△♄	12:45 am
ΨsD	5:49 am
☽ApG	10:59 am
☉⚹☽	11:04 pm

---

octobre

♌  ⟩⟩⟩ _____

☽ ♂ ♂   4:23 am   v/c

lundi
7

© *Billie Miracle 1994*

♌
♍ ♂♂♂ _____

☽→♍   6:50 am
☽□♇   9:23 am
☽♂♀   6:15 pm
☿→♎   8:14 pm

mardi
8

♍ ☿☿☿ _____

☽△♃   2:22 am
☿△♅   6:24 am
♅sD   3:15 pm
☿⚹♇   4:51 pm

mercredi
9

♍
♎ ♃♃♃ _____

☽△♆   8:16 am   v/c
☿☍♄   4:46 pm
☽→♎   6:01 pm
☽△♅   7:16 pm
☽⚹♇   8:38 pm
☽☍♄   11:32 pm

jeudi
10

♎ ♀♀♀ _____

☽♂☿   12:35 am
☽□♃   1:20 pm

vendredi
11

_____

All aspects in Pacific Daylight Time; add 3 hours for EDT; add 7 hours for GMT

© Billie Miracle 1994

open the window to
the blessed night air.

Rainbringer
begins her
thigh-slapping dance

with small waterbell
movements

she comes
(and comes and comes).
¤ *Marna 1992*

ħħħ

♎ ● **samedi**

12

☉☌☽ 7:15 am
☽✶♂ 7:58 am
♀△♃ 1:42 pm
☽□♆ 5:28 pm v/c
♂✶♄ 11:09 pm

Partial Solar Eclipse 7:14 am PDT (.758 mag.)
New Moon in ♎ Libra 7:15 am PDT, 14:15 GMT

⊙⊙⊙

♎ ● **dimanche**
♏

13

☉☌♄ 1:51 am
☽→♏ 2:47 am
☽□♅ 3:58 am
☉✶♂ 4:45 am
♄ApG 11:10 am
☽✶♃ 9:44 pm

Once

I come once more
without words.
The moon appears
shy as a heifer,
her horns gleaming
over woolly mountains.

And so we have waded
through ashes.
It is time to enjoy the fire.

I come once more
without words.
The moon has
many names.
Yours the quickest,
the most potent.

And so the Milky Way pours
over our shoulders.
We do not feel the dark.

I come once more
without words.
The moon's slow arms
imagine us,
Isis sifting for pieces
of Osiris.

And so the margins of tomorrow
can be no obstacle.
Hungry are the wings of dawn.

¤ *Marcia Cohee 1994*

XI. SEXY MAMA MOON

Erotic in Nature: Vulva Tree–Vulva Spirit

octubre

ⅅⅅⅅ

♏︎ **lunes**
14

☽✶♀ 12:34 am
☽□♂ 5:37 pm

♂♂♂

♏︎
♐︎ **martes**
15

☽✶♆ 12:13 am v/c
♅□♃ 7:13 am
☽→♐︎ 9:08 am
☽✶♅ 10:18 am
☽☌♇ 11:48 am
☽△♄ 1:37 pm

☿☿☿

♐︎ **miércoles**
16

☽✶♅ 6:36 am
☽□♀ 11:11 am

♃♃♃

♐︎
♑︎ **jueves**
17

☽△♂ 12:54 am
☉✶☽ 3:51 am v/c
☽→♑︎ 1:38 pm
☽□♄ 5:44 pm
☉□♆ 7:58 pm

♀♀♀

♑︎ **viernes**
18

☽☌♃ 8:20 am
☽□♅ 5:43 pm
☽△♀ 7:45 pm

All aspects in Pacific Daylight Time; add 3 hours for EDT; add 7 hours for GMT

Mudwrestling

© *Nance Paternoster 1993*

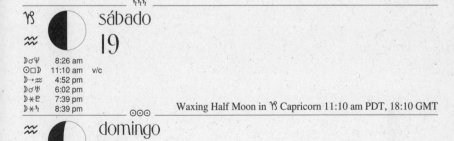

♑
♒ ♄♄♄

sábado
19

☽☌♆	8:26 am	
☉□☽	11:10 am	v/c
☽→♒	4:52 pm	
☽☌♅	6:02 pm	
☽⚹♇	7:39 pm	
☽⚹♄	8:39 pm	

♒

⊙⊙⊙

domingo
20

Waxing Half Moon in ♑ Capricorn 11:10 am PDT, 18:10 GMT

October

© Sonja Shahan 1994

For Annie

♒ ☽ Monday ☾☾☾
♓ 21

☽△♅	3:25 am
♂⊼♆	4:50 am
☽☍♂	11:19 am
☉△☽	5:31 pm v/c
☿♂♄	6:23 pm
☽→♓	7:23 pm
☽□♇	10:15 pm

♓ ☽ Tuesday ♂♂♂
22

☽PrG	1:44 am
☽⚹♃	2:37 pm
☉→♏	8:20 pm

Sun in Scorpio 8:20 pm PDT
3:20 GMT

♏

♓ ○ Wednesday ☿☿☿
♈ 23

☽☍♀	10:07 am
☽⚹♆	1:30 pm v/c
☉□♅	1:47 pm
☿□♆	7:46 pm
☽→♈	9:51 pm
☽⚹♅	11:05 pm

♈ ○ Thursday ♃♃♃
24

☽△♇	12:52 am
☽♂♄	1:10 am
☽□♃	5:48 pm
☉⊼♄	6:30 pm

♈ ○ Friday ♀♀♀
25

♀△♆	2:46 am
☿⚹♂	3:01 am
☽□♀	4:41 pm
♄△♇	8:17 pm
☽△♂	9:12 pm
☽☍♅	10:53 pm v/c

All aspects except Oct. 27 in Pacific Daylight Time; add 3 hours for EDT; add 7 hours for GMT

Year at a glance for SCORPIO ♏ (Oct. 22–Nov. 21)

Pluto has completed its fierce transit through your sign (1983–1995) and won't touch it again for a couple hundred years! Pluto brings transformation through crisis; twelve years of breakdown/breakthrough have endowed you with deep perceptions, powerful convictions, and an ability to weather anything. Soon you will be helping others, using these tools you unearthed in your own struggles. Baby Blue Eyes essence (FES) helps rebuild trust after trauma.

Uranus, at the base of your solar horoscope from 1995 to 2002, indicates a search for your best location, circumstances, or "tribe." Change will bring out qualities which would have remained undeveloped in your old setting. Your home could become a gathering place for those with common utopian, progressive, or spiritual values. You may add rooms to your home or unexpected members to the family, or live communally.

Your relationship with a parent changes; interactions are on a new, equal basis, even if the parent is no longer alive. Intuitive insights into childhood scripts can liberate you from the bondage of eternally repeating old patterns. Use Chestnut Bud (Bach) to release from outdated modes or California Wild Rose essence (FES) to transform the parent/child relationship. Forget-Me-Not essence (FES) assists the healing of relationships with those who have passed on.

Jupiter brings short, purposeful journeys, inspires education and writing. Saturn brings increased productivity. Creative blocks experienced in the last two years lift by April 1996. Iris essence (FES) is good for writer's block. For the next two years, improve skills and efficiency in preparation for future public exposure. If you are already a shining star, watch your health and develop a support team—it will pay off later.

¤ Gretchen Lawlor 1995

♈
♉

Saturday
26

☽→♉	1:12 am
☽□♅	2:31 am
☉☍☽	7:12 am
☿→♏	6:02 pm
☽△♃	10:23 pm

Full Moon in ♉ Taurus 7:12 am PDT, 14:12 GMT

♉

Sunday
27

♉□♅	5:06 am
♉☍♄	6:56 pm
☽△♆	9:42 pm

Daylight Savings Time ends 2:00 am PDT

MOON XI

Oktober

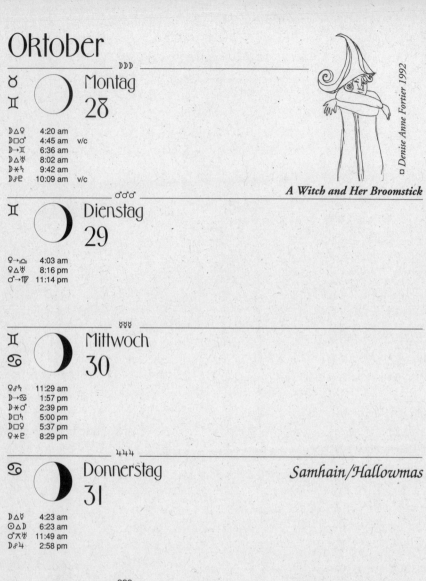

🜨 ♉ ◯ **Montag**
♊ ◯ **28**

☽△♀	4:20 am	
☽□♂	4:45 am	v/c
☽→♊	6:36 am	
☽△♅	8:02 am	
☽⚹♄	9:42 am	
☽☍♇	10:09 am	v/c

♂♂♂

♊ ◖ **Dienstag**
29

♀→♎	4:03 am
♀△♅	8:16 pm
♂→♍	11:14 pm

☿☿☿

♊ ◗ **Mittwoch**
♋ ◗ **30**

♀☍♄	11:29 am
☽→♋	1:57 pm
☽⚹♂	2:39 pm
☽□♄	5:00 pm
☽□♀	5:37 pm
♀⚹♇	8:29 pm

♄♄♄

♋ ◗ **Donnerstag**
31

Samhain/Hallowmas

☽△♉	4:23 am
☉△☽	6:23 am
♂☌♅	11:49 am
☽☍♃	2:58 pm

♀♀♀

♋ ◗ **Freitag**
1

November

☽☍♆	3:35 pm	v/c
☉☌♉	3:56 pm	

A Witch and Her Broomstick

□ *Denise Anne Fortier 1992*

All aspects in Pacific Standard Time; add 3 hours for EST; add 8 hours for GMT

□ *Webber 1993*

Samhain/ Hallowmas

"Enlightenment ... is a metaphor that skewers us firmly back into the story of duality; it negates the dark, the earth, the body, the dark womb, the night."—Starhawk, *from* Dreaming the Dark

"If the severing of our intimate connectedness to the Earth, the sky, the dead, the unseen, and our ancestors was the accomplishment of the Enlightenment, then ecofeminism calls for an endarkenment— a bonding with the Earth and the invisible that will reestablish our sense of interconnectedness with all things, phenomenal and spiritual, that make up the totality of life in our cosmos."—Gloria Feman Orenstein, *from* Reweaving the World

Samhain is pronounced by orthodox pagans "sow-wain." Not having benefit of the oral tradition, my own coven has called it "Sam-hain" for nine years. Most commonly we use Halloween, from All Hallows' Eve. It is the night of returning souls.

In northern climes, October, like a slippery cellar stairway, plunges us into the dark. By Samhain—October 31, the Witches' New Year—crisp round apples are being pressed into cider as linear time and linear thought unravel. At midnight on Samhain five women on hickory brooms fly through the loops. Wispy clouds illuminate, with silver-blue moonlight, five postmodern cowgirls riding giant mammoths with gleaming tusks through the shimmery grassland where Grangeville used to be. When ready, the mammoth riders dismount and form a circle. The spell is cast. Then, like female shamans in China, the timetravelers cover their faces with handkerchiefs and dance on one foot until they go into trance and fall over. Slowly, with lots of stretching and groaning, the warmth of crackling fire, the flickering orange glow of candlelit pumpkins, and the smell of pumpkin seeds roasting in olive oil and tamari bring the charm casters back to the Samhain kitchen. The glasses are filled with cider and a toast is made ... to the age of endarkenment!

□ *Peggy Sue McRae 1994, reprinted from* Earth First! Journal *(Samhain 1993 and 1994)*

Wind Women

Smooth and strong
are the fingers of the night
that pull my hair and part my thighs.
Cinnamon and cocoa
drips the tongue of the dark,
the voice of the sisters
calling me skyclad.
Coming as cats,
as owls,
as howls
of wolves
gathering
wind women
banshee.
Lilith.
Medea.

Scudding and screaching.
Spittle and spite.
Footstamping fury.
Shape shifting
shadow figures
weaving with leaves,
winging with bats,
webbing our jewels
of the spidery silvery
Cygnus.
Rising from ashes, the ashes.
Uprising from dust, the dust.
Writhing our rhythms
against your safe houses.
Pressing our indigo lips
to convention.
Cavorting, contorting,
cackling crones.
Wind women
banshee
flying
free.

© Claire Marshall 1994

Womb Print

© *Lucy Steel 1993*

Vitex

Vitex agnus-castus

Scorpio rules the reproductive organs. In today's polluted world our reproductive systems are vulnerable. Occasional mild liver herbs can help, but more may be required. Vitex has a long history and is currently being used as a hormone balancer. It's particularly helpful for women who show symptoms of excess estrogen or low progesterone, such as fibroids

or certain kinds of PMS. Many women have had success using vitex on a daily basis to shrink or regulate fibroid growth. Generally, long-term use is needed as well as other supporting therapies. The seeds are the part used.

© *Colette Gardiner 1995*

♋︎
♌︎

Samstag

2

☽→♌︎	1:17 am		
☽☍♅	3:03 am		
☽△♄	4:11 am		
☽△♇	5:33 am	♂□♇	8:33 pm
☽✳♀	11:50 am	☉□☽	11:51 pm

◯◯◯

Waning Half Moon in ♌︎ Leo 11:51 pm PST
7:59 GMT

♌︎

Sonntag

3

☽□☿	1:48 am	v/c
☽ApG	5:40 am	
☿✳♃	7:21 pm	

---

novembre

♌
♍

lundi
4

☽→♍ 1:58 pm
☽□♇ 6:26 pm
☽☌♂ 8:29 pm

Madonna and Pregnant Woman

□ *Denise Anne Fortier 1992*

♍

mardi
5

☉⚹♃ 9:26 am
☽△♃ 5:18 pm
☉⚹☽ 5:54 pm
☽⚹♅ 11:37 pm

♍

mercredi
6

☽△♆ 4:14 pm v/c

♍
♎

jeudi
7

☽→♎ 1:30 am
☿ApG 3:21 am
☽△♅ 3:24 am
☽☍♄ 3:49 am
☽⚹♇ 5:58 am

♎

vendredi
8

☽☌♀ 12:25 am
☽□♃ 4:24 am

All aspects in Pacific Standard Time; add 3 hours for EST; add 8 hours for GMT

¤ *J. Morrigan 1993*

Woman in Waiting

☌☌☌

♎︎
♏︎

samedi
9

☽□♆ 1:24 am v/c
☽→♏︎ 10:03 am
☽□♅ 11:57 am
☽✶♂ 8:50 pm

⊙⊙⊙

♏︎

dimanche
10

♀□♃ 12:04 am
♄✶♅ 8:50 am
☽✶♃ 12:08 pm
⊙☌☽ 8:17 pm

Lunar Samhain
New Moon in ♏︎ Scorpio 8:17 pm PST
4:17 GMT (Nov. 11)

MOON XI

The trees say
Look, Look
We are here
Green in this morning.
We grow taller every year.
Look, you too
Can survive.
But I, I wonder.
Touch is my touchstone.

Yes, you have survived
I say
Looking at the cut madrone
Drying beside the road.
Yes, you have survived
Until the chain saw
Dropped you
Severed you from the earth.

Look, says the mountain
I have survived.
Yes, you have survived
I say
I see you have survived
With patches of earth
Bare to the sun.
With deep gulleys
Cut by the rains.
With forest fires
And windfalls.
Yes, you have survived.

As I have survived
With deep gulleys
Cut by tears,
With bare nerves
Laced by fire
With hurricanes
Blowing through my mind.
Yes, I have survived.

□ *Ruth Mountaingrove 1984*

XII. INTERCONNECTEDNESS MOON

Our pain for the world is a very immediate way of recognizing and bowing to our interconnectedness.

—Joanna Macy

Collage and handlettering © Rashani 1991, quote © Joanna Macy 1991

noviembre

DDD

♏
♐
lunes
11

☽☌♅	7:08 am
☽⚹♆	7:20 am v/c
☿⚹♆	8:53 am
☽→♐	3:27 pm
☽△♄	5:13 pm
☽⚹♅	5:22 pm
☽☌♇	7:46 pm

♂♂♂

♐
martes
12

☽□♂	3:49 am
☽⚹♀	10:19 pm v/c

☿☿☿

♐
♑
miércoles
13

☽→♑	6:45 pm
☽□♄	8:20 pm

♃♃♃

♑
jueves
14

☿→♐	8:37 am
☽△♂	8:45 pm
☽☌♃	8:26 pm
☿△♄	10:35 pm

♀♀♀

♑
≈
viernes
15

☿⚹♅	3:11 am
☽□♀	5:44 am
☉⚹☽	10:37 am
☽☌♆	1:33 pm v/c
☽PrG	8:45 pm
☽→≈	9:15 pm
☽⚹♄	10:43 pm
☽☌♅	11:19 pm

'Cause you know our tears are healing
to the one whose pain we're feeling
We know our tears are healing
to the one who gave us birth
Sweet Mama Earth

© *Alice Di Micele 1989, excerpted from*
"Julie's Song" from the album It's a Miracle

All aspects in Pacific Standard Time; add 3 hours for EST; add 8 hours for GMT

We let the flesh of our Mother be coated with pavement
so we could walk all over her
without getting our feet wet or dirty
Sealed safely in our cars
So we can't hear her scream

When we let the flesh of our Mother
be coated in pavement
we let our own flesh become pavement
And before we know it
we let the whole world
DRIVE ALL OVER US
without getting its feet wet or dirty
Without hearing us Scream

© Loba G. Hardin 1994

		sábado 16
D✶♅	1:43 am	
D✶♇	1:43 am	
♅♂♇	1:44 am	

		domingo 17
☉✶♆	4:52 am	
D△♀	1:09 pm	
☉□D	5:10 pm	v/c

Waxing Half Moon in ≈ Aquarius 5:10 pm PST
1:10 GMT (Nov. 18)

November

♒︎
♓︎
Monday
18

☽→♓︎	12:01 am
☽□♇	4:41 am
☽□♅	10:48 am
☽☍♂	6:05 pm
♆□⚷	9:39 pm

♓︎
Tuesday
19

♀□♆	1:58 am
♀☌⚷	2:24 am
☽✶♃	3:29 am
☽✶♆	7:49 pm

♓︎
♈︎
Wednesday
20

☉△☽	12:39 am	v/c
☽→♈︎	3:35 am	
☽☌♄	4:54 am	
☽✶♅	5:57 am	
☽△♇	8:29 am	
☽△♅	9:03 am	

♈︎
Thursday
21

| ☽□♃ | 8:19 am |
| ☉→♐︎ | 4:50 pm |

♐︎

Sun in Sagittarius 4:50 pm PST
0:50 GMT

♈︎
♉︎
Friday
22

☽□♆	12:22 am	
☽☍♀	7:16 am	v/c
☽→♉︎	8:13 am	
☉△♄	9:46 am	
☽□♅	10:46 am	
♅☌♂	11:02 am	
♀→♏︎	5:35 pm	

All aspects in Pacific Standard Time; add 3 hours for EST; add 8 hours for GMT

Year at a glance for SAGITTARIUS ♐ (Nov. 21–Dec. 21)

Sagittarians are beginning a major cycle of metamorphosis, which surfaced when Pluto moved into your sign in 1995. Pluto symbolizes the forces of transformation, and will be with you for fourteen years. In the next couple of years you will be encouraged to take risks and do things you've always maintained you wouldn't. Utter sincerity and a respect for a process beyond your present comprehension help. Use Walnut (Bach) for guidance and assistance during major changes or Sage essence (FES) for wisdom and acceptance.

Under Pluto's influence you will become more profoundly Sagittarian in the next few years—more philosophical, more idealistic, more adventurous, and hopefully wiser. The changes that occur now are giving you opportunities to become a deeper, more powerful person.

Saturn indicates you will make a deeper impression on others by way of disciplined efforts rather than through dramatic displays in 1996. You may have more impact (and money) by teaching others to handle their creative processes; you see tangible proof of your ability to inspire others. Cosmos essence (FES) lends ability to articulate inspirations.

You benefit from exploring your town or city; you will discover people and activities that stimulate new interests. Flashes of insight free you from habitual thought-patterns and modes of expression. Heightened mental energy may leave you occasionally nervous, unable to settle. A program of physical exercise, a sport, or yoga helps to siphon off excess. Lady's Slipper essence (FES) helps harness excess nervous energy; Cosmos essence (FES) helps the mind keep up with insights.   ▢ *Gretchen Lawlor 1995*

♉ ◯ **Saturday**
23

☉✶♅	3:39 am
♀⊼♄	7:08 am
☽△♂	7:13 am
☽△♃	2:30 pm
♀□♅	10:39 pm

♉ ◯ **Sunday**
♊
24

☽△♆	6:20 am	v/c
☽→♊	2:21 pm	
☽✶♄	3:35 pm	♁ApG	6:38 pm
☉♂♇	3:56 pm	☽♂♇	7:52 pm
☽△♅	5:08 pm	☉♂☽	8:11 pm

Epona
▢ *Monica Sjöö 1990*

Full Moon in ♊ Gemini 8:11 pm PST
4:11 GMT (Nov. 25)

November

DDD

♊   ◐   ## Montag
☽   ## 25

☽□♂   4:24 pm
☽☍♅   11:23 pm   v/c

Wild Salmon

□ *S. J. Hugdahl 1994*

♂♂♂

♊   ◑   ## Dienstag
♋   ## 26

☽→♋   10:38 pm
☽□♄   11:53 pm

☿☿☿

♋   ◑   ## Mittwoch
          ## 27

☽△♀   9:46 am

♄♄♄

♋   ◑   ## Donnerstag
          ## 28

☽✶♂   4:17 am
☽☍♃   9:25 am

♀♀♀

♋   ◑   ## Freitag
♌   ## 29

☽☍♆   1:02 am   v/c
☽→♌   9:31 am
☽△♄   10:46 am
☽☍♅   12:56 pm
☽△♇   3:55 pm

All aspects in Pacific Standard Time; add 3 hours for EST; add 8 hours for GMT

Cleavers *Galium aparine*

What happens to Earth happens to us. Our blood, veins, and lymph system are microcosms of her waterways. There are many ways to support immunity, but one way is to support lymph drainage. The lymph system filters what is too big or too small for the veins to absorb directly and creates white blood cells for im-

Testimony of Faith

mune response. Exercise and hydrotherapy stimulate lymph circulation. Cleavers can support lymph drainage. Its mild nutritive action makes it ideal for regular use, unlike some of the stronger lymphatics such as echinacea or chaparral. It helps us adapt to the arrival of spring and summer and is a slight diuretic. Eat it steamed or make a tea from fresh tops.

© Colette Gardiner 1995

♌ ☽ **Samstag**
30

⊙△☽ 2:37 am
☽□♀ 4:00 am

♌ ☽ **Sonntag**
♍   **1**

Dezember

☽ApG 2:30 am
☽△♅ 2:23 pm v/c
☽→♍ 10:12 pm

MOON XII

décembre

♍ **lundi**
2

☽□♇	4:53 am
☿⚹⚷	7:28 am
☉□☽	9:07 pm
☽⚹♀	11:54 pm

 ♍ **mardi**
3

Waning Half Moon in ♍ Virgo 9:07 pm PST

5:07 GMT

♄sD	3:44 am
☽♂♂	10:04 am
☽△♃	12:25 pm

♍ ♎ **mercredi**
4

☽△♆	2:18 am	v/c
☿→♑	5:49 am	
☽→♎	10:24 am	
☽□☿	11:01 am	
☽☍♄	11:36 am	
☽△♅	2:11 pm	
☿□♄	4:01 pm	
☽⚹♇	5:04 pm	

♎ **jeudi**
5

☉⚹☽	1:41 pm
☽□♃	11:58 pm

 ♎ ♏ **vendredi**
6

☽□♆	12:12 pm	v/c
☽→♏	7:40 pm	
☽□♅	11:23 pm	

All aspects in Pacific Standard Time; add 3 hours for EST; add 8 hours for GMT

Earthquake Woman

¤ *Kellie Rae Cantwell (Bird) 1993*

earthquake

even California shook
I awoke in my sleep
it could have been another
rainforest burial
or the flight of a spotted owl
to her grave
but instead it was you
dancing your dance
beauty so bare upon your altar
the world
     ¤ *Brenwyn 1989*

♏ 🌑   ♄♄♄

samedi
7

☽✶☿   3:10 am

♏ 🌑   ☉☉☉

dimanche
8

♂△♃	1:44 am	
☽♂♀	6:18 am	
☽✶♃	7:31 am	
☽✶♂	7:38 am	
☽✶♆	6:10 pm	v/c
♀✶♃	10:21 pm	

this cabin is lushly forest-surrounded, and i sit here, strangely some-times, thinking of the homes we all build. i think of how many creatures take the world and shape it into something to wrap around themselves. —take these sticks, this hair, some moss; break them into pieces, mold it all into a shape like cupped hands for laying eggs in. —take this hillside; burrow tough little hands into dirt, expand holes in Earth into tunnels, doorways and rooms for long hours of sleeping. —take this mud and spit and leaves like papier-mâché; pack it all into a big hanging ball, lantern-like, full of chambers for flying in and out of.

OR take these trees and cut them down, crash all over everything, change the trees into boards, bang it all loudly together in a square with pointed corners, light it up at night when the rest of the forest is dark.

we have been stumbling. i send blessings for surefootedness in our steps towards quieter and humbler ways.

□ *Pandora Cate 1994*

□ *Becky Bee 1994*

XIII. SHELTER MOON

Becky Bee 1994

Earth Houses
joining millennia of women,
sculpting each other temples of
embracing earth
for our goddess selves.
Becky Bee 1994

diciembre

⟩⟩⟩

 ♏ ♐ **lunes**
9

☽→♐ 12:59 am
☽△♄ 2:05 am
♀✶♂ 4:23 am
☽✶♅ 4:38 am
☽♂♇ 7:06 am

Nest
© *Cilla Ericson 1993*

♂♂♂

 ♐ **martes**
10

☉♂☽ 8:57 am
☽□♂ 12:22 pm v/c

New Moon in ♐ Sagittarius 8:57 am PST, 16:57 GMT

☿☿☿

 ♐ ♑ **miércoles**
11

☽→♑ 3:16 am
☽□♄ 4:21 am
☽♂☿ 8:11 pm

♄♄♄

♑ **jueves**
12

☽♂♃ 1:21 pm
☽△♂ 3:02 pm
☽✶♀ 7:59 pm
☽PrG 8:10 pm
☽♂♆ 10:00 pm v/c

♀♀♀

♑ ♒ **viernes**
13

☽→♒ 4:15 am
☽✶♄ 5:23 am
☽♂♅ 8:02 am
☽✶♇ 10:20 am
☉□♂ 6:43 pm
♀✶♆ 8:31 pm

All aspects in Pacific Standard Time; add 3 hours for EST; add 8 hours for GMT

humeda tierra y
calido abrazo del
ramaje que enreda y
protege sus tiernos
sueños secretos

damp earth and
warm embrace of the
boughs which surround
     and
protect your tender
secret dreams

¤ *Isabel F. Vargas 1994*   © *Isabel F. Vargas 1994*

dreaming from earth

≈ ◗ **sábado**
           14

☉∗☽ 6:45 pm

≈ ◗ **domingo**
♓   **15**

☽□♀ 1:57 am   v/c
☽→♓ 5:45 am
☽□♇ 12:08 pm

December

DDD

♓ **Monday**
16

D ✱ ♉   7:40 am
D ✱ ♃   6:44 pm
♀ → ♐   9:35 pm
D ☍ ♂   10:02 pm

roofing the adobe

□ *zana 1985*

♂♂♂

♓
♈ **Tuesday**
17

☉ □ D   1:32 am
D ✱ ♅   2:32 am   v/c
D → ♈   8:56 am
D △ ♀   10:04 am
D ♂ ♄   10:19 am
♀ △ ♄   12:54 pm
D ✱ ♅   1:20 pm
D △ ♇   3:43 pm

Waxing Half Moon in ♓ Pisces 1:32 am PST, 9:32 GMT

♅♅♅

♈ **Wednesday**
18

D □ ♉   3:25 pm
♀ ✱ ♅   11:32 pm

♃♃♃

♈
♉ **Thursday**
19

D □ ♃   12:18 am
D □ ♆   7:40 am
☉ △ D   10:52 am   v/c
D → ♉   2:11 pm
D □ ♅   6:57 pm

♀♀♀

♉ **Friday**
20

♀ ♂ ♇   2:06 am

All aspects in Pacific Standard Time; add 3 hours for EST; add 8 hours for GMT

Year at a glance for CAPRICORN ♑ (Dec. 21–Jan. 20)

Jupiter, planet of optimism and abundance, is in Capricorn all of 1996—a good year to be adventurous. You inspire confidence and seize opportunities that will continue to benefit you for the next twelve years.

Uranus brings unsettled financial conditions; in 1996 you are likely to experience a windfall. Don't expect increased cash flow to stick around. You surprise even yourself with magnanimous gestures. Saturn in good aspect to Uranus from April to December indicates benefit through buying a home or property. Don't invest wildly. On a deeper level, you are finding ways to establish yourself on your own terms, free from old dependencies. Sunflower essence (FES) nourishes a healthy sense of self and heals early ego wounding.

You may experience a change in finances as you leave an unsatisfying job to pursue something more stimulating and meaningful. It's a good time to take stock of unused talents and abilities and develop them. It is less disruptive at this time to find ways to make an existing job more interesting and exciting, but if this can't be done, it's a good year to go looking. Buttercup essence (FES) helps you to acknowledge unique talents; Scleranthus (Bach) aids decisiveness.

Pluto, planet of transformation, will bring to the surface hidden or suppressed sides of yourself in the next few years, especially parts that went astray during your childhood. In your actions this year you may be trying to recreate the perfect past that you didn't have. Evening Primrose essence (FES) helps process early rejection or abandonment; Golden Ear Drops essence (FES) connects you with strength and wisdom from your past.

□ Gretchen Lawlor 1995

♉ ☽ Saturday
♊   21

☽△♉	12:19 am	
☉→♑	6:07 am	
☽△♃	7:56 am	
☽△♂	1:02 pm	☽→♊ 9:18 pm
☽△♆	2:43 pm	v/c ☽✱♄ 11:02 pm

Solstice

♑

Sun in Capricorn 6:07 am PST, 14:07 GMT

♊ ☽ Sunday
           22

☽△♅	2:27 am
☉□♄	4:10 am
☽☌♇	4:53 am
☽☌♀	10:14 am

Angeline's Dream

© Mara Friedman 1994

Winter Solstice/Yule

Yule celebrates the returning light. Hanukkah candles and Christmas lights both have deeper roots in pagan celebrations honoring the returning sun.

Sacred plants of the season are the evergreens, trees that retain their life and vitality throughout the year. A reverence for evergreens as a symbol of life everlasting is the history of today's Christmas tree. Cutting the tree down and bringing it inside to dry up and die defeats the sacred meaning. In an era of unprecedented deforestation there are better ways to honor evergreens than to kill them. Using driftwood or boughs taken from windfall are a few alternatives.

□ *Peggy Sue McRae, reprinted from*
Earth First! Journal *(Yule 1993)*

© *Beth Freewomon 1995*

from her deep well
springs abundant
Life
In loving & being free
we allow
the ancient
to thrive
in their
wise
deep
ways
Let us enter
the darkness
in strength
&
harmonious
song

Will Well

□ *Alea Brage 1994*

Dezember

♊ ◯ Montag
23

♅sR   11:40 am
☽□♂ 11:30 pm v/c

♊
♋ ◯ Dienstag
24

♂△♆ 3:12 am
☽→♋ 6:15 am
☽□♄ 8:13 am
☉☌☽ 12:42 pm

Full Moon in ♋ Cancer 12:42 pm PST, 20:42 GMT

♋ ◯ Mittwoch
25

☽☌♅ 6:47 pm

♋
♌ ◖ Donnerstag
26

☽☌♃ 5:03 am
☽☌♆ 10:28 am
☽✶♂ 12:03 pm v/c
☽→♌ 5:10 pm
☽△♄ 7:23 pm
☽☌♅ 11:11 pm

♌ ◖ Freitag
27

☽△♇ 1:37 am
☽△♀ 8:39 pm v/c

All aspects in Pacific Standard Time; add 3 hours for EST; add 8 hours for GMT

A Small Stone Knows

I have tried
this and that
here and there

still haven't hit
a niche that fits

but a small stone
that I let go
from my grip

knows where
to find its
place on Earth

¤ Nasira Alma 1994

¤ Marie Theodore 1993

Mnadra Temple, Malta

♌ Samstag
28

)ApG   9:23 pm

♌ Sonntag
♍ 29

♇→♏   4:10 am
)→♍   5:46 am
)☐♇   2:33 pm
☉△)   11:53 pm

décembre ♌♌♌

♍ **lundi**
30

☽△♅ 11:32 am
☽□♀ 4:49 pm

♂♂♂

♍
♎ **mardi**
31

☽△♃ 8:42 am
☽△♆ 12:10 pm
☽♂♂ 5:03 pm v/c
☽→♎ 6:33 pm
☽☍♄ 9:14 pm

☿☿☿

♎ **mercredi**
1

janvier 1997

☽△♅ 1:07 am
☽⚹♇ 3:20 am
☉♂♅ 5:23 pm
☽□♅ 5:42 pm
☉□☽ 5:46 pm

♃♃♃

Waning Half Moon in ♎ Libra 5:46 pm PST
1:46 GMT

♎ **jeudi**
2

☿PrG 9:13 am
☽⚹♀ 11:18 am
☽□♃ 8:51 pm
☽□♆ 11:12 pm v/c

♀♀♀

♎
♏ **vendredi**
3

♂→♎ 12:11 am
☽→♏ 5:03 am
☽□♅ 11:29 am
☽⚹♅ 9:27 pm

All aspects in Pacific Standard Time; add 3 hours for EST; add 8 hours for GMT

Owl Treehouse

□ *Julia Doughty 1987*

Protective Herbs for Our Shelters

The pollution of Earth is not just physical but psychic. Magical protection is important. An old European tradition recommends taking mistletoe and placing it inside a ball of hawthorn branches. Tie it above your door with a red ribbon at the winter solstice and keep it up all year for protection and good luck. Burn it the following winter solstice.

© *Colette Gardiner 1995*

♏  samedi

4

☉⚹☽ 7:35 am

♏ ♐ dimanche

5

☽⚹♃ 4:51 am
☽⚹♆ 6:13 am v/c
☽→♐ 11:28 am
☽⚹♂ 12:50 pm   ☽⚹♅ 5:38 pm
☽△♄ 2:16 pm   ☽☌♇ 7:22 pm

enero

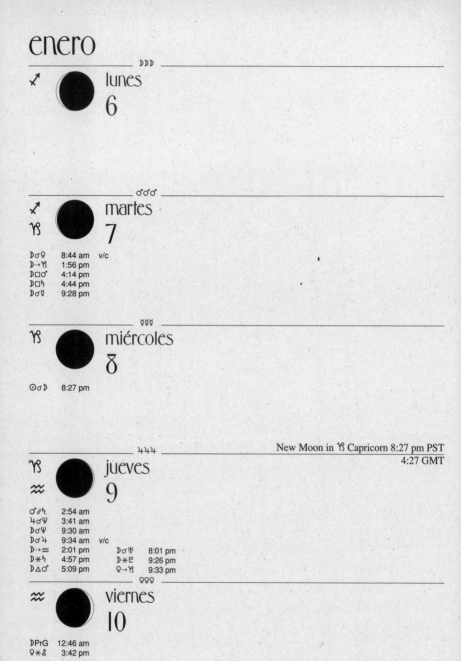

♐ **lunes**
6

⫶⫶⫶ ♂♂♂

♐
♑ **martes**
7

☽☌♀	8:44 am	v/c
☽→♑	1:56 pm	
☽□♂	4:14 pm	
☽□♄	4:44 pm	
☽☌♅	9:28 pm	

☿☿☿

♑ **miércoles**
8

| ☉☌☽ | 8:27 pm | |

♄♄♄

New Moon in ♑ Capricorn 8:27 pm PST
4:27 GMT

♑
♒ **jueves**
9

♂☍♄	2:54 am				
♃☌♆	3:41 am				
☽☌♆	9:30 am				
☽☌♃	9:34 am	v/c	☽☌♅	8:01 pm
☽→♒	2:01 pm		☽✶♇	9:26 pm
☽✶♄	4:57 pm		♀→♑	9:33 pm
☽△♂	5:09 pm			

♀♀♀

♒ **viernes**
10

| ☽PrG | 12:46 am | |
| ♀✶♆ | 3:42 pm | |

___

All aspects in Pacific Standard Time; add 3 hours for EST; add 8 hours for GMT

Cradled in the
Womb of
the
Woods

Cradled in the Womb of the Woods

□ Becca 1993

COVER NOTES

Front cover by Michelle Waters, Tahoma—Spirit of the Cascades © *1993*

Tahoma—Spirit of the Cascades was painted while I lived in northern Washington State. It is inspired by the North Cascades and by the spirit of wild salmon which lives strongly there, even though the salmon runs have all but been destroyed by human greed. *Tahoma* is one of a series of womb paintings which celebrate womyn's bodies as part of the earth. If we learn to recognize our human selves as being of this earth, we are more likely to treat her with respect. I want my art to serve as a reminder that humans are part of the web of life, and we need to reconnect!

May we all gather enough wisdom and courage to turn back the tide of planetary destruction and embrace all beings with love and protection.

© Michelle Waters 1995

ACKNOWLEDGMENTS

We'Moon '96 has been born, and I have undergone an initiation of sorts. Musawa, thanks for letting me care for your precious baby while you were away. Thank you, Margarita, for guiding me through the bizness end of things and for always having an answer. Linda, I appreciate how you hopped right in and harmonized with the We'Moon way. Pandora, thanks for hagging. Thanks, land sisters, for flexing with me.

Sincere thanks to all who helped in the weaving/selection process: Carruch, Deanne, C.J., Linda, Amy, diana, Lori, Bethroot, Madrone, Guida, Becky Bee, Korë, Marti, Kaseja, Ila, Judith, Hallie, Marna, Ann, Vivian, Patience, Emma, Jill, Catherine, Dayna, Raina, Leslie, Mychelle, Laura, Viki, Micki, Margarita, Lois, and Darryla. Special thanks to Catherine, Judith, Bethroot, and Madrone for hosting weaving circles. Thank you, Pandora, for co-organizing and co-facilitating the circles with me; it was great to weave and edit with you again.

Justine, thank you for your copyediting and proofing expertise. Wimmin at Rainbow's End and Other End, thank you for sharing your homes during production. Francis, thanks for opening your home/office to We'Moon and for sharing incredible bytes of pagemaking wisdom. Thanks, Ní Aódigaín, proof-mom, and other proofing wimmin: Annie, gani et se, Maria, Kasha, and Alex. Nicole, your food was an awesome way to connect with the abundant and delectable Mother while working!

Thank you, Gisela, Rosemarie, and Monica, for putting so much love into producing the German edition.

□ *Beth Freewomon 1995*

Copyrights/Contacts

Copyrights of individual works belong to each **We'Moon** contributor. Please honor the copyrights: © means "do not reproduce without the expressed permission of the artist or author." Some we'moon prefer to free the copyright on their work. ¤ means "this work may be passed on among women who wish to reprint it 'in the spirit of We'Moon,' with credit given and a copy sent to the author/artist." Contributors can be contacted directly when their addresses are given in the bylines, or by sending a letter *with a stamped envelope plus $1 handling fee for each contributor to be contacted*. **We'Moon** networking is awesome.

Contributor Bylines

Alea Brage (Portland, OR): Being a city gal, I must make it my daily practice to feel of the earth through song, dance, ritual, and with we'moons' love.

Alice Di Micele (Ashland, OR): I sing from my soul with reverence for all life. My goal is to inspire and to do my part in healing hearts, souls, and our world. Music is my spiritual path.

Amy Schutzer (Portland, OR): Writing, for me, is a divining rod that unearths what is hidden. When not writing, I garden. Both activities require lots of composting. I also love to schmooze with my friends.

Anne Paley (Manchester, England): I am a poet and astrologer, discovering how to heal myself and align with the flow of life.

Annie Ocean (Roseburg, OR): A long-time country lesbian, naturalist-herbalist-witch. A quintuplet water sign, age 46, photographing since she was 7, singing since she was born!

Audrey Nichols (Vienna, ME): The art quilts of Audrey Nichols reflect the cycles of nature; interrelationships between the cosmos, earth, and her inhabitants; and the myths and histories of various cultures from around the world. Her quilts are often inspired by her research into history from the feminine perspective.

Barbara J. Raisbeck (Eugene, OR) is an Herbalist and an Educator of Wholistic Health and Living. She is the mother of two children, and believes that each womb'an is a mother of the earth.

Becca (Gambrills, MD): Illustrator, graphic designer, teacher, helping partner Judy with painted furniture business in country, feeling truly blessed.

Becky Bee (Grants Pass, OR): Offer ♀ only workshops on earth house building as my service to mother earth and myself and others. Presently living in Oregon—shareholder at Aradia, New Zealand, open ♀♀ land.

Beth Freewomon (Cascadia, OR): I am living in intentional community with wimmin, guiding the **We'Moon** through her cycles. Recently a newlywed: I created an Imbolc commitment ceremony, dedicating myself to my Self, the Earth, and the Goddess. I am an eco-nerd: zealously refilling all sorts of containers instead of using virgin disposable cups, bags, and bottles. Thrift shopping is my passion!

Bethroot Gwynn (Myrtle Creek, OR): I have been living on lesbian land for 19 years—growing food, art, poetry, ritual. We offer summer workshops for women in Tai Chi, Personal Theater, Writing. Write for details: Fly Away Home, PO Box 593, Myrtle Creek, OR 97457.

Bev Severn (BC, Canada): Originally from England—Essex, Bristol, Brighton and the Wye Valley (Gwent). I now live on Denman Island with my daughter, Alana. My sculptural and decorative clay work reflect my love of nature and the creativity of the goddess within.

Billie Miracle (Grants Pass, OR) is a pastel and graphic artist living on women's land for 19 years. She is a founder of WomanShare and is a community/cultural worker. She is 50 now!

Brenwyn (Billings, MT) is a lesbian writer, artist, and musician currently living in Montana.

Carruch (Estacada, OR) lives in community at We'Moon. Interstellar Angel just visiting, but quite willing to help out around the planet.

Cary E. Rector (Pensacola, FL): Photographer, painter, sculptor, artist of life. Recently two elves made my sixfoot wingspan and antenna so that I could become the Fairy I always knew I was. I live my life with the purpose of waking others up to the true loving spirit within. I am currently writing a book for other free spirited women. Correspondence welcome! 2105 Magnolia Ave., Pensacola, FL 32503.

Cilla Ericson (Drottningholm, Sweden): I am an artist, mother, founder of The Painting Academy for Children in Stockholm. Presently working on a series of life forms titled "Bearing Fruit" (exhibition 94/95). Artists can still see with the eyes of a child.

Claire Marshall (Yorkshire, England): I am a poet and short story writer. I love Steve & my manic cat & cookery & painting & words & fragrance & moonlit nights & music.

Colette Gardiner (Eugene, OR): Colette Gardiner is a witch, herbalist, gardener, astrologer, and is quite attached to her feline familiars. She offers classes, herbwalks, and apprentice programs.

Corre Mott (Pender Island, BC, Canada): I am a woman who lives in the woods on an island off the BC coast. I am the mother of 3 sons. I am a Baha'i. It was important for me to paint this so that at least one piece of historic art made sense.

Corvus Conjunctio (Falls, PA) lives with her mate in eastern PA. Her Bone & Crow Studio produces mixed media art and fine crafts centered on spiritual and esoteric principles. Fabric collage a specialty.

Debby Earthdaughter (Saguaroland, Tucson, AZ): 32, european heritage, from middle class, living on SSI with multiple chemical sensitivity. Emerging from satanic ritual abuse.

Deborah Koff-Chapin (Langley, WA): As an artist and teacher, Deborah has been developing the process of Touch Drawing since she discovered it in revelatory play in 1974. Her artwork has been featured in *Parabola, Shaman's Drum, Psychological Perspectives,* and *Creation Spirituality.* Her book *At the Pool of Wonder* (co-authored with Marcia Lauck) is a selection of visionary dreams and images. She is also the creator of *Soul Cards* and founder of the Center for Touch Drawing.

Denise Anne Fortier (Eugene, OR): I am a womyn/artist/teacher/student living with my partner and my cat and a baby-to-be in a house in the country.... I am lucky to be surrounded by the beauty of nature.

Durga Bernhard (Woodstock, NY) is a painter, printmaker, designer, and illustrator of numerous children's books. Her work has been influenced by ancient and tribal art from all over the world. Greeting cards of her work are available from Amber Lotus, 1241 21st St., Oakland, CA 94607, (800) 326-2375.

Earth First! Journal (Eugene, OR) is a forum for the no-compromise environmental movement. *EF!* is published eight times a year on the solstices, equinoxes, and cross-quarter days. Subscriptions are available: PO Box 1415, Eugene, OR 97440, (503) 741-9191.

Elizabeth Hunter (Clifton, Bristol, England): For the past 5 years the Sumerian Goddess Inanna has been the source mythology for my work. The progress of Inanna through her descent into the underworld, the gaining of wisdom and her subsequent renewal provide a timeless mirror for the stages in a modern woman's life.

Ellen Marie Hinchcliffe (Minneapolis, MN): Named for both my Grandmas. Born on the Day of the Dead, 1968. Scorpio! I am a bisexual poet, actively trying to decolonize myself through Art, practicing anti-racism, loving our Mama (in the city!), and living with cats and womyn.

Gail D. Whitter (Coquitlam, BC, Canada) is a Canadian poet/haikuist whose work has appeared in numerous literary journals in North America. Gail is also editor of Trabarni Productions, a small press.

Georgiann Carlson (Arlington Heights, IL): Writer/artist/political cartoonist. Masters in wimmin's studies, feminist and animal rights activist. Also, witch and ritual maker. Blessed be—

Gretchen Lawlor (Langley, WA): Astrologer and naturopath. I use flower essences, herbs and homeopathy to support unfolding strengths and release outworn habits. Yes, I do astrological work, in person or by mail. Box 753, Langley, WA 98260.

Guida Veronda (Carpinteria, CA and Yellowstone National Park, WY): I am another woman committed to living within the resources of our Mother Earth, respecting the interconnections of all, and interpreting planet to people through writing, photography, slide programs, hikes, walks and talks in national parks of the western U.S.

Harvest McCampbell (Carmichael, CA) is a poet and herbalist of Native American and Northern European descent. She lives and works in Sacramento County, CA.

Hawk Madrone (Myrtle Creek, OR): The camera is another eye that reminds me: the goddess is everywhere!

The Holy Hemp Sisters (Santa Cruz, CA) are a **circle** of Co-Inspirators Reforming Cannabis Laws Everywhere, especially in Santa Cruz, where our spiritual/political changework is grounded in rituals for personal and community empowerment. If you are ready to just say "no more" and would like to know more, contact Theodora Kerry and Sandra Pastorius at PO Box 2344, Santa Cruz, CA 95063.

Hope Swann (Charlotte, NC): I am a Sagittarius Buddheo-Christian Green Witch embracing the mystery of my Crone Years with roller-coaster hormones and anticipation. Still don't know what I want to do when I grow up but I try to live mindfully and creatively.

Ila Suzanne (Portland, OR): Pisces, working class, white, lesbian, witch, poet, now turning toward crone.

Isabel F. Vargas (Bilboa, Spain): Freelance artist healing myself and getting in touch with my indigenous Colombian mother's background through my artwork, private rituals, visions, and dreams; priestess of the goddess; lover of Gaia rituals, myth, yoga, and vegetarian food.

Janet Taylor (Trin, CA): Living the Goddess in the Redwoods, growing with her image. Providing for me thru the clay, offering her out to you.

J. Morrigan (Devon, England): Awakening my Dream. My wish is to instill truth, beauty and goodness in all these arts I may birth into this time/space.

Jen Breese (Chula Vista, CA): i am a poet and a witch. i'm looking for someone who wants to talk about poetry and/or wicca—PO Box 772, Bonita, CA 91908.

Jullian Player (Victoria, BC, Canada): I live, work, and love in the witches' way. I am an herbalist in the wise woman tradition, and teach the blood mysteries to empower and connect women.

Jill Smith (Tigh-A-Ghlinne, Gravir, Isle of Lewis, Scotland), artist and poet, lives alone with her youngest son exhibiting her images of the spirit of the sacred landscape, standing stones, etc., in her own non-electric gallery.

Jo Pacsoo (Tarewaste, Cornwall, England): Growing food and trees, teaching Circle Dancing, learning to live sustainably and tread lightly upon the earth.

Joanna Tamar (Keston, Kent, England): My work is a continual mystery and discovery.

Jody Turner (Portland, OR): It is a beautiful and horrific experience being here on this earth. Being with the energy of the earth brings me to myself and a love of my choice to be here. My artwork brings me into this same reverence. I use the colors of the earth and the flowers in my awe, honor, and respect of her.

Joules (Lopez Island, WA) is a singer/songwriter and drummer who dwells in the woods of Lopez Island off the coast of northern Washington. Her work delves into the natural world and speaks out for the Earth Mother. Her tape *Wildcrafted* is available for $11. Write to Joules, PO Box 153, Lopez Island, WA 98261.

Judith Anderson (East Lansing, MI): I make the images I need to see. Reinterpreting various myths, legends, and religious traditions in my etchings, I want to express women's power and feelings and the sacred nature of ordinary experience.

Judith Brooks Summers (Mendocino, CA): I am a long-time resident of the Mendocino Coast working in the dirt, with paint, with words. Recently out and mated to a woman of my dreams, I practice blessing the goddess for all her gifts to me and all, PRACTICE, PRACTICE, PRACTICE!

Judith Burros (Portland, OR): Artist, quilter, photographer, survivor, searcher, finder of memories . . .

Julia Doughty (San Diego, CA) writes poetry and performance art and explores the wild spaces of the West Coast.

Julie Higgins (Mendocino, CA): I see the landscape, earth, and the body as vessels of life. Images of Ravens as goddess protectors express my concern for and connection with the planet. Contact Julie at PO Box 1562, Mendocino, CA 95460.

Kate Cartwright (Graton, CA): Artist, astrologer, gardener, a young crone unfolding into the lap of the Goddess. Increasingly my work reflects her influence and inspiration.

Kellie Rae Cantwell, aka **Bird** (Elmira, OR): True art is the **process** of creation. I sculpt, write, paint, and create music from deep within; gaining wisdom with each creation. I am extremely proud to be a "wild womon."

Kim Antieau (White Salmon, WA): My short stories have been published in over 30 magazines & anthologies. I am publisher & editor of *Daughters of Nyx: A Magazine of Goddess Stories, Mythmaking and Fairy Tales.* When I feel as though I am about to scatter into a million pieces, writing keeps me Earth bound.

Kit Sugrue (Seal Rock, OR): I am a mother, artist, and herbalist. I'm in a transitional period of life and finally allowing my art to take me where it will.

Laila Wah (Philadelphia, PA) has been writing poetry since grade school. Her life has centered around the arts— the performing arts (dance and music) coupled with painting and poetry. These are shared with a 23-year service in the field of Chinese medicine. She is a healer in acupuncture, herbology, etc. She is also a mother.

Laurie York (Albion, CA) is a painter who lives on the Mendocino Coast.

Leeala (Edinburgh, Scotland), born in New York City, is an award-winning poet & playwright who transforms old myths into new forms of Shamanic Poetry-Theatre.

Leslie Foxfire Stager (Portland, OR): Rights of Passages guide in birthing, deathing, calling LIFE into OUR BODIES & LIVING IT! I draw strength from images of women grounded with Earth.

Lin Karmon (San Diego, CA): When I clear my brain and see through my heart all things are Buddha-full. (619) 222-5415.

Liz Tree (Portland, OR): I am a wild witchy wemoon living in the beautiful NW. My family are the organic farmers who nourish all of us and the witch sisters scattered in sacred places. Every day is a ritual filled with acts of magik.

Llinora Milner (Liskeard, Cornwall, England): I am Gemini with Sagittarius rising working in Shiatsu and creative self healing, wherever my footsteps lead me. Currently, they begin to tread the medicine wheel.

Loba G. Hardin (Reserve, NM): I live with my husband Wolf and many other wild animals on an Anasazi ruin in a canyon, 7 river crossings from the nearest road, tending to the spirits of our magic home.

Lori Nicolosi (Hainesport, NJ): Art is my way of communicating deep feelings. I express being alive through my sculpture. All our beauty and shape as wommin always seems to shine right through.

Lorraine Lucie Lagimodière (Denman Island, BC, Canada): Person practicing the manifestation of inner vision through walking, talking, thinking, feeling, drawing, writing, meeting, and transforming materials already extracted from mother earth: may we rest in her peace.

Lucy Steel (Canterbury, Kent, England): I live in a tipi in Devon, enjoying living on the Earth making herbal paper, prints, and Goddess works.

Lycia Trouton (Vancouver, BC, Canada): Living in the Pacific Northwest; born in Ireland—working with my celtic roots and immersing myself in the Goddess tradition. Rediscovering myself after 12 years of girls school and 6 years of art school training! At present, enjoying working on outdoor organic installations and community-based public art.

Mara Friedman (Lorane, OR) is a scorpio artist, who spends much time in the quiet of her forest studio. There she creates magic in the form of paintings that arise from our deeply mysterious feminine within. For a brochure of cards and prints, write her c/o New Moon Visions, PO Box 23, Lorane, OR 97451.

Marcia Cohee (Laguna Beach, CA): I live in Laguna Canyon, a place more ancient and sacred than words. It is impossible to be silent.

Mari Susan Selby (Santa Fe, NM): Hopefully by the time the next **We'Moon** is in print, *The Power of Safety* (my book on sexual abuse recovery) will be published. I'm a therapist/witch who loves women, the earth, laughing and poetry in no particular order.

Marie Theodore (London, England): I am an actress, singer,and dancer. I have a desire to explore sacred drama in the context of healing our fragmented selves. I am taking a course to train as a priestess and devotee of Isis—the Great Goddess.

Marna (Portland, OR—Pacific Cascadia Bioregion) is an ecolesbian feminist who frolics and dances in the zany benevolent mysteries. Art, poetry, Wicca, Gaia, and ♀ delight her. Welcoming ♀ly connection/corresponDANCE: PO Box 14194, Portland, OR 97214. Blessings on the spiral journeys.

Marsha A. Gómez (Austin, TX): Clay sculptor, environmental/human rights activist for 20 years. Currently director of Alma de Mujer Retreat Center for Social Change. Contact her at La Madre Productions, PO Box 3870, Austin, TX 78764.

Mau Blossom (Doniphan, MO): I am a 60-year-old country womon. I am a healer with a private practice that is based in Ayurveda, a 5,000-year-old tradition. I am a musician and love piano, saxophone, flute, clarinet, penny whistle, guitar and lately a psaltry, an ancient stringed instrument. My ancestry is both Celtic and Italian. I love to be in nature and live in a womon-built yurt in the deep woods of Missouri.

Michelle Waters (Santa Cruz, CA) is an ecofeminist, artist, and animal liberation activist who hopes her artwork contributes to the fall of the patriarchy. She communes with whales, cats, and redwood trees, at home on the shores of Monterey Bay.

Monica Sjöö (Bristol, England): I am currently exhibiting in both Sweden, my motherland and where I am rediscovering my roots up north, and the UK. Author of *New Age and Armageddon* and coauthor of *The Great Cosmic Mother.*

Musawa/Radha (Estacada, OR): I am reentering Oregon We'Moon land community with new energy and perspective after taking a year of "matriarchy leave." Feels like I am still in "virtual reality" getting ready to leap orbits. Am changing my relation to everything in my life: Mother Tongue Ink, We'Moon land, my healing work, my writing, my home—all is transforming.

Nance Paternoster (San Francisco, CA): I'm a computer graphics artist/animator & instructor. I teach at the Academy of Art College & do freelance animation work.

Nancy Ann Jones (La Crescenta, CA) is a witch, Metis elder, grandmother, artist, and cranky old lady. She hangs out as elder priestess of Virago: a compatible company of contentious crones.

Nancy Bright (Eugene, OR): Much of Nancy's work is a biography reflecting spiritual and emotional growth and transitions. She distributes cards and posters of her work nationwide.

Nasira Alma (Portland, OR) is studying for the priesthood in an independent Catholic church. She is a freelance editor and consultant to authors.

New Society Publishers (Philadelphia, PA) is a not-for-profit, worker-controlled publishing house, dedicated to promoting fundamental social change through non-violent action. *Healing the Wounds,* along with other books that are building a new society, is available from them at 4527 Springfield Ave., Philadelphia, PA 19143, (800) 333-9093.

Nic Beechsquirrel (Dyfed, Cymru, UK): I am a feminist artist seeking to celebrate the goddess in women and all of nature, through my work. I enjoy being with other women and sharing our creations.

Oshun Coyotë (Brighton, East Sussex, England): I feel honored that the Goddess channels these images thru me. Much love to all we'moon everywhere; I often feel isolated in my beliefs, but thru the pages of this diary each year, I know I'm not alone! Thank you!

Pandora Cate (We'Moon Healing Ground, Estacada, OR): i am a grinning piece of motion with my feet all over the land; leo dyke writing witch explorer, joining the swing of spirit always.

Peggy Sue McRae (Pullman, WA) is an artist and an activist. She works with Idaho Earth First!. She is completing a Fine Arts degree at Washington State University.

Priya Prasad (Victoria, BC, Canada): Born in Fiji, immigrated to Vancouver when 3 years old, now in Victoria, soon someplace else. Like insects, plants, bad TV shows, earrings, my family and Margret Laurence.

Rachel Bachman (Cheney, WA) has delusions of goddess-hood and creates because it makes her happy.

Rae Keegan (Olympia, WA) is a Dianic priestess and artist. Her work and dedicated to mirroring the Goddess and celebrating the beauty and power of the Divine in ALL things.

Rana Belshe (Fairchild, WI) balances her work around the country as an energy conservation consultant with a simple home life, rich in the gifts of earth, spirit, and sister-travelers.

Rashani (Na'alehu, Ka'ū, HI) is a musician and artist currently based in Hawaii where she is co-creating a women's retreat center and facilitating ♀♀'s councils. She also travels the world gathering and sharing songs.

Red Raven (Torrance, CA): Spiral journaler, mural painter, channeler of poetry, creatrix of Goddess images for Her altar, Heaver of Mountains—Digger of Spirit in the Circle of the Wild Yoni Hairs.

Ruth Mountaingrove (Arcata, CA): Have been a poet since I was 18, a photographer since I was 16, a songwriter since I was 44, a writer all my life, an artist since 1988.

S. J. Hugdahl (Forks of Salmon, CA): I'm living in northern California with my family, my horse, the foxes, the salmon, the bear, the cougar, the jays, the eagles, the toads, my cat, the ringtails, the deer, the blackberries and my art.

Sandra Calvo (Oakland, CA): I enjoy doing my art to connect to, explore, and express the spiritual/emotional/cultural/sexual dimensions of my life. I am especially fond of collages that let me piece many parts into a cohesive whole.

Sandra Pastorius AKA Laughing Giraffe (Santa Cruz, CA): With awe and inspiration, I continue my practice of astrological counseling, metaphysical bookselling at Gateways Book & Gift, and spiritual/political work with the Holy Hemp Sisters. Write me at PO Box 2344, Santa Cruz, CA 95063.

Sandra Stanton (Farmington, ME): An artist whose paintings are centered around Goddess mythology—ancient & future—& all Her beautiful creatures.

Sierra Lonepine Briano (Portland, OR): I am a 47-year-old Lesbian artist, loudmouth and troublemaker. I recently survived the L.A. earthquake, so there shouldn't be much left to scare me. My astrologer says I'm a late bloomer and I like that because it means I can choose from my whole life experience when I paint. I am working on a new series of Goddesses I Have Known.

Sonja Shahan (Santa Cruz, CA): i am weeks away from the exciterrifying transplant of myself to the cement soil of the city, to live, for a time, a life of education, excavation, eradication . . . fostering freedom by telling the truth, in the name of justice, i go. a prayer that my art be ever inspired by my delve into the depth of diversity.

Starhawk (San Francisco, CA) is the author of *The Spiral Dance, Dreaming the Dark, Truth or Dare,* and *The Fifth Sacred Thing.* A feminist and peace activist, Starhawk is one of the foremost voices of ecofeminism, and travels widely in North America and Europe giving lectures and workshops. She also works with the Reclaiming Collective which offers classes, workshops, and public rituals in earth-based spirituality.

Stephanie Gaydos (San Diego, CA): Student of Mother Earth and all her relations, spirited and/or of form. Lover, healer, and nurturer of land; artist, musician, and writer of much; gifted and giving of her tender touch. I live my daily bread.

Sudie Rakusin (Hillsborough, NC): I live in the woods with my 3 dog companions. My work these days seems to be pure exploration as I experiment in 3-dimensional media. I am feeling gently guided and reassured as I make my way into the complete unknown. This feels like the work of the goddess and I am grateful.

Sue Rice (Little Britain, ON, Canada): Surviving & living in the cuntree with dog & cat companions. Harvesting my vulva-shaped garden. Longing for connection with other rural ♀♀—please write Box 137, Little Britain, ON, Canada, KOM 2CO.

Sun Crow (Olympia, WA): I am a Firewalker emerging from Death. I'm learning to live from the Truth in My Heart and my own True Being. I'm heading to Arizona with my beloved cats and living and following my Dreams! Blessed Be!

Susan Levitt (Sausalito, CA) is a fey tarot-reading mermaid priestess living in watery bliss by the sea.

Susun S. Weed (Woodstock, NY), friend of the fairies, speaker for the earth, green witch, goat herder, best-selling author, and high priestess of the goddess, invites you to play with joy and thankfulness in the wild world of weeds and magic.

Terry Lee (Kenesaw, NE): I live in a cabin on the south bank of the Platte River with my three children. We co-inhabit this space with the sandhill cranes, coyotes, white-tailed deer, eagles, and other assorted creatures that enrich our lives.

Virginia Neale (Pender Island, BC, Canada) is a white lesbian feminist trying to crack the conundrum of how to live in balance in an unbalanced world. Beginning to emerge from a 5-year reclusion of healing, grieving, yearning on a glorious (but straining) island. Eager to connect with other soul-Earth-sisters from near & far: RR #1, Pender Island, BC, Canada, VON 2MO.

The Weaving Project (Kykotsmovi, AZ), also known as Women in Resistance, the Sovereign Diné Nation Textile Industry Weaving Collective, directly supports the Diné (Navaho) women's resistance to forced relocation and genocide through the sale of the collective's weavings. For more information contact: Weaving Resource Center, c/o Sheila Keith, PO Box 3445, Flagstaff, AZ 86003, (602) 779-1956.

Webber (San Cristobal, NM) is an artist who weaves spells of astral magic and erotic imagination with words, color, and song. May these offerings awaken your memory and power.

Ynestra King (New York, NY) is a writer, social thinker and political activist whose work in originating and developing the perspective of "ecofeminism" is widely recognized as germinal for what has become a multicultural, international movement. Born in Selma, Alabama, she got her start in the civil rights movement. She is a single mother and is currently completing a book entitled *Ecofeminism and the Reenchantment of Nature: Women, Ecology and Peace* (Beacon Press, forthcoming).

zana (Tucson, AZ): 48, jewish, disabled, sharing land with other lesbians for many years now. my book of poetry and art, *herb womon*, is available for $7 (more or less) from me at MSC 044, zana, HCO4 Box 6872, Tucson, AZ 85735.

How to Become a *We'Moon* Contributor

We'Moon is an exploration of a world created in Her image. We welcome artwork by, for, and about womyn. Our focus on womyn is an affirmation of the range and richness of a world where womyn are whole unto themselves. Many earth-based cultures traditionally have womyn-only spaces and times, which, through deepening the female experience, are seen to enhance womyn's contributions to the whole of society. **We'Moon** invites all womyn who love and honor womyn to join us in this spirit, and we offer what we create from such a space for the benefit of all beings.

Presently in production (due date past): We'Moon '97: Womyn in Community

Now accepting contributions for: We'Moon '98: Wise Womyn Ways

We welcome your art and brief writings DUE DATE: SEPTEMBER 21, 1996

If you are interested in being a **We'Moon** contributor, **please** send an SASE (self-addressed stamped # 10 envelope) and/or international postal coupon to Mother Tongue Ink, and we will send you a Call for Contributions and a Release form (which will include specific information about the theme, as well as how to submit your art and writing).

How to Order a *We'Moon*

We'Moon '96s are available directly from the publisher. They are $13.95 plus $2.05 for surface shipping and handling for *each* calendar ordered ($16.00 ppd). Order 3 or more to the same address and pay no surface shipping charges. Please call or write for 1st class/air mail charges.

When ordering please include:

Check or money order in U.S. funds made out to Mother Tongue Ink

Your name, address, phone number and how many **We'Moons** you want (written on a separate piece of paper from your payment)

Mother Tongue Ink
P.O. Box 1395-A, Estacada, OR 97023

Our Cosmic Clock:
Astrological Life Cycles

We all share common rites of passage at certain ages in our life cycles. Using the guidance of the planet allies during these times can help us to understand the stresses, challenges, and unique opportunities that emerge.

Our own planetary cosmic clock is set in motion at birth when all the planets begin their cycles. The time it takes for each planet to then circle the sun and return to its originating position determines one full cycle. These "return" times sound an "alarm" for us, and catalyze new phases of growth, change, and development throughout our ages and stages of life. Each planet symbolizes certain life energies.

☉ When the SUN, symbol of the self, returns to its original position each year we celebrate our birthday. We may enjoy some extra attention and a personal sense of renewal each year.

♂ The MARS cycle activates our ambitions every 2 years when it returns to the birth position. During these times we can reenergize our physical bodies, assert our passions, begin new projects, set business goals, and start therapies and programs for personal growth.

♃ JUPITER makes its first return at age 12 when we are at puberty and beginning a new phase of social development. JUPITER then returns at ages 24, 36, 48, 60, 72, and 84. These ages offer us new confidence and opportunities for social growth and skill expansion. Career changes are best made at these times.

♄ SATURN takes 28–29 years for its first return to occur, at which time our adulthood may be tested as we settle accounts, make commitments, and claim true inner authority. Saturn then returns at ages 56 and 84.

♅ URANUS has an orbit cycle of 84 years, completing one full revolution during what could be the complete human lifetime. Uranus catalyzes us to express our uniqueness, unfettered by conventions. It comes into trine (120°) aspect in its cycle every 28 years. We must respond to this call for creativity, while Saturn tempers these times with constraints, conditions, and responsibilities. With a restless, and often divine, discontent, we may break up old patterns and liberate ourselves from outworn situations. At approximately age 42, when Uranus comes into the 180° opposition phase, we may experience our own versions of the midlife crisis.

Since we grow in spirals, these ages are often symbolically linked, and often we must deal with the new face of our life issues each time we experience a planetary return.

© Sandra Pastorius 1993

A RETURN TO SOURCE:
THE MERCURY RETROGRADE ☿ ℞ CYCLE

The cycle of the wing-footed messenger, Mercury, represents our mental and communicative life processes. This companion dancer to the sun (never traveling more than 28° away) inspires mobility and adaptability within our environment. Through Mercury, we express ourselves with language, writing, speaking, and reasoning. At times, Mercury emerges in us as nimble jester or creative genius, or when in retrograde, the coyote trickster/teacher within. To this Muse of the Mind, we give thanks for our ability to grow in symbolic and intellectual connection with each other, and with ourselves.

Mercury turns retrograde three or four times a year, always when the sun is in signs of the same element. Due to the motion of the earth's orbit, the planet *appears* to be moving backwards through zodiacal territory. During this passage lasting 20 to 28 days, our attentions move towards unfinished business. Since all backward movement symbolizes a return to source, we can use these times to attend to our inner perceptions, and reconnect with the spiritual source of our thoughts. This introversion can bring about a critical purification process that can help us gain new insights based on prior knowledge. These are good times for completing projects, connecting with old friends, and settling accounts. Delays often point towards the need for more attention to detail and rethinking priorities. Be patient and thorough. Take advantage of this ebb in the cycle. Daydream and rest more. When we linger longer to relish the ground beneath us, we can see the flowers blooming in the dust raised during our busy recent past.

In 1996, Mercury retrogrades four times; the retrograde periods begin when the sun is in each of the earth signs. During Capricorn, from January 9 to 30, when Mercury retreats we get turned around as soon as the new year begins. Wait on serious resolutions until February when our intentions can move forward. During Taurus, from May 3 to 27, when Mercury retraces her steps we get back to essentials in practical matters, catch up with spring cleaning, and reconsider excess possessions. During Virgo, from September 3 to 26, we get resourceful and think ecologically, with a critical eye on the trails we leave behind. Go back over details often, and research projects thoroughly. During Capricorn, from December 23 to January 12, Mercury takes us reluctantly into 1997. Double-check holiday travel plans, and clear up old business with family or friends.

This change in polarity of our mental life can be used consciously; we can turn our thoughts towards healing and renewal. When Mercury goes direct we can move ahead with new projects, and put any mental values gleaned into play. Remember, Mercury is the channel through which we send messages to our future selves, and create the collaborative mental sharing to which we attribute our humanness.

© *Sandra Pastorius 1995*

ECLIPSES 1996

A solar eclipse is a conjunction of the sun and the moon. This occurs only at the time of the new moon. A solar eclipse can be either partial, total, or annular. An annular eclipse occurs when the moon is at apogee and the surface of the moon is not large enough to completely block out the sun. As a result, the sun leaves a light ring around the moon.

A lunar eclipse is an opposition of the sun and the moon. This occurs only during the time of the full moon. A lunar eclipse only occurs 14 days before or after a solar eclipse. Total, partial, and appulse eclipses are the forms of lunar eclipse. During an appulse eclipse, the body of the moon only receives the light of the sun from one side of the earth. This produces a darkening of the moon's surface.

□ *Monica Sjöö 1990*

Mawu—African Mother of Us All

Since ancient times, astrologers have used the eclipse as a form of prediction and delineation of events. Eclipses bring us in touch with our dark side: fears, wild woman selves, emotional patterns, animal natures. During the time of the eclipse a crack in ordinary reality appears. We can use this information to create a window for change, on any level, and specifically to evolve our emotional consciousness.

To determine the effect of an eclipse, check your natal chart. In what house does the eclipse fall? This will determine the specific emphasis of the eclipse (e.g., 1st house—body, 7th house—relationships). If the eclipse is in opposition or conjunction to any planets, the emphasis becomes a crisis (i.e., a requirement for us to devote more time and attention to whatever area of our life the eclipse emphasizes). The more personal the planets, the stronger the influence.

© *Mari Susan Selby 1993*

1996 eclipses occur April 3, April 17, September 26, and October 12.

WHY ASTEROIDS?

The discovery of the first asteroids points to the rebirth of the goddess in women's spirituality. Traditional astrology uses only two planets to symbolize female archetypes: Moon as mother and Venus as mate. As a result, astrological language has tried to fit all other women's experiences into male-defined archetypes.

When a heavenly body is prominent in the sky at the time of a person's birth, the mythological story of the god or goddess who shares the same name as the planet or asteroid becomes a major theme in that individual's life.

Ceres, the Great Mother, provides a model to understand the causes of eating disorders, co-dependency, child sexual abuse and incest, the wounded child, dysfunctional families, the trauma of separation between parents and children due to the breakup of families and challenges of single-parenting. Ceres also encompasses the ancient knowledge of conscious dying and the psychological death and rebirth transformation process.

Pallas Athena, Goddess of Wisdom, refers to the dilemma of professional women who sacrifice relationship or children for career, sexism in the professional world, the wounds from the father-daughter interaction, androgyny, and taking responsibility for creating our reality. Pallas also provides insights into the causes of disease due to breakdown of the auto-immune system, and is a key to understanding learning disorders.

Vesta, the Temple Priestess, illuminates the need to reintegrate spiritual and sexual energies, focus on self-healing, find our vocation or meaningful work, and develop a deeper relationship with our own soul. Vesta symbolizes the importance of following a spiritual path to heal addictions and offers a clue to the spread of sexually transmitted diseases.

Juno, the Goddess of Marriage, speaks to the redefinition of meaningful relationships, lesbian and gay couples, changing sexual roles, and the plight of powerless and battered women. Juno's story provides a foundation to understand the issues of projection, love addiction, dependency, domination, obsession, jealousy, betrayal, trust, and power themes in relationships.

In addition, the asteroids help clarify and enhance the horoscope's existing astrological themes. It is not unusual for the asteroids to group around the major points of focus in the chart and complete major aspect patterns.

© *Demetra George 1991, author of* Asteroid Goddesses

1996 ASTEROID EPHEMERIS

Reprinted with permission from Astro Communications Services, Inc.

1996	Ceres 1	Pallas 2	Juno 3	Vesta 4
JAN 1	21♏57.0	27♎51.6	25♉10.4	02♏16.9
11	25 45.4	00♏53.5	29 13.2	06 21.8
21	29 22.2	03 32.0	03♊20.3	10 12.7
31	02♐45.2	05 42.7	07 30.8	13 46.0
FEB 10	05 51.9	07 20.6	11 43.7	16 58.3
20	08 39.6	08 20.3	15 58.5	19 45.2
MAR 1	11 04.9	08R36.0	20 14.4	22 01.0
11	13 04.4	08 03.7	24 30.4	23 40.4
21	14 34.3	06 41.6	28 46.2	24 37.6
31	15 30.6	04 32.9	03♋00.9	24R47.6
APR 10	15 50.2	01 48.5	07 13.5	24 08.4
20	15♐31.0	28♎45.3	11 23.4	22 41.9
30	14 33.3	25 45.1	15 29.6	20 38.0
MAY 10	13 01.3	23 08.4	19 31.0	18 13.9
20	11 03.0	21 10.1	23 26.3	15 50.5
30	08 51.2	19 58.4	27 13.8	13 49.8
JUN 9	06 40.5	19D34.4	00♌52.0	12 27.7
19	04 44.9	19 55.3	04 18.7	11 52.6
29	03 16.1	20 56.6	07 30.8	12D07.1
JUL 9	02 21.1	22 32.5	10 25.2	13 08.2
19	02D02.6	24 37.8	12 57.7	14 51.0
29	02 20.4	27 07.8	15 03.8	17 10.0
AUG 8	03 12.1	29 58.3	16 37.9	19 59.6
18	04 34.2	03♏06.1	17 33.7	23 15.2
28	06 23.5	06 28.1	17R46.1	26 52.4
SEP 7	08 35.3	10 01.9	17 12.3	00♏47.5
17	11 07.3	13 45.7	15 52.2	04 57.8
27	13 56.3	17 37.6	13 53.9	09 21.0
OCT 7	16 59.5	21 36.0	11 33.5	13 54.6
17	20 15.1	25 39.7	09 12.9	18 37.2
27	23 40.9	29 47.5	07 15.6	23 27.2
NOV 6	27 15.2	03♐58.3	05 59.8	28 23.4
16	00♏56.7	08 11.1	05D36.2	03♐24.6
26	04 43.9	12 24.8	06 08.5	08 29.8
DEC 6	08 35.6	16 38.4	07 33.1	13 38.2
16	12 30.9	20 51.0	09 45.6	18 49.0
26	16 28.4	25 01.5	12 39.3	24 01.2
JAN 5	20♏27.4	29♐08.9	16♌07.4	29♐14.1

1996	Sappho 80	Amor 1221	Pandora 55	Icarus 1566
JAN 1	04♏22.8	04♎13.3	21♒34.0	29♈49.0
11	07 22.6	14 21.5	26 06.1	04♉38.1
21	10 05.8	25 21.1	00♓44.7	09 44.3
31	12 28.9	07♏15.1	05 28.6	15 10.7
FEB 10	14 28.3	19 20.8	10 16.6	21 01.8
20	15 59.6	01♐42.8	15 06.0	27 24.6
MAR 1	16 56.0	13 43.7	20 01.6	04♉28.8
11	17 19.4	25 01.0	24 56.8	12 29.0
21	16R59.8	05♑18.6	29 52.6	21 48.2
31	15 57.8	14 27.0	04♈48.8	03♊01.8
APR 10	14 15.8	22 23.3	09 44.1	17 10.7
20	12 00.7	29 05.3	14 38.3	05♋55.1
30	09 25.9	04♒29.9	19 30.4	18 29.8
MAY 10	06 48.3	08 34.3	24 19.4	14♈47.0
20	04 25.6	11 12.1	29 06.1	07 10.1
30	02 32.8	12 16.3	03♉48.2	23♈10.0
JUN 9	01 19.4	11R43.6	08 25.3	06♉06.3
19	00 49.4	09 35.8	12 56.7	00♊41.5
29	01D03.0	06 10.7	17 20.9	11♊58.5
JUL 9	01 57.1	02 03.2	21 37.1	06 26.3
19	03 27.7	27♑56.3	25 43.5	04 51.3
29	05 30.7	24 29.6	29 36.3	05♋03.5
AUG 8	08 01.7	22 05.5	03♊16.6	06 15.3
18	10 57.2	20 49.1	06 44.8	08 05.7
28	14 14.1	20D36.5	09 50.6	10 23.6
SEP 7	17 49.5	21 17.6	12 33.6	13 01.6
17	21 41.5	22 42.6	14 49.5	15 55.6
27	25 48.0	24 43.0	16 33.5	19 02.8
OCT 7	00♐07.5	27 10.9	17 40.9	22 20.6
17	04 38.9	00♒01.0	18 06.9	25 48.1
27	09 20.9	03 08.5	17R48.6	29 23.9
NOV 6	14 12.6	06 29.7	16 46.4	03♓07.3
16	19 13.3	10 02.0	15 14.8	06 57.8
26	24 22.1	13 43.1	12 55.8	10 55.0
DEC 6	29 38.4	17 30.9	10 35.2	14 58.7
16	05♑01.6	21 24.3	08 22.5	19 09.1
26	10 31.1	25 21.8	06 34.7	23 26.2
JAN 5	16♑08.3	29♒22.2	05♈23.5	27♈50.4

1996	Psyche 16	Eros 433	Lilith 1181	Toro 1685
JAN 1	08R39.4	09♈47.2	28♉15.4	04♑21.4
11	07♊40.2	16 04.6	00♊41.2	09 20.5
21	07D20.6	22 59.0	03 39.4	14 17.8
31	07 40.8	00♉25.7	07 04.5	19 12.9
FEB 10	08 37.8	08 19.8	10 51.6	24 06.1
20	10 07.3	16 37.6	14 56.5	28 57.4
MAR 1	12 05.0	25 15.8	19 15.9	03♒46.6
11	14 26.3	04♊10.4	23 46.6	08 34.0
21	17 07.2	13 18.0	28 26.4	13 20.0
31	20 04.4	22 35.6	03♋13.3	18 04.4
APR 10	23 14.6	01♋58.8	08 05.5	22 48.4
20	26 35.7	11 24.5	13 01.8	27 32.7
30	00♋05.3	20 49.1	18 00.6	02♓18.5
MAY 10	03 41.8	00♌08.8	23 01.2	07 08.9
20	07 23.6	09 20.8	28 02.8	12 07.6
30	11 09.6	18 22.4	03♌04.6	17 21.3
JUN 9	14 58.5	27 11.3	08 05.9	23 02.6
19	18 49.6	05♍46.3	13 06.2	29 32.4
29	22 41.8	14 06.8	18 05.1	07♈31.1
JUL 9	26 34.4	22 12.1	23 01.9	18 18.8
19	00♌26.9	00♍03.0	27 56.4	04♉25.7
29	04 18.3	07 39.9	02♍47.9	29 10.9
AUG 8	08 08.0	15 03.6	07 36.0	00♊11.7
18	11 55.3	22 15.4	12 20.4	26 11.6
28	15 39.3	29 16.3	17 00.2	13♊39.7
SEP 7	19 19.1	06♎07.2	21 34.9	25 57.2
17	22 53.9	12 49.6	26 03.9	05♋50.5
27	26 22.9	19 24.4	00♎26.1	14 43.9
OCT 7	29 42.9	25 52.4	04 40.6	23 14.2
17	02♍54.4	02 14.7	08 46.1	01♌30.1
27	05 54.0	08 31.9	12 41.1	09 28.4
NOV 6	08 42.3	14 44.8	16 24.0	17 04.2
16	11 14.1	20 54.2	19 52.7	24 12.2
26	13 27.5	27 00.4	23 04.5	00♍48.7
DEC 6	15 19.5	03♏03.9	25 57.0	06 51.8
16	16 46.4	09 05.3	28 26.4	12 18.7
26	17 44.9	15 04.8	00♏29.0	17 06.1
JAN 5	18♍11.8	21♏02.7	02♏00.9	21♍10.3

1996	Diana 78	Hidalgo 944	Urania 30	Chiron 2060
JAN 1	08♊27.8	28♋15.0	29♐12.7	13♋34.7
11	12 11.3	29 14.3	03♑44.8	14 01.7
21	15 52.4	00♌05.9	08 16.6	14 16.9
31	19 30.0	00 48.2	12 47.2	14R20.0
FEB 10	23 03.0	01 20.0	17 15.8	14 11.3
20	26 30.3	01 40.4	21 41.7	13 51.5
MAR 1	29 50.5	01 48.3	26 03.7	13 21.6
11	03♋02.3	01R33.3	00♒20.8	12 43.6
21	06 04.2	01 25.1	04 31.9	11 59.8
31	08 54.3	00 54.1	08 35.6	11 12.9
APR 10	11 30.7	00 11.2	12 30.2	10 25.8
20	13 51.3	29♋18.1	16 14.1	09 41.3
30	15 53.3	28 16.8	19 44.8	09 02.1
MAY 10	17 34.2	27 10.3	22 59.9	08 30.5
20	18 50.7	26 01.4	25 58.0	08 08.0
30	19 39.6	24 53.6	28 29.3	07 56.1
JUN 9	19 58.3	23 49.9	00♓35.5	07D55.2
19	19R44.2	22 53.1	02 00.5	08 05.6
29	18 56.5	22 05.5	03♓20.1	08 27.1
JUL 9	17 36.9	21 28.8	03R20.1	08 59.3
19	15 49.7	21 04.0	02 48.7	09 41.4
29	13 43.3	20 51.8	01 32.4	10 32.7
AUG 8	11 28.9	20D51.9	29♒37.7	11 32.1
18	09 18.8	21 04.3	27 17.4	12 38.6
28	07 25.2	21 28.0	24 31.3	13 51.4
SEP 7	05 57.4	22 02.3	22 40.2	15 09.2
17	05 01.1	22 46.1	21 02.3	16 31.0
27	04 39.2	23 38.3	20 00.9	17 55.7
OCT 7	04D51.3	24 37.7	20D07.2	19 22.2
17	05 35.5	25 43.1	20 54.0	20 49.5
27	06 49.0	26 53.1	22 26.6	22 16.3
NOV 6	08 28.5	28 06.7	24 39.3	23 41.5
16	10 30.8	29 22.4	27 27.0	25 04.0
26	12 52.9	00♌38.9	00♓44.4	26 22.4
DEC 6	15 31.9	01 55.0	04 26.8	27 35.6
16	18 25.5	03 09.3	08 30.0	28 42.4
26	21 31.3	04 20.4	12 50.9	29 41.3
JAN 5	24♋47.4	05♌27.0	17♓25.4	00♌31.5

Giving the positions of asteroids every
ten days in LONGITUDE at 00:00 GMT

NOON EPHEMERIS: GMT* — JANUARY 1996

Day	Sid.Time	☉	0 hr ☽	Noon ☽	True ☊	☿	♀	♂	♃	♄	♅	♆	♇
1 M	18 41 44	10♑20 58	16♉41 32	22♉44 28	23♎25.7	29♑42.9	13♒14.2	24♑33.6	29♐35.5	19♓25.7	29♑22.7	24♑41.8	1♐57.9
2 Tu	18 45 40	11 22 7	28 45 24	4♊44 45	23R19.4	0♒48.3	14 27.9	25 20.4	29 49.1	19 29.9	29 26.1	24 44.1	1 59.9
3 W	18 49 37	12 23 16	10♊42 54	16 40 9	23 9.9	1 48.3	15 41.7	26 7.3	0♑ 2.6	19 34.1	29 29.5	24 46.3	2 1.8
4 Th	18 53 33	13 24 24	22 36 48	28 33 5	22 57.7	2 42.2	16 55.4	26 54.1	0 16.2	19 38.4	29 32.9	24 48.5	2 3.8
5 F	18 57 30	14 25 33	4♋29 12	10♋25 21	22 43.5	3 29.1	18 9.0	27 41.0	0 29.7	19 42.8	29 36.4	24 50.8	2 5.7
6 Sa	19 1 26	15 26 41	16 21 41	22 18 21	22 28.4	4 8.2	19 22.6	28 28.0	0 43.2	19 47.2	29 39.8	24 53.0	2 7.5
7 Su	19 5 23	16 27 49	28 15 29	4♌13 15	22 13.6	4 38.5	20 36.2	29 14.9	0 56.6	19 51.8	29 43.3	24 55.3	2 9.4
8 M	19 9 19	17 28 58	10♌11 49	16 11 22	22 0.4	4 59.1	21 49.7	0♒ 1.9	1 10.1	19 56.4	29 46.7	24 57.5	2 11.2
9 Tu	19 13 16	18 30 6	22 12 9	28 14 23	21 49.7	5R 9.2	23 3.1	0 48.9	1 23.5	20 1.1	29 50.2	24 59.8	2 13.1
10 W	19 17 13	19 31 14	4♍18 24	10♍24 32	21 42.1	5 8.2	24 16.5	1 36.0	1 36.9	20 5.9	29 53.7	25 2.1	2 14.9
11 Th	19 21 9	20 32 22	16 33 11	22 44 46	21 37.6	4 55.5	25 29.9	2 23.0	1 50.3	20 10.8	29 57.2	25 4.3	2 16.6
12 F	19 25 6	21 33 30	28 59 46	5♎18 41	21 35.6	4 30.9	26 43.2	3 10.1	2 3.6	20 15.7	0♒ 0.7	25 6.6	2 18.4
13 Sa	19 29 2	22 34 38	11♎42 1	18 10 19	21D35.3	3 54.8	27 56.5	3 57.2	2 16.9	20 20.7	0 4.2	25 8.9	2 20.1
14 Su	19 32 59	23 35 46	24 44 5	1♏23 48	21R35.3	3 7.5	29 9.7	4 44.4	2 30.2	20 25.8	0 7.7	25 11.2	2 21.8
15 M	19 36 55	24 36 54	8♏ 9 54	15 2 43	21 34.2	2 10.3	0♓22.8	5 31.5	2 43.4	20 31.0	0 11.2	25 13.4	2 23.4
16 Tu	19 40 52	25 38 1	22 2 27	29 9 10	21 31.0	1 4.7	1 35.9	6 18.7	2 56.7	20 36.2	0 14.8	25 15.7	2 25.1
17 W	19 44 48	26 39 9	6♐22 44	13♐42 48	21 25.1	29♑52.6	2 49.0	7 5.9	3 9.8	20 41.5	0 18.3	25 18.0	2 26.7
18 Th	19 48 45	27 40 16	21 8 49	28 39 58	21 16.5	28 36.3	4 2.0	7 53.2	3 23.0	20 46.9	0 21.8	25 20.3	2 28.3
19 F	19 52 42	28 41 23	6♑15 12	13♑53 18	21 5.8	27 18.1	5 14.9	8 40.4	3 36.1	20 52.3	0 25.4	25 22.6	2 29.8
20 Sa	19 56 38	29 42 30	21 32 52	29 12 27	20 54.2	26 0.5	6 27.8	9 27.7	3 49.1	20 57.8	0 28.9	25 24.8	2 31.4
21 Su	20 0 35	0♒43 35	6♒50 32	14♒25 41	20 42.9	24 45.9	7 40.6	10 15.0	4 2.1	21 3.4	0 32.4	25 27.1	2 32.9
22 M	20 4 31	1 44 40	21 56 36	29 22 8	20 33.2	23 36.0	8 53.3	11 2.3	4 15.1	21 9.1	0 36.0	25 29.4	2 34.3
23 Tu	20 8 28	2 45 45	6♓41 24	13♓53 42	20 26.0	22 32.7	10 6.0	11 49.6	4 28.0	21 14.8	0 39.5	25 31.6	2 35.8
24 W	20 12 24	3 46 48	20 58 37	27 55 57	20 21.6	21 37.0	11 18.6	12 37.0	4 40.8	21 20.6	0 43.0	25 33.9	2 37.2
25 Th	20 16 21	4 47 50	4♈45 42	11♈28 4	20 19.7	20 49.7	12 31.1	13 24.3	4 53.7	21 26.4	0 46.6	25 36.2	2 38.6
26 F	20 20 17	5 48 51	18 3 23	24 32 6	20D19.4	20 11.4	13 43.6	14 11.7	5 6.4	21 32.3	0 50.1	25 38.4	2 39.9
27 Sa	20 24 14	6 49 51	0♉54 46	7♉11 58	20R19.6	19 42.2	14 55.9	14 59.1	5 19.1	21 38.2	0 53.6	25 40.7	2 41.2
28 Su	20 28 11	7 50 49	13 24 21	19 32 33	20 19.1	19 21.9	16 8.2	15 46.5	5 31.8	21 44.3	0 57.1	25 42.9	2 42.5
29 M	20 32 7	8 51 47	25 37 13	1♊38 58	20 16.7	19 10.2	17 20.4	16 33.8	5 44.4	21 50.3	1 0.6	25 45.1	2 43.8
30 Tu	20 36 4	9 52 43	7♊38 24	13 36 6	20 11.9	19D 6.8	18 32.5	17 21.2	5 56.9	21 56.5	1 4.2	25 47.4	2 45.0
31 W	20 40 0	10 53 39	19 32 33	25 28 15	20 4.2	19 11.2	19 44.5	18 8.7	6 9.4	22 2.6	1 7.7	25 49.6	2 46.2

LONGITUDE — FEBRUARY 1996

Day	Sid.Time	☉	0 hr ☽	Noon ☽	True ☊	☿	♀	♂	♃	♄	♅	♆	♇
1 Th	20 43 57	11♒54 33	1♋23 37	7♋19 2	19♎54.0	19♑22.8	20♓56.4	18♒56.1	6♑21.8	22♓ 8.9	1♒11.1	25♑51.8	2♐47.4
2 F	20 47 53	12 55 26	13 14 49	19 11 14	19R41.9	19 41.0	22 8.2	19 43.5	6 34.2	22 15.2	1 14.6	25 54.0	2 48.5
3 Sa	20 51 50	13 56 17	25 8 33	1♌ 6 58	19 28.7	20 5.5	23 19.9	20 30.9	6 46.5	22 21.5	1 18.1	25 56.2	2 49.6
4 Su	20 55 46	14 57 8	7♌ 6 37	13 7 40	19 15.7	20 35.5	24 31.6	21 18.4	6 58.7	22 27.9	1 21.6	25 58.4	2 50.7
5 M	20 59 43	15 57 57	19 10 14	25 14 27	19 3.9	21 10.8	25 43.1	22 5.8	7 10.9	22 34.3	1 25.0	26 0.6	2 51.7
6 Tu	21 3 40	16 58 45	1♍20 25	7♍28 16	18 54.3	21 50.7	26 54.5	22 53.2	7 23.0	22 40.8	1 28.5	26 2.7	2 52.7
7 W	21 7 36	17 59 32	13 38 9	19 50 15	18 47.5	22 35.0	28 5.8	23 40.7	7 35.0	22 47.3	1 31.9	26 4.9	2 53.7
8 Th	21 11 33	19 0 18	26 4 45	2♎21 53	18 43.6	23 23.2	29 17.0	24 28.1	7 47.0	22 53.9	1 35.3	26 7.0	2 54.6
9 F	21 15 29	20 1 3	8♎41 55	15 5 9	18D42.2	24 15.0	0♈28.1	25 15.6	7 58.9	23 0.5	1 38.7	26 9.1	2 55.5
10 Sa	21 19 26	21 1 47	21 31 55	28 2 32	18 42.5	25 10.1	1 39.1	26 3.0	8 10.7	23 7.2	1 42.1	26 11.3	2 56.4
11 Su	21 23 22	22 2 30	4♏37 23	11♏16 48	18 43.4	26 8.3	2 49.9	26 50.5	8 22.5	23 13.9	1 45.5	26 13.4	2 57.3
12 M	21 27 19	23 3 12	18 1 5	24 50 33	18R43.9	27 9.2	4 0.7	27 37.9	8 34.2	23 20.7	1 48.8	26 15.5	2 58.1
13 Tu	21 31 15	24 3 53	1♐45 22	8♐45 40	18 42.8	28 12.6	5 11.3	28 25.4	8 45.8	23 27.5	1 52.2	26 17.5	2 58.8
14 W	21 35 12	25 4 32	15 51 25	23 2 30	18 39.6	29 18.5	6 21.8	29 12.9	8 57.3	23 34.3	1 55.5	26 19.6	2 59.6
15 Th	21 39 9	26 5 11	0♑18 34	7♑39 8	18 34.3	0♒26.5	7 32.2	0♓ 0.3	9 8.7	23 41.2	1 58.8	26 21.6	3 0.3
16 F	21 43 5	27 5 48	15 3 31	22 30 53	18 27.2	1 36.6	8 42.5	0 47.8	9 20.1	23 48.1	2 2.1	26 23.7	3 0.9
17 Sa	21 47 2	28 6 24	0♒ 0 14	7♒30 27	18 19.1	2 48.5	9 52.6	1 35.2	9 31.4	23 55.0	2 5.4	26 25.7	3 1.6
18 Su	21 50 58	29 6 59	15 0 20	22 28 43	18 11.2	4 2.3	11 2.6	2 22.7	9 42.5	24 2.0	2 8.6	26 27.7	3 2.2
19 M	21 54 55	0♓ 7 32	29 54 25	7♓16 20	18 4.4	5 17.7	12 12.5	3 10.1	9 53.6	24 9.0	2 11.9	26 29.7	3 2.7
20 Tu	21 58 51	1 8 4	14♓33 31	21 45 12	17 59.5	6 34.7	13 22.2	3 57.6	10 4.6	24 16.0	2 15.1	26 31.6	3 3.2
21 W	22 2 48	2 8 33	28 50 44	5♈49 44	17 56.7	7 53.2	14 31.8	4 45.0	10 15.6	24 23.1	2 18.3	26 33.6	3 3.7
22 Th	22 6 44	3 9 1	12♈41 57	19 27 19	17D55.9	9 13.1	15 41.2	5 32.4	10 26.4	24 30.2	2 21.4	26 35.5	3 4.2
23 F	22 10 41	4 9 27	26 5 58	2♉38 8	17 56.6	10 34.4	16 50.5	6 19.8	10 37.1	24 37.3	2 24.6	26 37.4	3 4.6
24 Sa	22 14 37	5 9 52	9♉ 4 9	15 24 30	17 58.1	11 57.0	17 59.6	7 7.2	10 47.7	24 44.5	2 27.7	26 39.3	3 5.0
25 Su	22 18 34	6 10 14	21 39 42	27 50 19	17 59.4	13 20.9	19 8.5	7 54.6	10 58.3	24 51.6	2 30.8	26 41.2	3 5.3
26 M	22 22 31	7 10 35	3♊56 57	10♊ 0 14	17R59.7	14 46.1	20 17.3	8 42.0	11 8.7	24 58.8	2 33.8	26 43.0	3 5.6
27 Tu	22 26 27	8 10 53	16 0 47	21 59 13	17 58.6	16 12.4	21 25.9	9 29.3	11 19.1	25 6.1	2 36.9	26 44.9	3 5.9
28 W	22 30 24	9 11 10	27 56 9	3♋52 9	17 55.7	17 39.9	22 34.3	10 16.7	11 29.3	25 13.3	2 39.9	26 46.7	3 6.2
29 Th	22 34 20	10 11 24	9♋47 45	15 43 29	17 51.1	19 8.5	23 42.6	11 4.0	11 39.4	25 20.6	2 42.9	26 48.5	3 6.4

Ephemeris reprinted with permission from Astro Communications Services, Inc.

*Giving the positions of planets daily at noon, in LONGITUDE Greenwich Mean Time

Noon Ephemeris: GMT*

March 1996

Day	Sid.Time	☉	0 hr ☽	Noon ☽	True ☊	☿	♀	♂	♃	♄	♅	♆	♇
1 F	22 38 17	11♓11 36	21♋39 48	27♋37 8	17♎45.2	20♒38.3	24♈50.6	11♓51.3	11♑49.4	25♓27.9	2♒45.9	26♑50.2	3♐ 6.5
2 Sa	22 42 13	12 11 47	3♌35 51	9♌36 17	17R38.6	22 9.2	25 58.5	12 38.6	11 59.4	25 35.2	2 48.8	26 52.0	3 6.7
3 Su	22 46 10	13 11 55	15 38 43	21 43 24	17 31.9	23 41.3	27 6.1	13 25.9	12 9.2	25 42.5	2 51.7	26 53.7	3 6.8
4 M	22 50 6	14 12 2	27 50 30	4♍ 0 11	17 25.8	25 14.4	28 13.6	14 13.1	12 18.9	25 49.8	2 54.6	26 55.4	3 6.8
5 Tu	22 54 3	15 12 7	10♍12 34	16 27 45	17 20.9	26 48.6	29 20.8	15 0.4	12 28.5	25 57.2	2 57.4	26 57.1	3R 6.9
6 W	22 58 0	16 12 9	22 45 46	29 6 43	17 17.6	28 24.0	0♉27.9	15 47.6	12 37.9	26 4.5	3 0.2	26 58.7	3 6.9
7 Th	23 1 56	17 12 10	5♎30 36	11♎57 28	17D16.1	0♓ 0.5	1 34.7	16 34.8	12 47.3	26 11.9	3 3.0	27 0.4	3 6.8
8 F	23 5 53	18 12 10	18 27 21	25 0 18	17 16.2	1 38.0	2 41.3	17 21.9	12 56.5	26 19.3	3 5.7	27 2.0	3 6.7
9 Sa	23 9 49	19 12 7	1♏36 22	8♏15 36	17 17.3	3 16.7	3 47.6	18 9.1	13 5.7	26 26.7	3 8.5	27 3.5	3 6.6
10 Su	23 13 46	20 12 3	14 58 4	21 43 50	17 19.0	4 56.6	4 53.8	18 56.2	13 14.7	26 34.1	3 11.1	27 5.1	3 6.5
11 M	23 17 42	21 11 57	28 32 56	5♐25 25	17 20.5	6 37.6	5 59.7	19 43.4	13 23.6	26 41.5	3 13.8	27 6.6	3 6.3
12 Tu	23 21 39	22 11 50	12♐21 18	19 20 31	17R21.3	8 19.7	7 5.3	20 30.5	13 32.3	26 49.0	3 16.4	27 8.1	3 6.1
13 W	23 25 35	23 11 41	26 23 0	3♑28 36	17 21.1	10 3.0	8 10.7	21 17.6	13 41.0	26 56.4	3 19.0	27 9.6	3 5.9
14 Th	23 29 32	24 11 30	10♑37 3	17 48 3	17 19.7	11 47.5	9 15.9	22 4.6	13 49.5	27 3.8	3 21.6	27 11.1	3 5.6
15 F	23 33 29	25 11 18	25 1 10	2♒15 55	17 17.4	13 33.2	10 20.8	22 51.6	13 57.9	27 11.3	3 24.1	27 12.5	3 5.3
16 Sa	23 37 25	26 11 4	9♒31 41	16 47 49	17 14.5	15 20.1	11 25.4	23 38.7	14 6.1	27 18.7	3 26.5	27 13.9	3 4.9
17 Su	23 41 22	27 10 48	24 3 35	1♓18 15	17 11.6	17 8.2	12 29.7	24 25.6	14 14.3	27 26.2	3 29.0	27 15.3	3 4.6
18 M	23 45 18	28 10 30	8♓31 2	15 41 13	17 9.2	18 57.5	13 33.8	25 12.6	14 22.2	27 33.6	3 31.4	27 16.6	3 4.1
19 Tu	23 49 15	29 10 10	22 48 6	29 51 3	17 7.6	20 48.1	14 37.6	25 59.5	14 30.1	27 41.1	3 33.7	27 17.9	3 3.7
20 W	23 53 11	0♈ 9 48	6♈49 32	13♈43 8	17D 7.0	22 39.9	15 41.0	26 46.4	14 37.8	27 48.5	3 36.1	27 19.2	3 3.2
21 Th	23 57 8	1 9 25	20 31 31	27 14 29	17 7.2	24 32.9	16 44.2	27 33.3	14 45.4	27 56.0	3 38.3	27 20.5	3 2.7
22 F	0 1 4	2 8 59	3♉51 57	10♉23 58	17 8.2	26 27.1	17 47.0	28 20.2	14 52.8	28 3.4	3 40.6	27 21.7	3 2.1
23 Sa	0 5 1	3 8 30	16 50 39	23 12 15	17 9.5	28 22.6	18 49.5	29 7.0	15 0.1	28 10.8	3 42.8	27 22.9	3 1.6
24 Su	0 8 58	4 8 0	29 29 4	5♊41 30	17 10.8	0♈19.3	19 51.7	29 53.8	15 7.3	28 18.3	3 45.0	27 24.1	3 1.0
25 M	0 12 54	5 7 27	11♊50 1	17 55 5	17 11.8	2 17.1	20 53.5	0♈40.5	15 14.3	28 25.7	3 47.1	27 25.2	3 0.3
26 Tu	0 16 51	6 6 52	23 57 16	29 57 6	17 12.4	4 16.0	21 54.9	1 27.2	15 21.1	28 33.1	3 49.2	27 26.3	2 59.7
27 W	0 20 47	7 6 15	5♋55 11	11♋52 6	17R12.5	6 16.0	22 56.0	2 13.9	15 27.8	28 40.5	3 51.2	27 27.4	2 59.0
28 Th	0 24 44	8 5 36	17 48 26	23 44 46	17 12.0	8 16.9	23 56.7	3 0.5	15 34.4	28 47.9	3 53.2	27 28.4	2 58.2
29 F	0 28 40	9 4 54	29 41 40	5♌39 41	17 11.2	10 18.7	24 57.0	3 47.2	15 40.8	28 55.3	3 55.2	27 29.5	2 57.5
30 Sa	0 32 37	10 4 9	11♌39 19	17 41 3	17 10.3	12 21.2	25 56.8	4 33.7	15 47.1	29 2.6	3 57.1	27 30.5	2 56.7
31 Su	0 36 33	11 3 23	23 45 20	29 52 33	17 9.3	14 24.4	26 56.2	5 20.3	15 53.2	29 10.0	3 58.9	27 31.4	2 55.8

Longitude

April 1996

Day	Sid.Time	☉	0 hr ☽	Noon ☽	True ☊	☿	♀	♂	♃	♄	♅	♆	♇
1 M	0 40 30	12♈ 2 34	6♍ 3 3	12♍17 7	17♎ 8.5	16♈27.9	27♉55.2	6♈ 6.8	15♑59.1	29♓17.3	4♒ 0.8	27♑32.3	2♐55.0
2 Tu	0 44 26	13 1 43	18 34 59	24 56 49	17R 8.0	18 31.6	28 53.7	6 53.2	16 4.9	29 24.6	4 2.5	27 33.2	2R54.1
3 W	0 48 23	14 0 50	1♎22 43	7♎52 43	17 7.7	20 35.4	29 51.8	7 39.6	16 10.5	29 31.9	4 4.3	27 34.1	2 53.2
4 Th	0 52 20	14 59 55	14 26 50	21 4 56	17D 7.7	22 38.8	0♊49.3	8 26.0	16 16.0	29 39.2	4 6.0	27 34.9	2 52.3
5 F	0 56 16	15 58 58	27 46 56	4♏32 36	17 7.8	24 41.5	1 46.3	9 12.4	16 21.3	29 46.5	4 7.6	27 35.7	2 51.3
6 Sa	1 0 13	16 57 59	11♏21 44	18 14 3	17 7.9	26 43.4	2 42.9	9 58.7	16 26.5	29 53.7	4 9.2	27 36.5	2 50.3
7 Su	1 4 9	17 56 58	25 9 17	2♐ 7 6	17R 8.0	28 44.0	3 38.9	10 45.0	16 31.4	0♈ 1.0	4 10.8	27 37.2	2 49.3
8 M	1 8 6	18 55 55	9♐ 7 10	16 9 11	17 7.9	0♉43.1	4 34.3	11 31.2	16 36.3	0 8.2	4 12.3	27 37.9	2 48.3
9 Tu	1 12 2	19 54 51	23 12 46	0♑17 38	17 7.8	2 40.1	5 29.2	12 17.4	16 40.9	0 15.3	4 13.8	27 38.6	2 47.2
10 W	1 15 59	20 53 45	7♑23 26	14 29 51	17 7.7	4 34.8	6 23.5	13 3.6	16 45.4	0 22.5	4 15.2	27 39.3	2 46.1
11 Th	1 19 55	21 52 37	21 36 34	28 43 17	17D 7.6	6 26.8	7 17.1	13 49.7	16 49.7	0 29.6	4 16.5	27 39.9	2 45.0
12 F	1 23 52	22 51 27	5♒49 42	12♒55 30	17 7.8	8 15.7	8 10.2	14 35.8	16 53.9	0 36.7	4 17.9	27 40.5	2 43.9
13 Sa	1 27 49	23 50 16	20 0 23	27 4 2	17 8.1	10 1.3	9 2.6	15 21.9	16 57.8	0 43.8	4 19.1	27 41.0	2 42.7
14 Su	1 31 45	24 49 3	4♓ 6 9	11♓ 6 25	17 8.6	11 43.3	9 54.3	16 7.9	17 1.6	0 50.8	4 20.4	27 41.5	2 41.5
15 M	1 35 42	25 47 48	18 4 31	25 0 7	17 9.2	13 21.3	10 45.3	16 53.8	17 5.2	0 57.9	4 21.6	27 42.0	2 40.3
16 Tu	1 39 38	26 46 31	1♈52 56	8♈42 41	17 9.6	14 55.2	11 35.6	17 39.7	17 8.7	1 4.8	4 22.7	27 42.4	2 39.1
17 W	1 43 35	27 45 13	15 29 5	22 11 54	17R 9.6	16 24.6	12 25.2	18 25.6	17 11.9	1 11.8	4 23.8	27 42.8	2 37.8
18 Th	1 47 31	28 43 53	28 50 56	5♉26 2	17 9.1	17 49.5	13 14.0	19 11.5	17 15.0	1 18.7	4 24.8	27 43.2	2 36.5
19 F	1 51 28	29 42 30	11♉57 6	18 24 5	17 8.0	19 9.7	14 2.0	19 57.3	17 17.9	1 25.6	4 25.8	27 43.6	2 35.2
20 Sa	1 55 24	0♉41 6	24 47 0	1♊ 5 57	17 6.5	20 25.0	14 49.1	20 43.0	17 20.6	1 32.4	4 26.7	27 43.9	2 33.9
21 Su	1 59 21	1 39 39	7♊21 3	13 32 31	17 4.5	21 35.2	15 35.4	21 28.7	17 23.2	1 39.3	4 27.6	27 44.2	2 32.6
22 M	2 3 18	2 38 11	19 40 38	25 45 42	17 2.4	22 40.3	16 20.7	22 14.4	17 25.5	1 46.0	4 28.4	27 44.4	2 31.2
23 Tu	2 7 14	3 36 40	1♋48 7	7♋48 19	17 0.5	23 40.2	17 5.1	22 60.0	17 27.7	1 52.8	4 29.2	27 44.6	2 29.8
24 W	2 11 11	4 35 8	13 46 46	19 43 58	16 59.0	24 34.7	17 48.6	23 45.5	17 29.7	1 59.5	4 30.0	27 44.8	2 28.5
25 Th	2 15 7	5 33 33	25 40 29	1♌36 51	16 58.2	25 23.9	18 31.0	24 31.0	17 31.5	2 6.1	4 30.7	27 44.9	2 27.0
26 F	2 19 4	6 31 56	7♌33 40	13 31 31	16D58.2	26 7.5	19 12.3	25 16.5	17 33.1	2 12.7	4 31.3	27 45.1	2 25.6
27 Sa	2 23 0	7 30 17	19 31 0	25 32 42	16 58.9	26 45.7	19 52.5	26 1.9	17 34.5	2 19.3	4 31.9	27 45.1	2 24.2
28 Su	2 26 57	8 28 36	1♍37 10	7♍44 59	17 0.2	27 18.3	20 31.6	26 47.3	17 35.8	2 25.8	4 32.4	27 45.2	2 22.7
29 M	2 30 53	9 26 52	13 56 38	20 12 35	17 1.7	27 45.3	21 9.5	27 32.6	17 36.8	2 32.3	4 32.9	27R45.2	2 21.2
30 Tu	2 34 50	10 25 7	26 33 15	2♎58 58	17 3.0	28 6.8	21 46.2	28 17.8	17 37.7	2 38.7	4 33.3	27 45.2	2 19.7

*Giving the positions of planets daily at noon, in LONGITUDE Greenwich Mean Time

NOON EPHEMERIS: GMT*

MAY 1996

Day	Sid.Time	☉	0 hr ☽	Noon ☽	True ☊	☿	♀	♂	♃	♄	♅	♆	♇
1 W	2 38 46	11♉23 20	9♎29 58	16♎ 6 25	17♎ 3.7	28♉22.7	22♊21.6	29♈ 3.0	17♑38.4	2♈45.1	4♒33.7	27♑45.1	2♐18.2
2 Th	2 42 43	12 21 31	22 48 22	29 35 46	17R 3.3	28 33.1	22 55.6	29 48.2	17 38.9	2 51.5	4 34.1	27R45.0	2R16.7
3 F	2 46 40	13 19 40	6♏28 26	13♏26 2	17 1.7	28R38.1	23 28.2	0♉33.3	17 39.2	2 57.8	4 34.3	27 44.9	2 15.2
4 Sa	2 50 36	14 17 48	20 28 11	27 34 21	16 58.9	28 37.8	23 59.4	1 18.4	17R39.3	3 4.0	4 34.6	27 44.8	2 13.7
5 Su	2 54 33	15 15 54	4♐43 55	11♐56 11	16 55.2	28 32.4	24 29.1	2 3.4	17 39.2	3 10.2	4 34.8	27 44.6	2 12.1
6 M	2 58 29	16 13 58	19 10 24	26 25 50	16 51.2	28 22.2	24 57.3	2 48.4	17 39.0	3 16.3	4 34.9	27 44.4	2 10.5
7 Tu	3 2 26	17 12 1	3♑41 42	10♑57 18	16 47.4	28 7.3	25 23.9	3 33.3	17 38.6	3 22.4	4 35.0	27 44.1	2 9.0
8 W	3 6 22	18 10 3	18 11 57	25 25 4	16 44.4	27 48.1	25 48.8	4 18.2	17 37.9	3 28.5	4R35.0	27 43.9	2 7.4
9 Th	3 10 19	19 8 3	2♒36 7	9♒44 43	16 42.6	27 25.1	26 12.0	5 3.0	17 37.1	3 34.4	4 35.0	27 43.6	2 5.8
10 F	3 14 16	20 6 2	16 50 33	23 53 21	16D42.2	26 58.7	26 33.4	5 47.8	17 36.1	3 40.4	4 35.0	27 43.2	2 4.2
11 Sa	3 18 12	21 3 59	0♓52 58	7♓49 20	16 42.9	26 29.3	26 53.0	6 32.5	17 34.9	3 46.2	4 34.9	27 42.9	2 2.6
12 Su	3 22 9	22 1 55	14 42 25	21 32 12	16 44.3	25 57.5	27 10.8	7 17.2	17 33.5	3 52.0	4 34.7	27 42.5	2 1.0
13 M	3 26 5	22 59 50	28 18 43	5♈ 2 2	16 45.5	25 23.9	27 26.5	8 1.8	17 31.9	3 57.8	4 34.5	27 42.0	1 59.3
14 Tu	3 30 2	23 57 44	11♈42 11	18 19 14	16R46.0	24 49.0	27 40.3	8 46.4	17 30.2	4 3.5	4 34.2	27 41.6	1 57.7
15 W	3 33 58	24 55 37	24 53 12	1♉24 8	16 45.0	24 13.6	27 52.0	9 30.9	17 28.2	4 9.1	4 33.9	27 41.1	1 56.1
16 Th	3 37 55	25 53 28	7♉52 4	14 17 0	16 42.1	23 38.2	28 1.7	10 15.3	17 26.1	4 14.7	4 33.6	27 40.5	1 54.4
17 F	3 41 51	26 51 17	20 38 57	26 57 57	16 37.4	23 3.5	28 9.1	10 59.8	17 23.8	4 20.2	4 33.2	27 40.0	1 52.8
18 Sa	3 45 48	27 49 6	3♊14 3	9♊27 16	16 31.1	22 30.0	28 14.3	11 44.1	17 21.3	4 25.7	4 32.7	27 39.4	1 51.1
19 Su	3 49 44	28 46 53	15 37 42	21 45 28	16 23.6	21 58.2	28 17.2	12 28.4	17 18.6	4 31.0	4 32.2	27 38.8	1 49.5
20 M	3 53 41	29 44 38	27 50 43	3♋53 38	16 15.8	21 28.8	28R17.8	13 12.7	17 15.7	4 36.3	4 31.7	27 38.1	1 47.8
21 Tu	3 57 38	0♊42 22	9♋54 28	15 53 30	16 8.4	21 2.2	28 16.0	13 56.9	17 12.7	4 41.6	4 31.1	27 37.5	1 46.2
22 W	4 1 34	1 40 5	21 51 4	27 47 35	16 2.0	20 38.7	28 11.9	14 41.0	17 9.5	4 46.8	4 30.4	27 36.8	1 44.5
23 Th	4 5 31	2 37 45	3♌43 27	9♌39 11	15 57.3	20 18.7	28 5.3	15 25.1	17 6.1	4 51.9	4 29.7	27 36.0	1 42.9
24 F	4 9 27	3 35 25	15 35 16	21 32 17	15 54.4	20 2.6	27 56.3	16 9.1	17 2.5	4 56.9	4 29.0	27 35.3	1 41.2
25 Sa	4 13 24	4 33 3	27 30 49	3♍31 28	15D53.4	19 50.5	27 44.8	16 53.1	16 58.8	5 1.9	4 28.2	27 34.5	1 39.6
26 Su	4 17 20	5 30 39	9♍34 51	15 41 37	15 53.7	19 42.6	27 31.0	17 37.0	16 54.9	5 6.8	4 27.4	27 33.7	1 37.9
27 M	4 21 17	6 28 14	21 52 23	28 7 44	15 54.7	19D39.1	27 14.7	18 20.9	16 50.8	5 11.6	4 26.5	27 32.8	1 36.3
28 Tu	4 25 13	7 25 47	4♎28 15	10♎54 25	15R55.6	19 40.1	26 56.0	19 4.7	16 46.6	5 16.4	4 25.6	27 32.0	1 34.6
29 W	4 29 10	8 23 19	17 26 42	24 5 24	15 55.5	19 45.5	26 35.1	19 48.4	16 42.2	5 21.0	4 24.6	27 31.1	1 33.0
30 Th	4 33 7	9 20 50	0♏50 47	7♏42 53	15 53.6	19 55.4	26 11.9	20 32.1	16 37.7	5 25.6	4 23.6	27 30.1	1 31.4
31 F	4 37 3	10 18 20	14 41 39	21 46 50	15 49.5	20 9.7	25 46.5	21 15.8	16 33.0	5 30.2	4 22.6	27 29.2	1 29.7

LONGITUDE

JUNE 1996

Day	Sid.Time	☉	0 hr ☽	Noon ☽	True ☊	☿	♀	♂	♃	♄	♅	♆	♇
1 Sa	4 41 0	11♊15 48	28♏57 58	6♐14 27	15♎43.3	20♉28.6	25♊19.2	21♉59.3	16♑28.1	5♈34.6	4♒21.5	27♑28.2	1♐28.1
2 Su	4 44 56	12 13 16	13♐35 29	21 0 6	15R35.5	20 51.8	24R49.9	22 42.9	16R23.1	5 39.0	4R20.3	27R27.2	1R26.5
3 M	4 48 53	13 10 42	28 27 16	5♑55 49	15 27.0	21 19.3	24 18.9	23 26.3	16 17.9	5 43.3	4 19.2	27 26.2	1 24.9
4 Tu	4 52 49	14 8 8	13♑24 37	20 52 31	15 18.8	21 51.0	23 46.4	24 9.8	16 12.6	5 47.5	4 17.9	27 25.2	1 23.3
5 W	4 56 46	15 5 33	28 18 29	5♒41 34	15 12.0	22 26.9	23 12.4	24 53.1	16 7.2	5 51.7	4 16.7	27 24.1	1 21.7
6 Th	5 0 43	16 2 57	13♒ 0 58	20 16 4	15 7.2	23 6.8	22 37.3	25 36.4	16 1.6	5 55.7	4 15.4	27 23.0	1 20.1
7 F	5 4 39	17 0 21	27 26 25	4♓31 43	15 4.6	23 50.7	22 1.2	26 19.7	15 55.9	5 59.7	4 14.0	27 21.9	1 18.5
8 Sa	5 8 36	17 57 44	11♓31 51	18 26 47	15D 3.9	24 38.5	21 24.4	27 2.9	15 50.0	6 3.6	4 12.7	27 20.8	1 16.9
9 Su	5 12 32	18 55 6	25 16 37	2♈ 1 34	15 4.3	25 30.0	20 47.1	27 46.0	15 44.1	6 7.4	4 11.2	27 19.6	1 15.4
10 M	5 16 29	19 52 28	8♈41 52	15 17 48	15R 4.8	26 25.2	20 9.5	28 29.1	15 37.9	6 11.1	4 9.8	27 18.4	1 13.8
11 Tu	5 20 25	20 49 50	21 49 40	28 17 48	15 4.2	27 24.0	19 31.9	29 12.2	15 31.7	6 14.8	4 8.3	27 17.2	1 12.3
12 W	5 24 22	21 47 11	4♉42 28	11♉ 3 58	15 1.5	28 26.4	18 54.5	29 55.2	15 25.4	6 18.3	4 6.7	27 16.0	1 10.8
13 Th	5 28 18	22 44 31	17 22 33	23 38 25	14 56.2	29 32.3	18 17.6	0♊38.1	15 18.9	6 21.8	4 5.2	27 14.7	1 9.3
14 F	5 32 15	23 41 51	29 51 47	6♊ 2 49	14 48.1	0♊41.5	17 41.4	1 21.0	15 12.3	6 25.2	4 3.5	27 13.5	1 7.8
15 Sa	5 36 12	24 39 11	12♊11 39	18 18 25	14 37.5	1 54.2	17 6.0	2 3.8	15 5.7	6 28.5	4 1.9	27 12.2	1 6.3
16 Su	5 40 8	25 36 30	24 23 14	0♋26 14	14 25.3	3 10.1	16 31.8	2 46.5	14 58.9	6 31.7	4 0.2	27 10.9	1 4.8
17 M	5 44 5	26 33 48	6♋27 31	12 27 15	14 12.5	4 29.3	15 58.9	3 29.2	14 52.0	6 34.8	3 58.5	27 9.5	1 3.4
18 Tu	5 48 1	27 31 6	18 25 36	24 22 44	14 0.1	5 51.8	15 27.5	4 11.9	14 45.1	6 37.9	3 56.8	27 8.2	1 1.9
19 W	5 51 58	28 28 23	0♌18 55	6♌14 25	13 49.1	7 17.4	14 57.8	4 54.5	14 38.0	6 40.8	3 55.0	27 6.8	1 0.5
20 Th	5 55 54	29 25 39	12 9 34	18 4 43	13 40.3	8 46.3	14 29.8	5 37.0	14 30.9	6 43.6	3 53.2	27 5.5	0 59.1
21 F	5 59 51	0♋22 55	24 0 17	29 56 45	13 34.2	10 18.3	14 3.8	6 19.4	14 23.7	6 46.4	3 51.3	27 4.1	0 57.7
22 Sa	6 3 47	1 20 10	5♍54 37	11♍54 26	13 30.7	11 53.4	13 39.9	7 1.8	14 16.5	6 49.0	3 49.4	27 2.7	0 56.3
23 Su	6 7 44	2 17 24	17 56 48	24 2 19	13 29.2	13 31.5	13 18.1	7 44.2	14 9.1	6 51.6	3 47.5	27 1.2	0 55.0
24 M	6 11 41	3 14 38	0♎11 38	6♎25 23	13D29.1	15 12.8	12 58.5	8 26.5	14 1.7	6 54.1	3 45.6	26 59.8	0 53.7
25 Tu	6 15 37	4 11 51	12 44 12	19 8 41	13R29.1	16 57.0	12 41.2	9 8.7	13 54.3	6 56.5	3 43.6	26 58.3	0 52.3
26 W	6 19 34	5 9 4	25 39 24	2♏16 51	13 28.2	18 44.1	12 26.2	9 50.9	13 46.8	6 58.7	3 41.6	26 56.9	0 51.0
27 Th	6 23 30	6 6 16	9♏ 1 23	15 53 17	13 25.3	20 34.1	12 13.7	10 33.0	13 39.3	7 0.9	3 39.6	26 55.4	0 49.8
28 F	6 27 27	7 3 28	22 52 39	29 59 22	13 19.9	22 26.8	12 3.5	11 15.0	13 31.7	7 3.0	3 37.6	26 53.9	0 48.5
29 Sa	6 31 23	8 0 39	7♐13 9	14♐33 27	13 12.0	24 22.2	11 55.7	11 57.0	13 24.1	7 5.0	3 35.5	26 52.4	0 47.3
30 Su	6 35 20	8 57 50	21 59 33	29 30 26	13 2.1	26 20.0	11 50.3	12 39.0	13 16.4	7 6.9	3 33.4	26 50.9	0 46.1

*Giving the positions of planets daily at noon, in LONGITUDE Greenwich Mean Time

Noon Ephemeris: GMT* July 1996

Day	Sid.Time	☉	0 hr ☽	Noon ☽	True ☊	☿	♀	♂	♃	♄	♅	♆	♇
1 M	6 39 16	9♋55 1	7♑ 4 57	14♑41 48	12♎51.4	28♊20.2	11♊47.3	13♊20.9	13♑ 8.8	7♈ 8.7	3♒31.3	26♑49.4	0♐44.9
2 Tu	6 43 13	10 52 12	22 19 34	29 56 53	12R 41.0	0♋22.5	11D 46.6	14 2.7	13R 1.1	7 10.4	3R 29.2	26R 47.8	0R 43.7
3 W	6 47 10	11 49 23	7♒32 20	15♒ 4 42	12 32.0	2 26.7	11 48.2	14 44.5	12 53.4	7 12.0	3 27.0	26 46.3	0 42.6
4 Th	6 51 6	12 46 34	22 32 53	29 55 58	12 25.4	4 32.5	11 52.2	15 26.2	12 45.7	7 13.5	3 24.8	26 44.7	0 41.5
5 F	6 55 3	13 43 45	7♓13 17	14♓24 22	12 21.4	6 39.8	11 58.4	16 7.8	12 38.0	7 14.9	3 22.6	26 43.2	0 40.4
6 Sa	6 58 59	14 40 56	21 28 57	28 26 59	12 19.7	8 48.1	12 6.7	16 49.4	12 30.3	7 16.2	3 20.4	26 41.6	0 39.3
7 Su	7 2 56	15 38 8	5♈18 32	12♈ 3 49	12D 19.5	10 57.2	12 17.2	17 31.0	12 22.6	7 17.4	3 18.2	26 40.0	0 38.3
8 M	7 6 52	16 35 20	18 43 11	25 17 0	12R 19.6	13 6.8	12 29.8	18 12.5	12 15.0	7 18.5	3 15.9	26 38.4	0 37.3
9 Tu	7 10 49	17 32 33	1♉45 42	8♉ 9 45	12 18.6	15 16.7	12 44.4	18 53.9	12 7.3	7 19.5	3 13.6	26 36.8	0 36.3
10 W	7 14 45	18 29 46	14 29 37	20 45 45	12 15.6	17 26.5	13 0.9	19 35.3	11 59.7	7 20.5	3 11.4	26 35.2	0 35.3
11 Th	7 18 42	19 26 59	26 58 34	3♊ 8 30	12 9.9	19 36.0	13 19.3	20 16.6	11 52.1	7 21.3	3 9.1	26 33.6	0 34.4
12 F	7 22 39	20 24 13	9♊15 53	15 21 3	12 1.3	21 44.8	13 39.6	20 57.9	11 44.5	7 22.0	3 6.7	26 32.0	0 33.5
13 Sa	7 26 35	21 21 28	21 24 18	27 25 54	11 50.1	23 52.9	14 1.6	21 39.1	11 37.0	7 22.6	3 4.4	26 30.4	0 32.6
14 Su	7 30 32	22 18 42	3♋26 4	9♋25 0	11 37.2	26 0.1	14 25.3	22 20.2	11 29.5	7 23.1	3 2.1	26 28.8	0 31.7
15 M	7 34 28	23 15 57	15 22 53	21 19 53	11 23.6	28 6.0	14 50.6	23 1.3	11 22.1	7 23.5	2 59.7	26 27.2	0 30.9
16 Tu	7 38 25	24 13 13	27 16 11	3♌11 57	11 10.4	0♌10.7	15 17.5	23 42.4	11 14.7	7 23.7	2 57.4	26 25.5	0 30.1
17 W	7 42 21	25 10 29	9♌ 7 22	15 2 39	10 58.7	2 13.9	15 46.0	24 23.4	11 7.4	7 23.9	2 55.0	26 23.9	0 29.3
18 Th	7 46 18	26 7 45	20 58 2	26 53 47	10 49.3	4 15.7	16 15.9	25 4.3	11 0.2	7R 24.0	2 52.6	26 22.3	0 28.6
19 F	7 50 14	27 5 1	2♍50 13	8♍47 41	10 42.7	6 15.8	16 47.2	25 45.1	10 53.1	7 24.0	2 50.2	26 20.7	0 27.8
20 Sa	7 54 11	28 2 18	14 46 35	20 47 21	10 38.8	8 14.3	17 19.9	26 25.9	10 46.0	7 23.9	2 47.9	26 19.0	0 27.2
21 Su	7 58 8	28 59 35	26 50 28	2♎56 27	10 37.2	10 11.2	17 53.8	27 6.7	10 39.0	7 23.7	2 45.5	26 17.4	0 26.5
22 M	8 2 4	29 56 52	9♎ 5 51	15 19 14	10D 37.2	12 6.3	18 29.1	27 47.3	10 32.1	7 23.4	2 43.1	26 15.8	0 25.9
23 Tu	8 6 1	0♌54 10	21 37 12	28 0 19	10R 37.6	13 59.7	19 5.5	28 27.9	10 25.3	7 22.9	2 40.7	26 14.2	0 25.3
24 W	8 9 57	1 51 28	4♏29 10	11♏ 4 15	10 37.3	15 51.4	19 43.2	29 8.5	10 18.6	7 22.4	2 38.3	26 12.6	0 24.7
25 Th	8 13 54	2 48 46	17 46 2	24 34 52	10 35.3	17 41.4	20 21.9	29 49.0	10 11.9	7 21.8	2 35.9	26 11.0	0 24.2
26 F	8 17 50	3 46 5	1♐30 58	8♐34 24	10 31.2	19 29.6	21 1.8	0♋29.4	10 5.4	7 21.1	2 33.5	26 9.3	0 23.7
27 Sa	8 21 47	4 43 24	15 45 4	23 2 37	10 24.8	21 16.0	21 42.7	1 9.8	9 59.1	7 20.2	2 31.1	26 7.7	0 23.2
28 Su	8 25 43	5 40 44	0♑26 29	7♑55 54	10 16.6	23 0.8	22 24.6	1 50.1	9 52.8	7 19.3	2 28.7	26 6.1	0 22.8
29 M	8 29 40	6 38 4	15 29 50	23 7 6	10 7.6	24 43.8	23 7.5	2 30.4	9 46.6	7 18.3	2 26.3	26 4.6	0 22.4
30 Tu	8 33 37	7 35 25	0♒46 22	8♒26 11	9 58.7	26 25.2	23 51.3	3 10.6	9 40.6	7 17.2	2 23.9	26 3.0	0 22.0
31 W	8 37 33	8 32 47	16 5 7	23 41 48	9 51.1	28 4.8	24 36.0	3 50.7	9 34.7	7 16.0	2 21.5	26 1.4	0 21.6

Longitude August 1996

Day	Sid.Time	☉	0 hr ☽	Noon ☽	True ☊	☿	♀	♂	♃	♄	♅	♆	♇
1 Th	8 41 30	9♌30 9	1♓14 55	8♓43 23	9♎45.5	29♌42.7	25♊21.6	4♋30.8	9♑28.9	7♈14.6	2♒19.1	25♑59.8	0♐21.3
2 F	8 45 26	10 27 33	16 6 16	23 22 53	9R 42.3	1♍18.9	26 8.1	5 10.9	9R 23.3	7R 13.2	2R 16.8	25R 58.3	0R 21.0
3 Sa	8 49 23	11 24 58	0♈32 45	7♈35 36	9D 41.2	2 53.5	26 55.4	5 50.8	9 17.7	7 11.7	2 14.4	25 56.7	0 20.8
4 Su	8 53 19	12 22 24	14 31 23	21 20 11	9 41.6	4 26.3	27 43.5	6 30.7	9 12.4	7 10.1	2 12.0	25 55.2	0 20.6
5 M	8 57 16	13 19 51	28 2 14	4♉37 54	9 42.4	5 57.5	28 32.3	7 10.6	9 7.1	7 8.4	2 9.7	25 53.6	0 20.4
6 Tu	9 1 12	14 17 19	11♉ 7 35	17 31 47	9R 42.6	7 26.9	29 21.9	7 50.4	9 2.1	7 6.6	2 7.4	25 52.1	0 20.2
7 W	9 5 9	15 14 49	23 51 1	0♊ 5 49	9 41.4	8 54.7	0♋12.1	8 30.2	8 57.1	7 4.7	2 5.0	25 50.6	0 20.1
8 Th	9 9 6	16 12 21	6♊16 43	12 24 13	9 38.1	10 20.7	1 3.1	9 9.8	8 52.4	7 2.7	2 2.7	25 49.1	0 20.0
9 F	9 13 2	17 9 53	18 28 50	24 31 2	9 32.6	11 44.9	1 54.7	9 49.5	8 47.7	7 0.6	2 0.4	25 47.6	0 20.0
10 Sa	9 16 59	18 7 27	0♋31 15	6♋29 54	9 25.1	13 7.4	2 46.9	10 29.1	8 43.3	6 58.5	1 58.1	25 46.1	0D 20.0
11 Su	9 20 55	19 5 2	12 27 19	18 23 51	9 16.3	14 28.0	3 39.7	11 8.6	8 39.0	6 56.2	1 55.9	25 44.6	0 20.0
12 M	9 24 52	20 2 39	24 19 47	0♌15 23	9 6.8	15 46.8	4 33.2	11 48.0	8 34.8	6 53.8	1 53.6	25 43.2	0 20.0
13 Tu	9 28 48	21 0 16	6♌10 55	12 6 34	8 57.7	17 3.7	5 27.2	12 27.4	8 30.9	6 51.4	1 51.4	25 41.8	0 20.1
14 W	9 32 45	21 57 55	18 2 35	23 59 9	8 49.6	18 18.6	6 21.7	13 6.7	8 27.1	6 48.9	1 49.2	25 40.3	0 20.2
15 Th	9 36 41	22 55 35	29 56 28	5♍54 45	8 43.3	19 31.5	7 16.8	13 46.0	8 23.5	6 46.2	1 47.0	25 38.9	0 20.4
16 F	9 40 38	23 53 16	11♍54 15	17 55 11	8 39.1	20 42.3	8 12.3	14 25.2	8 20.0	6 43.5	1 44.8	25 37.5	0 20.6
17 Sa	9 44 35	24 50 59	23 57 51	0♎ 2 32	8 37.0	21 50.9	9 8.4	15 4.4	8 16.7	6 40.7	1 42.7	25 36.2	0 20.8
18 Su	9 48 31	25 48 43	6♎ 9 34	12 19 19	8D 36.7	22 57.3	10 5.0	15 43.4	8 13.6	6 37.9	1 40.5	25 34.8	0 21.0
19 M	9 52 28	26 46 27	18 32 10	24 48 32	8 37.6	24 1.3	11 2.0	16 22.5	8 10.7	6 34.9	1 38.4	25 33.5	0 21.3
20 Tu	9 56 24	27 44 13	1♏ 8 50	7♏33 32	8 39.0	25 2.8	11 59.4	17 1.4	8 8.0	6 31.9	1 36.3	25 32.2	0 21.6
21 W	10 0 21	28 42 0	14 3 2	20 37 45	8 40.1	26 1.7	12 57.3	17 40.3	8 5.4	6 28.8	1 34.3	25 30.9	0 22.0
22 Th	10 4 17	29 39 49	27 18 5	4♐ 4 19	8R 40.2	26 57.8	13 55.6	18 19.1	8 3.0	6 25.6	1 32.3	25 29.6	0 22.4
23 F	10 8 14	0♍37 38	10♐56 42	17 55 21	8 38.8	27 51.1	14 54.4	18 57.9	8 0.9	6 22.3	1 30.2	25 28.3	0 22.8
24 Sa	10 12 10	1 35 29	25 0 15	2♑11 13	8 35.9	28 41.3	15 53.5	19 36.6	7 58.9	6 19.0	1 28.3	25 27.1	0 23.2
25 Su	10 16 7	2 33 20	9♑27 56	16 49 51	8 31.8	29 28.3	16 53.0	20 15.2	7 57.1	6 15.6	1 26.3	25 25.9	0 23.7
26 M	10 20 4	3 31 14	24 16 16	1♒46 18	8 27.0	0♎11.8	17 52.9	20 53.8	7 55.4	6 12.1	1 24.4	25 24.7	0 24.3
27 Tu	10 24 0	4 29 8	9♒18 54	16 52 55	8 22.2	0 51.7	18 53.2	21 32.3	7 54.0	6 8.5	1 22.5	25 23.5	0 24.8
28 W	10 27 57	5 27 4	24 27 8	2♓ 0 18	8 18.2	1 27.7	19 53.8	22 10.8	7 52.7	6 4.9	1 20.7	25 22.3	0 25.4
29 Th	10 31 53	6 25 1	9♓31 13	16 58 46	8 15.4	1 59.6	20 54.8	22 49.2	7 51.7	6 1.2	1 18.8	25 21.2	0 26.0
30 F	10 35 50	7 23 0	24 21 56	1♈39 53	8D 14.1	2 27.1	21 56.2	23 27.5	7 50.8	5 57.5	1 17.0	25 20.1	0 26.7
31 Sa	10 39 46	8 21 1	8♈51 57	15 57 39	8 14.2	2 49.9	22 57.9	24 5.8	7 50.1	5 53.6	1 15.3	25 19.0	0 27.4

*Giving the positions of planets daily at noon, in LONGITUDE Greenwich Mean Time

Noon Ephemeris: GMT*

September 1996

Day	Sid.Time	☉	0 hr ☽	Noon ☽	True ☊	☿	♀	♂	♃	♄	♅	♆	♇
1 Su	10 43 43	9♍19 3	22♈56 42	29♈48 57	8♎15.2	3♎ 7.8	23♋59.9	24♋44.0	7♑49.6	5♈49.8	1♒13.5	25♑18.0	0♐28.1
2 M	10 47 39	10 17 7	6♉34 28	13♉13 23	8 16.7	3 20.5	25 2.2	25 22.1	7R49.3	5R45.8	1R11.8	25R16.9	0 28.8
3 Tu	10 51 36	11 15 14	19 46 0	26 12 41	8 17.9	3 27.7	26 4.8	26 0.2	7D49.2	5 41.8	1 10.2	25 15.9	0 29.6
4 W	10 55 32	12 13 22	2♊33 54	8♊50 6	8R18.6	3R29.2	27 7.8	26 38.2	7 49.3	5 37.8	1 8.6	25 14.9	0 30.4
5 Th	10 59 29	13 11 33	15 1 52	21 9 42	8 18.2	3 24.6	28 11.0	27 16.2	7 49.5	5 33.7	1 7.0	25 14.0	0 31.3
6 F	11 3 26	14 9 45	27 14 12	3♋15 55	8 16.7	3 13.7	29 14.5	27 54.1	7 50.0	5 29.6	1 5.4	25 13.0	0 32.2
7 Sa	11 7 22	15 8 0	9♋15 22	15 13 5	8 14.3	2 56.4	0♌18.3	28 31.9	7 50.6	5 25.4	1 3.9	25 12.1	0 33.1
8 Su	11 11 19	16 6 16	21 9 35	27 5 18	8 11.2	2 32.7	1 22.4	29 9.7	7 51.5	5 21.1	1 2.4	25 11.2	0 34.0
9 M	11 15 15	17 4 34	3♌ 0 41	8♌56 9	8 7.7	2 2.4	2 26.7	29 47.4	7 52.5	5 16.8	1 1.0	25 10.4	0 35.0
10 Tu	11 19 12	18 2 54	14 52 4	20 48 45	8 4.4	1 25.8	3 31.3	0♌25.0	7 53.7	5 12.5	0 59.6	25 9.6	0 36.0
11 W	11 23 8	19 1 17	26 46 31	2♍45 39	8 1.5	0 43.1	4 36.2	1 2.6	7 55.1	5 8.1	0 58.2	25 8.8	0 37.0
12 Th	11 27 5	19 59 41	8♍46 22	14 48 55	7 59.4	29♍54.8	5 41.3	1 40.1	7 56.7	5 3.7	0 56.9	25 8.0	0 38.1
13 F	11 31 1	20 58 7	20 53 30	27 0 18	7 58.2	29 1.4	6 46.6	2 17.5	7 58.5	4 59.2	0 55.6	25 7.2	0 39.2
14 Sa	11 34 58	21 56 34	3♎ 9 31	9♎21 17	7D57.9	28 3.9	7 52.1	2 54.9	8 0.5	4 54.8	0 54.4	25 6.5	0 40.3
15 Su	11 38 55	22 55 4	15 35 49	21 53 17	7 58.3	27 3.3	8 57.9	3 32.1	8 2.6	4 50.3	0 53.2	25 5.8	0 41.5
16 M	11 42 51	23 53 35	28 13 51	4♏37 42	7 59.2	26 0.7	10 3.9	4 9.3	8 5.0	4 45.7	0 52.1	25 5.2	0 42.7
17 Tu	11 46 48	24 52 8	11♏ 5 2	17 36 1	8 0.2	24 57.6	11 10.1	4 46.5	8 7.5	4 41.2	0 51.0	25 4.6	0 43.9
18 W	11 50 44	25 50 43	24 10 52	0♐49 44	8 1.1	23 55.5	12 16.5	5 23.5	8 10.2	4 36.6	0 49.9	25 4.0	0 45.2
19 Th	11 54 41	26 49 20	7♐32 47	14 20 9	8 1.7	22 55.9	13 23.2	6 0.5	8 13.2	4 32.0	0 48.9	25 3.4	0 46.5
20 F	11 58 37	27 47 58	21 11 54	28 8 5	8R 1.8	22 0.2	14 30.0	6 37.4	8 16.2	4 27.3	0 47.9	25 2.9	0 47.8
21 Sa	12 2 34	28 46 38	5♑ 8 39	12♑13 28	8 1.5	21 10.1	15 37.0	7 14.3	8 19.5	4 22.7	0 47.0	25 2.4	0 49.1
22 Su	12 6 30	29 45 19	19 22 21	26 34 56	8 1.0	20 26.7	16 44.2	7 51.1	8 23.0	4 18.0	0 46.1	25 1.9	0 50.5
23 M	12 10 27	0♎44 2	3♒50 49	11♒ 9 27	8 0.2	19 51.2	17 51.6	8 27.8	8 26.6	4 13.4	0 45.3	25 1.4	0 51.9
24 Tu	12 14 24	1 42 47	18 30 11	25 52 17	7 59.6	19 24.5	18 59.2	9 4.4	8 30.4	4 8.7	0 44.5	25 1.0	0 53.3
25 W	12 18 20	2 41 33	3♓14 57	10♓37 18	7 59.1	19 7.4	20 7.0	9 40.9	8 34.4	4 4.0	0 43.8	25 0.7	0 54.8
26 Th	12 22 17	3 40 22	17 58 28	25 17 35	7 58.9	19D 0.1	21 15.0	10 17.4	8 38.5	3 59.4	0 43.1	25 0.3	0 56.3
27 F	12 26 13	4 39 12	2♈33 47	9♈46 19	7D58.8	19 3.0	22 23.1	10 53.8	8 42.9	3 54.7	0 42.4	24 60.0	0 57.8
28 Sa	12 30 10	5 38 4	16 54 30	23 57 46	7 58.9	19 16.1	23 31.5	11 30.1	8 47.4	3 50.0	0 41.8	24 59.7	0 59.3
29 Su	12 34 6	6 36 59	0♉55 40	7♉47 51	7 59.0	19 39.1	24 40.0	12 6.4	8 52.0	3 45.3	0 41.3	24 59.5	1 0.9
30 M	12 38 3	7 35 56	14 34 10	21 14 32	7R59.1	20 11.6	25 48.6	12 42.5	8 56.9	3 40.7	0 40.8	24 59.2	1 2.5

Longitude

October 1996

Day	Sid.Time	☉	0 hr ☽	Noon ☽	True ☊	☿	♀	♂	♃	♄	♅	♆	♇
1 Tu	12 41 59	8♎34 55	27♉49 0	4♊17 45	7♎59.0	20♍53.3	26♌57.5	13♌18.6	9♑ 1.9	3♈36.0	0♒40.3	24♑59.0	1♐ 4.1
2 W	12 45 56	9 33 56	10♊41 4	16 59 16	7R58.8	21 43.4	28 6.5	13 54.6	9 7.1	3R31.3	0R39.9	24R58.9	1 5.7
3 Th	12 49 52	10 32 59	23 12 46	29 22 5	7 58.7	22 41.3	29 15.6	14 30.6	9 12.4	3 26.7	0 39.6	24 58.8	1 7.4
4 F	12 53 49	11 32 5	5♋27 42	11♋30 11	7D58.6	23 46.4	0♍25.0	15 6.4	9 17.9	3 22.1	0 39.3	24 58.7	1 9.1
5 Sa	12 57 46	12 31 13	17 30 6	23 28 2	7 58.7	24 57.9	1 34.4	15 42.2	9 23.6	3 17.5	0 39.0	24 58.6	1 10.8
6 Su	13 1 42	13 30 24	29 24 34	5♌20 17	7 59.1	26 15.0	2 44.1	16 17.9	9 29.5	3 12.9	0 38.8	24D58.6	1 12.5
7 M	13 5 39	14 29 37	11♌15 45	17 11 30	7 59.7	27 37.0	3 53.9	16 53.5	9 35.5	3 8.4	0 38.7	24 58.6	1 14.3
8 Tu	13 9 35	15 28 51	23 8 3	29 5 54	8 0.6	29 3.3	5 3.8	17 29.1	9 41.6	3 3.8	0 38.6	24 58.7	1 16.1
9 W	13 13 32	16 28 9	5♍ 5 30	11♍ 7 15	8 1.5	0♎33.3	6 13.8	18 4.5	9 47.9	2 59.3	0D38.5	24 58.7	1 17.9
10 Th	13 17 28	17 27 28	17 11 32	23 18 39	8 2.3	2 6.3	7 24.0	18 39.9	9 54.4	2 54.9	0 38.5	24 58.9	1 19.7
11 F	13 21 25	18 26 49	29 28 54	5♎42 28	8R 2.7	3 41.8	8 34.4	19 15.1	10 1.0	2 50.4	0 38.6	24 59.0	1 21.6
12 Sa	13 25 21	19 26 13	11♎59 33	18 20 15	8 2.6	5 19.3	9 44.8	19 50.3	10 7.8	2 46.0	0 38.7	24 59.2	1 23.5
13 Su	13 29 18	20 25 39	24 44 39	1♏12 44	8 1.8	6 58.5	10 55.4	20 25.4	10 14.8	2 41.7	0 38.8	24 59.4	1 25.3
14 M	13 33 15	21 25 6	7♏44 31	14 19 54	8 0.3	8 39.0	12 6.1	21 0.4	10 21.8	2 37.4	0 39.0	24 59.6	1 27.3
15 Tu	13 37 11	22 24 36	20 58 49	27 41 7	7 58.4	10 20.4	13 16.9	21 35.3	10 29.1	2 33.1	0 39.3	24 59.9	1 29.2
16 W	13 41 8	23 24 8	4♐26 39	11♐15 15	7 56.2	12 2.5	14 27.9	22 10.1	10 36.5	2 28.9	0 39.6	25 0.2	1 31.2
17 Th	13 45 4	24 23 41	18 6 44	25 0 55	7 54.3	13 45.1	15 38.9	22 44.8	10 44.0	2 24.7	0 39.9	25 0.6	1 33.2
18 F	13 49 1	25 23 16	1♑57 36	8♑56 36	7 52.8	15 27.9	16 50.1	23 19.4	10 51.7	2 20.6	0 40.4	25 1.0	1 35.2
19 Sa	13 52 57	26 22 53	15 57 42	23 0 41	7D52.2	17 10.8	18 1.4	23 53.9	10 59.5	2 16.5	0 40.8	25 1.4	1 37.2
20 Su	13 56 54	27 22 32	0♒ 5 19	7♒11 24	7 52.5	18 53.7	19 12.8	24 28.3	11 7.4	2 12.5	0 41.3	25 1.8	1 39.2
21 M	14 0 50	28 22 12	14 18 38	21 26 45	7 53.6	20 36.4	20 24.3	25 2.6	11 15.5	2 8.5	0 41.9	25 2.3	1 41.3
22 Tu	14 4 47	29 21 54	28 35 26	5♓44 20	7 55.0	22 18.9	21 35.9	25 36.8	11 23.8	2 4.7	0 42.5	25 2.8	1 43.3
23 W	14 8 44	0♏21 37	12♓53 4	20 1 13	7 56.4	24 1.1	22 47.6	26 10.9	11 32.1	2 0.8	0 43.2	25 3.4	1 45.4
24 Th	14 12 40	1 21 23	27 8 19	4♈13 54	7R57.1	25 42.9	23 59.4	26 44.9	11 40.6	1 57.0	0 43.9	25 4.0	1 47.5
25 F	14 16 37	2 21 10	11♈17 28	18 18 32	7 56.7	27 24.4	25 11.3	27 18.8	11 49.3	1 53.3	0 44.7	25 4.6	1 49.7
26 Sa	14 20 33	3 20 59	25 16 37	2♉11 16	7 55.0	29 5.4	26 23.3	27 52.5	11 58.0	1 49.7	0 45.5	25 5.2	1 51.8
27 Su	14 24 30	4 20 50	9♉ 2 4	15 48 40	7 52.0	0♏46.0	27 35.4	28 26.2	12 6.9	1 46.1	0 46.3	25 5.9	1 53.9
28 M	14 28 26	5 20 43	22 30 47	29 8 12	7 47.9	2 26.1	28 47.6	28 59.8	12 15.9	1 42.6	0 47.3	25 6.6	1 56.1
29 Tu	14 32 23	6 20 38	5♊40 48	12♊ 8 34	7 43.1	4 5.7	29 59.9	29 33.3	12 25.1	1 39.2	0 48.2	25 7.4	1 58.3
30 W	14 36 19	7 20 35	18 31 33	24 49 55	7 38.3	5 44.9	1♎12.3	0♍ 6.6	12 34.3	1 35.9	0 49.2	25 8.1	2 0.5
31 Th	14 40 16	8 20 35	1♋ 3 53	7♋13 48	7 34.1	7 23.6	2 24.8	0 39.9	12 43.7	1 32.6	0 50.3	25 8.9	2 2.7

*Giving the positions of planets daily at noon, in LONGITUDE Greenwich Mean Time

Noon Ephemeris: GMT* — November 1996

Day	Sid.Time	☉	0 hr ☽	Noon ☽	True ☊	☿	♀	♂	♃	♄	♅	♆	♇
1 F	14 44 13	9♏20 36	13♋20 3	19♋23 4	7♎30.9	9♏ 1.8	3♎37.4	1♍13.0	12♑53.2	1♈29.4	0♒51.4	25♑ 9.8	2♐ 4.9
2 Sa	14 48 9	10 20 40	25 23 22	1♌21 30	7R29.1	10 39.6	4 50.0	1 46.0	13 2.8	1R26.3	0 52.6	25 10.7	2 7.2
3 Su	14 52 6	11 20 45	7♌18 3	13 13 39	7D28.7	12 16.9	6 2.8	2 18.9	13 12.6	1 23.3	0 53.8	25 11.6	2 9.4
4 M	14 56 2	12 20 53	19 8 53	25 4 25	7 29.5	13 53.8	7 15.6	2 51.7	13 22.4	1 20.3	0 55.1	25 12.5	2 11.7
5 Tu	14 59 59	13 21 3	1♍ 0 53	6♍58 54	7 31.1	15 30.3	8 28.5	3 24.4	13 32.4	1 17.4	0 56.4	25 13.5	2 13.9
6 W	15 3 55	14 21 15	12 59 5	19 2 0	7 32.8	17 6.3	9 41.5	3 56.9	13 42.5	1 14.7	0 57.7	25 14.5	2 16.2
7 Th	15 7 52	15 21 29	25 8 11	1♎18 7	7 34.0	18 42.0	10 54.6	4 29.3	13 52.6	1 12.0	0 59.1	25 15.5	2 18.5
8 F	15 11 48	16 21 44	7♎32 15	13 50 55	7R34.0	20 17.3	12 7.7	5 1.6	14 2.9	1 9.4	1 0.6	25 16.6	2 20.8
9 Sa	15 15 45	17 22 2	20 14 24	26 42 52	7 32.2	21 52.2	13 20.9	5 33.7	14 13.4	1 6.9	1 2.1	25 17.7	2 23.1
10 Su	15 19 41	18 22 22	3♏16 26	9♏55 2	7 28.5	23 26.8	14 34.2	6 5.7	14 23.9	1 4.4	1 3.6	25 18.8	2 25.4
11 M	15 23 38	19 22 43	16 38 33	23 26 45	7 22.9	25 1.1	15 47.5	6 37.5	14 34.5	1 2.1	1 5.2	25 20.0	2 27.7
12 Tu	15 27 35	20 23 6	0♐19 17	7♐15 43	7 16.0	26 35.1	17 0.9	7 9.3	14 45.2	0 59.9	1 6.9	25 21.1	2 30.1
13 W	15 31 31	21 23 31	14 15 33	21 18 13	7 8.6	28 8.8	18 14.4	7 40.8	14 56.0	0 57.7	1 8.6	25 22.4	2 32.4
14 Th	15 35 28	22 23 57	28 23 7	5♑29 40	7 1.5	29 42.1	19 28.0	8 12.3	15 7.0	0 55.7	1 10.3	25 23.6	2 34.8
15 F	15 39 24	23 24 25	12♑37 16	19 45 22	6 55.8	1♐15.2	20 41.5	8 43.5	15 18.0	0 53.8	1 12.1	25 24.9	2 37.1
16 Sa	15 43 21	24 24 54	26 53 27	4♒ 1 6	6 51.9	2 48.1	21 55.2	9 14.7	15 29.1	0 51.9	1 13.9	25 26.2	2 39.5
17 Su	15 47 17	25 25 24	11♒ 7 56	18 13 39	6 50.1	4 20.7	23 8.9	9 45.6	15 40.3	0 50.2	1 15.8	25 27.5	2 41.8
18 M	15 51 14	26 25 56	25 18 2	2♓20 54	6D50.0	5 53.1	24 22.6	10 16.5	15 51.6	0 48.6	1 17.7	25 28.9	2 44.2
19 Tu	15 55 10	27 26 28	9♓22 8	16 21 38	6 51.1	7 25.2	25 36.4	10 47.1	16 3.0	0 47.0	1 19.7	25 30.3	2 46.6
20 W	15 59 7	28 27 2	23 19 20	0♈15 10	6R52.1	8 57.1	26 50.3	11 17.6	16 14.5	0 45.6	1 21.7	25 31.7	2 48.9
21 Th	16 3 4	29 27 37	7♈ 9 3	14 0 54	6 52.0	10 28.8	28 4.2	11 47.9	16 26.1	0 44.3	1 23.7	25 33.1	2 51.3
22 F	16 7 0	0♐28 13	20 50 37	27 38 2	6 49.8	12 0.2	29 18.1	12 18.1	16 37.7	0 43.0	1 25.8	25 34.6	2 53.7
23 Sa	16 10 57	1 28 51	4♉23 1	11♉ 5 22	6 45.1	13 31.4	0♏32.2	12 48.1	16 49.5	0 41.9	1 28.0	25 36.1	2 56.1
24 Su	16 14 53	2 29 30	17 44 53	24 21 22	6 37.8	15 2.4	1 46.2	13 18.0	17 1.3	0 40.9	1 30.1	25 37.6	2 58.4
25 M	16 18 50	3 30 10	0♊54 38	7♊24 29	6 28.2	16 33.2	3 0.3	13 47.6	17 13.2	0 40.0	1 32.3	25 39.1	3 0.8
26 Tu	16 22 46	4 30 52	13 50 47	20 13 27	6 17.3	18 3.6	4 14.5	14 17.1	17 25.2	0 39.2	1 34.6	25 40.7	3 3.2
27 W	16 26 43	5 31 35	26 32 25	2♋47 43	6 6.0	19 33.8	5 28.6	14 46.4	17 37.2	0 38.5	1 36.9	25 42.3	3 5.6
28 Th	16 30 39	6 32 19	8♋59 25	15 7 42	5 55.4	21 3.7	6 42.9	15 15.6	17 49.4	0 37.9	1 39.2	25 43.9	3 7.9
29 F	16 34 36	7 33 5	21 12 46	27 14 57	5 46.4	22 33.2	7 57.2	15 44.5	18 1.6	0 37.4	1 41.6	25 45.6	3 10.3
30 Sa	16 38 33	8 33 53	3♌14 36	9♌12 9	5 39.8	24 2.3	9 11.5	16 13.3	18 13.9	0 37.0	1 44.0	25 47.3	3 12.7

Longitude — December 1996

Day	Sid.Time	☉	0 hr ☽	Noon ☽	True ☊	☿	♀	♂	♃	♄	♅	♆	♇
1 Su	16 42 29	9♐34 41	15♌ 8 7	21♌ 3 2	5♎35.5	25♐31.0	10♏25.9	16♍41.8	18♑26.2	0♈36.8	1♒46.4	25♑48.9	3♐15.1
2 M	16 46 26	10 35 31	26 57 30	2♍52 7	5R33.6	26 59.1	11 40.3	17 10.2	18 38.6	0R36.6	1 48.9	25 50.7	3 17.4
3 Tu	16 50 22	11 36 23	8♍47 35	14 44 33	5D33.3	28 26.7	12 54.7	17 38.4	18 51.1	0D36.5	1 51.5	25 52.4	3 19.8
4 W	16 54 19	12 37 16	20 43 43	26 45 47	5 33.7	29 53.5	14 9.2	18 6.3	19 3.7	0 36.6	1 54.0	25 54.2	3 22.1
5 Th	16 58 15	13 38 10	2♎51 24	9♎ 1 14	5R33.8	1♑19.5	15 23.7	18 34.1	19 16.3	0 36.7	1 56.6	25 55.9	3 24.5
6 F	17 2 12	14 39 6	15 15 52	21 35 51	5 32.4	2 44.6	16 38.2	19 1.6	19 29.0	0 37.0	1 59.2	25 57.8	3 26.8
7 Sa	17 6 8	15 40 2	28 1 40	4♏33 38	5 28.9	4 8.6	17 52.8	19 28.9	19 41.8	0 37.4	2 1.9	25 59.6	3 29.2
8 Su	17 10 5	16 41 0	11♏12 1	17 56 55	5 22.6	5 31.3	19 7.4	19 56.0	19 54.6	0 37.9	2 4.6	26 1.4	3 31.5
9 M	17 14 2	17 41 59	24 48 15	1♐45 49	5 13.8	6 52.5	20 22.1	20 22.8	20 7.5	0 38.5	2 7.3	26 3.3	3 33.8
10 Tu	17 17 58	18 43 0	8♐49 11	15 57 47	5 2.9	8 11.9	21 36.7	20 49.4	20 20.5	0 39.2	2 10.1	26 5.2	3 36.2
11 W	17 21 55	19 44 1	23 10 54	0♑27 40	4 51.1	9 29.3	22 51.4	21 15.8	20 33.5	0 40.0	2 12.9	26 7.1	3 38.5
12 Th	17 25 51	20 45 3	7♑47 7	15 8 16	4 39.7	10 44.3	24 6.2	21 41.9	20 46.5	0 40.9	2 15.7	26 9.0	3 40.8
13 F	17 29 48	21 46 5	22 30 4	29 51 33	4 29.9	11 56.5	25 20.9	22 7.8	20 59.6	0 42.0	2 18.6	26 11.0	3 43.1
14 Sa	17 33 44	22 47 8	7♒11 49	14♒30 4	4 22.5	13 5.4	26 35.7	22 33.4	21 12.8	0 43.1	2 21.5	26 12.9	3 45.3
15 Su	17 37 41	23 48 12	21 45 38	28 58 1	4 18.0	14 10.6	27 50.5	22 58.7	21 26.0	0 44.4	2 24.4	26 14.9	3 47.6
16 M	17 41 38	24 49 15	6♓ 6 49	13♓11 49	4 16.0	15 11.4	29 5.3	23 23.8	21 39.3	0 45.7	2 27.3	26 16.9	3 49.9
17 Tu	17 45 34	25 50 20	20 12 54	27 10 3	4D15.7	16 7.3	0♐20.1	23 48.6	21 52.6	0 47.2	2 30.3	26 18.9	3 52.1
18 W	17 49 31	26 51 24	4♈ 3 22	10♈52 57	4R15.7	16 57.4	1 34.9	24 13.1	22 6.0	0 48.8	2 33.3	26 21.0	3 54.4
19 Th	17 53 27	27 52 29	17 38 58	24 21 38	4 14.7	17 41.0	2 49.8	24 37.3	22 19.4	0 50.4	2 36.3	26 23.0	3 56.6
20 F	17 57 24	28 53 34	1♉ 1 5	7♉37 30	4 11.5	18 17.3	4 4.6	25 1.3	22 32.8	0 52.2	2 39.4	26 25.1	3 58.8
21 Sa	18 1 20	29 54 39	14 11 3	20 41 48	4 5.2	18 45.3	5 19.5	25 25.0	22 46.3	0 54.1	2 42.5	26 27.2	4 1.0
22 Su	18 5 17	0♑55 45	27 9 51	3♊35 16	3 55.8	19 4.1	6 34.4	25 48.3	22 59.8	0 56.1	2 45.6	26 29.2	4 3.2
23 M	18 9 13	1 56 51	9♊58 2	16 18 10	3 43.6	19R13.0	7 49.3	26 11.4	23 13.4	0 58.2	2 48.7	26 31.3	4 5.3
24 Tu	18 13 10	2 57 58	22 35 39	28 50 29	3 29.5	19 11.0	9 4.3	26 34.2	23 27.0	1 0.4	2 51.9	26 33.5	4 7.5
25 W	18 17 7	3 59 5	5♋ 2 40	11♋12 11	3 14.8	18 57.6	10 19.2	26 56.6	23 40.7	1 2.7	2 55.0	26 35.6	4 9.6
26 Th	18 21 3	5 0 12	17 19 7	23 23 32	3 0.7	18 32.4	11 34.2	27 18.7	23 54.4	1 5.1	2 58.2	26 37.7	4 11.8
27 F	18 25 0	6 1 19	29 25 34	5♌25 24	2 48.3	17 55.4	12 49.2	27 40.5	24 8.1	1 7.6	3 1.4	26 39.9	4 13.9
28 Sa	18 28 56	7 2 27	11♌23 18	17 19 32	2 38.6	17 7.1	14 4.2	28 1.9	24 21.8	1 10.2	3 4.7	26 42.1	4 15.9
29 Su	18 32 53	8 3 35	23 14 29	29 8 33	2 31.8	16 8.3	15 19.2	28 23.0	24 35.6	1 12.9	3 7.9	26 44.2	4 18.0
30 M	18 36 49	9 4 44	5♍ 2 14	10♍56 3	2 27.9	15 0.5	16 34.2	28 43.8	24 49.4	1 15.7	3 11.2	26 46.4	4 20.1
31 Tu	18 40 46	10 5 53	16 50 34	22 46 25	2 26.3	13 45.7	17 49.3	29 4.2	25 3.2	1 18.6	3 14.5	26 48.6	4 22.1

*Giving the positions of planets daily at noon,
in LONGITUDE Greenwich Mean Time

January - Januar - janvier - enero

INANNA

Monday	Tuesday	Wednesday	Thursday	Friday	Saturday	Sunday
1	2	3	4	5	6	7
8	9	10	11	12	13	14
15	16	17	18	19	20	21
22	23	24	25	26	27	28
29	30	31				

February - Februar - février - febrero

FREYA

Monday	Tuesday	Wednesday	Thursday	Friday	Saturday	Sunday
			1	2	3	4
5	6	7	8	9	10	11
12	13	14	15	16	17	18
19	20	21	22	23	24	25
26	27	28	29			

March – März – mars – marzo

Monday	Tuesday	Wednesday	Thursday	Friday	Saturday	Sunday
PELE				1	2	3
4	5	6	7	8	9	10
11	12	13	14	15	16	17
18	19	20	21	22	23	24
25	26	27	28	29	30	31

April - April - avril - abril

Monday	Tuesday	Wednesday	Thursday	Friday	Saturday	Sunday
1	2	3	4	5	6	7
8	9	10	11	12	13	14
15	16	17	18	19	20	21
22	23	24	25	26	27	28
29	30					

TARA

May - Mai - mai - mayo

Monday	Tuesday	Wednesday	Thursday	Friday	Saturday	Sunday
		1	2	3	4	5
6	7	8	9	10	11	12
13	14	15	16	17	18	19
20	21	22	23	24	25	26
27	28	29	30	31		SAPPHO

June - Juni - juin - junio

	Monday	Tuesday	Wednesday	Thursday	Friday	Saturday	Sunday
	KWAN-YIN					1	2
	3	4	5	6	7	8	9
	10	11	12	13	14	15	16
	17	18	19	20	21	22	23
	24	25	26	27	28	29	30

July - Juli - juilliet - julio

Monday	Tuesday	Wednesday	Thursday	Friday	Saturday	Sunday
1	2	3	4	5	6	7
8	9	10	11	12	13	14
15	16	17	18	19	20	21
22	23	24	25	26	27	28
29	30	31				

OSHUN

August - August - août - agosto

Monday	Tuesday	Wednesday	Thursday	Friday	Saturday	Sunday
ARTEMIS			1	2	3	4
5	6	7	8	9	10	11
12	13	14	15	16	17	18
19	20	21	22	23	24	25
26	27	28	29	30	31	

September - septembre - septiembre

ISIS

	Monday	Tuesday	Wednesday	Thursday	Friday	Saturday	Sunday
							1
	2	3	4	5	6	7	8
	9	10	11	12	13	14	15
	16	17	18	19	20	21	22
	23 / 30	24	25	26	27	28	29

October – Oktober – octobre – octubre

Monday	Tuesday	Wednesday	Thursday	Friday	Saturday	Sunday
	1	2	3	4	5	6
7	8	9	10	11	12	13
14	15	16	17	18	19	20
21	22	23	24	25	26	27
28	29	30	31			

KALI

November - novembre - noviembre

BUFFALO WOMON

Monday	Tuesday	Wednesday	Thursday	Friday	Saturday	Sunday
				1	2	3
4	5	6	7	8	9	10
11	12	13	14	15	16	17
18	19	20	21	22	23	24
25	26	27	28	29	30	

December - décembre - diciembre

LILLITH

Monday	Tuesday	Wednesday	Thursday	Friday	Saturday	Sunday
						1
2	3	4	5	6	7	8
9	10	11	12	13	14	15
16	17	18	19	20	21	22
23	24	25	26	27	28	29
30	31